THE JEWISH FAITH

By the same author

The Jews of Canterbury
On Earth as it is in Heaven: Jews, Christians and Liberation
    Theology
The Jewish Heritage
Jewish Petitionary Prayer: A Theological Exploration
Holocaust Theology
Rabbinic Perspectives on the New Testament
Issues in Contemporary Judaism
The Blackwell Dictionary of Judaica
A Dictionary of Judaism and Christianity
The Crucified Jew: Twenty Centuries of Christian Anti-
    Semitism
Exodus: An Agenda for Jewish-Christian Dialogue
Israel: The History of an Idea
Not a Job for a Nice Jewish Boy
An Atlas of Jewish History
Judaism and Other Faiths
Exploring Reality (co-editor)
The Canterbury Papers: Essays on Religion and Society
    (editor)
The Salman Rushdie Controversy in Interreligious Perspective
    (editor)
Tradition and Unity: Sermons Published in Honour of Robert
    Runcie (editor)
Using the Bible Today: Contemporary Interpretations of
    Scripture (editor)
The Sayings of Moses (editor)
Islam in a World of Diverse Faiths (editor)
Torah and Revelation (editor)
World Religions and Human Liberation (editor)
Religion and Public Life (co-editor)
God: Experiencing the Divine (editor)
Problems in Contemporary Jewish Theology (editor)
Many Mansions: Interfaith and Religious Intolerance (editor)
Beyond Death (co-editor)
Divine Intervention and Miracles (editor)
A Traditional Quest: Essays in Honour of Louis Jacobs (editor)

The
Jewish Faith

DAN COHN-SHERBOK

First published in Great Britain 1993
Society for Promoting Christian Knowledge
Holy Trinity Church
Marylebone Road
London NW1 4DU

Second impression 1994

British Library Cataloguing in Publication Data

A catalogue record for this book is available
from the British Library

ISBN 0-281-04685-9

Typeset by Deltatype Ltd, Ellesmere Port, Cheshire
Printed and bound in Great Britain
by Mackays of Chatham plc, Chatham, Kent

For Lavinia, Herod and Dido

Contents

Contents

Part II

PRACTICES

Acknowledgements

In writing this study I am particularly indebted to a number of helpful books from which I have obtained information and source materials: Louis Jacobs, *A Jewish Theology*, Darton, Longman and Todd, 1973; Louis Jacobs, *The Book of Jewish Belief*, Behrman House, 1984; Louis Jacobs, *The Book of Jewish Practice*, Behrman House, 1987; Richard Siegel, Michael Strassfeld, Sharon Strassfeld (eds.), *The Jewish Catalog*, The Jewish Publication Society of America, 1973; Sharon Strassfeld, Michael Strassfeld (eds.), *The Second Jewish Catalog*, The Jewish Publication Society of America, 1976; Geoffrey Wigoder, *The Encyclopedia of Judaism*, The Jerusalem Publishing House, 1989; *Encyclopedia Judaica*, Keter Publishing House, 1972; Robert Seltzer, *Jewish People, Jewish Thought*, Macmillan, 1980. I would also like to thank Mollie Roots, Justine Clements, Val Swash, and Jane Wrench of the Rutherford College Secretarial Office for typing the manuscript.

Preface

For more than fifteen years I have taught courses in Jewish studies to both Jewish and non-Jewish students at the University of Kent at Canterbury, England. During this time I frequently directed students to such multi-volume encyclopedias as the *Jewish Encyclopedia* and the *Encyclopedia Judaica*. These vast repositories of material provide a wealth of information about all aspects of Jewish life. Nonetheless, students often find these works overwhelming, as well as difficult to gain access to if they are much in demand in the library.

Aware of these difficulties, I also suggested they look at more specific studies dealing with Jewish history, belief, and practice. Yet very few of these works deal in detail with both Jewish theology and the Jewish way of life. Increasingly I came to see that what was needed was a relatively succinct presentation which would serve as an introduction to the Jewish religion. This present volume, *The Jewish Faith*, is thus designed to provide students as well as general readers with a handy and accessible guide to the Jewish faith.

Beginning with a short overview of Jewish history, the book is divided into two main parts. In the first, dealing with Jewish belief, I outline the central principles of the Jewish religion through the centuries. The second part focuses on the major aspects of Jewish practice. Here the concentration is on traditional procedures, but I have also added some information about religious practice in the non-Orthodox branches of Judaism. The book concludes with a glossary and a list of further reading consisting of general studies as well as more specialised works arranged chronologically according to period.

Introduction

For over fifteen years I have taught an introductory course about Judaism to undergraduates at the University of Kent in Canterbury, England. During this time the majority of students have been Christians. Thus at the outset I always emphasize that Judaism is in one very fundamental sense different from Christianity: Jewish identity is ultimately based on descent rather than religious conviction. According to Jewish law, it is sufficient for someone to have been born of a Jewish mother for them to be regarded as a Jew. Conversely, however, a person born of a Jewish father and a non-Jewish mother is not Jewish – such an individual is a Gentile. For millennia this has been the traditional understanding of Jewish identification. This means that an agnostic or atheist as well as a non-practising person born of a Jewish mother is Jewish. Correct belief or observance is irrelevant.

As a result of this legal definition of Jewishness, there are many people today who though formally recognized as Jews are in no sense religious. Some of these individuals adamantly identify themselves as Jews; others refuse such identification. Yet, whatever their response, the Jewish community regards them as belonging to the Jewish fold and accords them religious rights (such as the right to be married in a synagogue or buried in a Jewish cemetery). Here, then, is a simple concrete criterion of Jewishness. In modern times, however, such a definition has been obscured for two major reasons. First, the Gentile world has not invariably applied this legal criterion of Jewishness to the Jewish community. Frequently – as occurred in Nazi Germany – individuals are deemed Jews even if they do not qualify by this internal Jewish classification. During the Third Reich, for example, the Citizen Laws defined someone as Jewish if they were simply of Jewish blood. This meant that some of the people who were massacred by the Nazis would not have been accepted as Jews by the Jewish community.

The second difficulty concerns the decision taken in 1983 by the Central Conference of American Rabbis (the central body of American Reform rabbis) that a child of either a Jewish mother or a Jewish father should be regarded as Jewish. By expanding the determination of Jewishness to include children of both matrilineal and patrilineal descent, the Reform movement defined as Jews individuals whom the other branches of Judaism regard as Gentiles; this means that neither these persons nor their descendants can be accepted as Jews by non-Reform religious establishment.

In addition to the legal (*halakhic*) ruling about biological descent, Judaism also permits Gentiles to become Jews by undergoing conversion. According to traditional Judaism, conversion is a ritual process involving immersion in a ritual bath (*mikveh*), and circumcision for males. The conversion is to take place in the presence of three rabbis who compose a court of law (*bet din*). This procedure has remained constant through the ages; however, within the Neo-Orthodox branches of Judaism, there have been various modifications to this process. Conservative Judaism generally follows the traditional procedure, but it does not always follow the precise legal requirements. For this reason, most Orthodox rabbis do not recognize Conservative conversions as valid. Similarly, since Reform Judaism has largely abandoned ritual immersion and does not conduct circumcision in the required form, its converts are not accepted by the Orthodox community. Thus Reform and Conservative converts and their offspring are deemed to be non-Jews by the Orthodox establishment, and in consequence there is considerable confusion in the Jewish world as to who should be regarded as legitimately Jewish.

A further complication about Jewish status concerns the remarriage of female Jews who, though divorced in civil law, have failed to obtain a Jewish bill of divorce (*get*). Orthodoxy does not recognize their divorces as valid, and any subsequent liaison, even when accompanied by a non-Orthodox Jewish marriage ceremony or civil marriage, is regarded as adulterous. Further, the children of such unions are stigmatized as illegitimate (*mamzerim*) and barred from marrying other Jews unless they are also *mamzerim*. These problems, produced by deviations from traditional Jewish practice, present contemporary Jewry with enormous perplexities, and highlight the fissures separating the various Jewish religious groupings. As is evident, in the modern world Jews themselves cannot reach universal agreement about who is a legitimate Jew.

Such a perplexity is due to the fragmentation of Jewish life which has taken place over the last two centuries. In the past, Judaism was essentially a unified structure embracing different interpretations of the same tradition. This was the case, for example, in Hellenistic times when the Jewish community was divided into three main parties: Pharisees, Sadducees and Essenes. Again in the early modern period the Hasidim and traditional rabbis (*Mitnagdim*) vied with one another for supremacy. But the modern period has witnessed an unprecedented fragmentation of the Jewish people into a wide variety of sub-groups with markedly different orientations. This development in Jewish life has been largely the result of the Enlightenment which began at the end of the eighteenth century. No longer were Jews insulated from non-Jewish currents of culture and thought, and this change led many Jews to seek a modernization of Jewish worship. The earliest reformers engaged in liturgical revision, but quickly the spirit of reform spread to other areas of Jewish existence. Eventually modernists convened a succession of rabbinical conferences in order to formulate a common policy. Such a radical approach to the Jewish tradition evoked a hostile response from a number of leading Orthodox rabbis, and stimulated the creation of Neo-Orthodoxy. Such opposition, however, did not stem the tide; the development of the scientific study of Judaism continued to inspire many reformers who were sympathetic to modern culture and learning. As a result of these events Judaism has ceased to be a monolithic structure; instead today it is divided into a variety of sects with profoundly different orientations.

Surveying these divisions within the Jewish community, the most conservative approach to the Jewish heritage is represented by traditional Orthodoxy which itself is composed of a number of diverse sub-groups. In the nineteenth century European Jews who refused to adopt radical changes to Jewish ritual and belief either continued to live in accordance with Jewish law or attempted to combine modernity with the Jewish way of life. The first approach led to extreme conservatism as espoused by Rabbi Moseh Sofer of Pressburg, who launched a ferocious attack on reformers. Another expression of such

Orthodoxy was formulated by the Hasidic leader Rabbi Schneur Zalman of Liady who supported the Tsar against Napoleon; according to Schneur Zalman, the Napoleonic policy of Jewish emancipation constituted a threat to Jewish existence. Both of these figures rejected secular culture and were anxious to steer the Jewish community away from reform. An alternative approach to emancipation, however, was propounded by the Neo-Orthodox thinker, Rabbi Samson Raphael Hirsch of Frankfurt. While affirming the validity of the *halakhah*, Hirsch embraced European culture and advocated secular education combined with traditional religious instruction. For Hirsch, the slogan of modern Jewish life was *'Torah im derekh eretz'* ('Torah with the way of the land'): by this he wished to emphasize that Judaism must be combined with modern culture and knowledge.

These two reactions to contemporary Jewish life have determined the nature of current Orthodoxy. A minority of Orthodox Jews, including the various Hasidic sects, reject modern culture and secular education. Although they have accepted a wide range of technological developments (such as electricity, cars, and aeroplanes), they have separated themselves from the rest of the community. They have as little contact with the outside world as possible, and categorically reject Gentile culture. The majority of Orthodox Jews, however, are followers of the Hirschian approach. For these individuals there is no objection to wearing Western clothes, attending secular schools and universities, and embracing many of the cultural values of the Gentile world. Although modern Orthodoxy is committed to the *halakhah*, it is flexible in its interpretation as well as implementation of the law. In addition, modern Orthodox rabbis have usually undergone university training, and preach sermons in the vernacular. Although women pray separately from men, the women's gallery is not usually curtained off, and frequently women play an active role in communal life. None the less, there are many lapsed Orthodox Jews, who while observing a wide range of Jewish practices, have substantially rejected the vast corpus of Orthodox law. Although they define themselves as Orthodox, they have readily parted from traditional belief and practice.

A middle position on the Jewish spectrum is occupied by Conservative Judaism. Initially this movement emerged from the ranks of Reform Judaism, but adherents of Conservatism opposed the radical alterations of the tradition advanced by reformers in the nineteenth century. In 1845 the leading figure of this approach, Zacharias Frankel, walked out of a Frankfurt Reform rabbinical conference in protest and founded the Jewish Theological Seminary in Breslau, which combined a traditional Jewish curriculum with historical scholarship. Later in the century a number of American rabbis adopted the approach of Frankel in their revision of Jewish liturgy and observance. Prominent among these moderates was Isaac Lesser who published the journal *Occident*, which espoused a revised form of traditionalism. Together with such immigrant scholars as Sabbato Morais, Marcus Jastrow and Alexander Kohut, Lesser strove to preserve Hebrew in the liturgy, maintain Sabbath observance, and observe the dietary laws. In addition, these thinkers stressed the importance of the messianic hope, Jewish national identity, and Zionism. In 1887 Morais founded the Jewish Theological Seminary in New York which continued the tradition of Frankel's Seminary in Breslau. In 1902 Solomon Schechter became the head of the Jewish Theological Seminary, and in 1913 founded a body of affiliated synagogues, the United Synagogue of America. Today Conservative Judaism continues to uphold the traditionalist position despite subscribing to a critical approach to the Bible. In contrast to Orthodoxy, Conservative synagogues have introduced mixed seating, abolished various restrictions, (such as that concerning levirate marriage), discontinued the use of the ritual bath (*mikveh*), and recently countenanced the ordination of women. Although most Conservative scholars reject the belief that the Five Books of Moses were revealed by God to Moses on Mount Sinai, they still regard the *Torah* as of divine origin. An offshoot of Conservative Judaism is the Reconstructionist movement founded by Mordecai Kaplan. According to Kaplan, Judaism should be understood as an evolving religious civilization rather than a supernaturally revealed religion. Currently Reconstructionists have their own rabbinical seminary and network of synagogues.

The third modern development of contemporary Judaism is the Reform movement, which emerged in Europe at the beginning of the nineteenth century. In 1810 Israel Jacobson introduced reforms into the synagogue liturgy in Westphalia, including a sermon and hymns in the vernacular, the use of an organ, a mixed choir, the shortening of prayers, and the institution of confirmation. Accompanying such liturgical revision, other reformers introduced ideological reforms in their conception of Judaism; no longer, they believed, should Jews long to return to Zion, rebuild the Temple in Jerusalem, or reinstitute sacrifice. As a result of such a revolution in attitudes, a new prayer book was produced for the Hamburg Temple in 1819, and in 1841 an even more radical revision was introduced, which reinterpreted the concept of the Messiah. Initially reformers defended their approach on the basis of the *halakhah*, but in time they argued the case for reform on ideological grounds.

The division between the early moderate reformers such as Abraham Geiger, and radical reformers such as Samuel Holdheim, has continued to the present. In Britain the first Reform congregation was founded in 1840 by a dissident group which had broken away from Orthodox synagogues. In general they were traditional in orientation despite their rejection of Orthodoxy. Other British reformers, however, advocated a more radical position and founded the Liberal movement. A similar division occurred in the United States. In the latter half of the nineteenth century Isaac Mayer Wise founded the Hebrew Union College in Cincinnati and was an instigator of the Cleveland Platform of Reform Judaism which recognized the divine nature of the Bible and the validity of the rabbinic tradition. More radical reformers however, such as David Einhorn and Kaufman Kohler, opposed Wise's moderate stance and advanced a more radical programme of reform. In 1885 the Pittsburg Platform was formulated under the leadership of Kohler. This Platform viewed the Bible as containing outmoded religious ideas; only the moral code of Judaism, these reformers argued, is binding, together with any rituals which are spiritually significant for the modern age. Reform Judaism, they continued, should abandon dietary laws, national aspirations, and such doctrines as the resurrection of the dead and reward and punishment in the hereafter. Throughout this century Reform Judaism has continued to espouse a fundamentally different lifestyle from Orthodox Judaism, although there has been a gradual return to tradition and a general acceptance of Zionism. Nonetheless, some Reform congregations, following the lead of radical reformers of the past, have continued to press for fundamental change to Jewish belief and practice.

Given these religious divisions within contemporary Judaism, it is not possible to isolate a core of beliefs and practices which are currently accepted by the Jewish community as a whole. Nonetheless, despite the variances of religious convictions and observances within the modern Jewish community, there remains a bedrock of inherited tradition – even the most radical reformers would acknowledge the pivotal importance of biblical and rabbinic teaching. The purpose of this book is thus to provide a framework for understanding the development of Jewish religious thought through the centuries, as well as the observances that have served as the foundation for Jewish existence. *The Jewish Faith* is hence a handbook of basic Jewish beliefs and practices as they have evolved throughout history. In the chapters which follow, readers are introduced to the theological reflections of many of the most important thinkers of the past as well as the essential elements of the Jewish faith. While I have also given some indications of current deviations from traditional Judaism within Conservative, Reconstructionist and Reform movements, the aim of the book is to present mainstream Judaism as it has been understood and practised for nearly 4000 years.

It should be noted, however, that Judaism should not be viewed as a religion like Christianity, Islam, Hinduism or Buddhism. Unlike many other traditions, there is no dichotomy between the religious and secular aspects of the Jewish faith. Historical awareness, cultural consciousness, and Jewish identity are all bound together within a unified religious framework. Thus the *Torah* and its attendant patterns of behaviour are inextricably bound up with the Jewish way of life. For Jewry the Covenant embraces God's dealing with his chosen people as well as a divinely prescribed path of living. In this light belief and practice are inseparable: the Jewish tradition teaches basic beliefs about God, revelation and humanity and also expresses these doctrines in ceremonies, rituals and laws which have given rise to various institutions and distinctive styles of Jewish culture. Being devoutly Jewish, therefore, involves correct belief as well as participation in the religious life of the community.

For this reason, I have divided this volume into two parts, each of which deals with the central dimension of the Jewish faith. Part I begins with an examination of the primary religious doctrines of Judaism from ancient times to the modern age: each chapter highlights biblical teaching and traces its development from rabbinic times to the present. Beginning with a survey of Jewish belief about God's unity, the book goes on to examine the traditional Jewish doctrines about God's nature, including such doctrines as divine transcendence, eternal existence, omniscience, and omnipotence. Turning to a consideration of God's action in the world, the subsequent chapters focus on creation, providence, divine goodness, and revelation. There then follows an examination of doctrines specifically connected with God's relation to Israel: *Torah, mitzvah,* sin and repentance, the chosen people, the promised land, prayer, and the love and fear of God. Part I concludes with an exploration of Jewish eschatology and the relationship between Judaism and the world's religions.

Part Two – dealing with Jewish practice – commences with a depiction of the Jewish community, its literature, and the process of education as it has emerged over the centuries. This is followed by an outline of the Jewish calendar, and Jewish worship embracing such institutions as the Sanctuary, Temple and Synagogue as well as the major festivals in the yearly cycle: Sabbath, Pilgrim festivals, New Year, Day of Atonement, Days of Joy, and Fast Days. The next chapters discuss major events in the Jewish life cycle including marriage, divorce, death and mourning. In the following chapter some of the central characteristics of Jewish morality are highlighted, and the book concludes with a depiction of the conversion procedure. Here then is an in depth introduction to the Jewish way as it has been lived through the centuries.

The Historical Background

Jews in the ancient world

The history of the Jewish people began in Mesopotamia where successive empires of the ancient world flourished and decayed before the Jews emerged as a separate people. The culture of these civilizations had a profound impact on the Jewish religion – ancient Near Eastern myths were refashioned to serve the needs of the Hebrew people. It appears that the Jews emerged in this milieu as a separate nation between the nineteenth and sixteenth centuries BC. According to the Bible, Abraham was the father of the Jewish people. Initially known as Abram, he came from Ur of the Chaldeans. Together with his family he went to Haran and subsequently to Canaan, later settling in the plain near Hebron. Abraham was followed by Isaac and Jacob, whose son Joseph was sold into slavery in Egypt. There he prospered, becoming a vizier in the house of Pharaoh. Eventually the entire Hebrew clan moved to Egypt where they remained and flourished for centuries until a new Pharaoh decreed that all male Hebrew babies should be put to death.

To persuade Pharaoh to let the Jewish people go, God sent a series of plagues upon the Egyptians. After this devastation Moses, the leader of the people, led his kinsfolk out of Egypt; after wandering in the desert for forty years, the Hebrews finally entered into the land that God had promised them. Under Joshua's leadership, the Hebrews conquered the existing inhabitants. After Joshua's death the people began to form separate groups. At first there were twelve tribes named after the sons of Jacob: Joseph, Benjamin, Levi, Simeon, Reuben, Judah, Issachar, Zebulun, Dan, Naphtali, Gad, and Asher. When Levi became a special priestly group excluded from this territorial division, the tribe of Joseph was divided into two and named after his sons, Ephraim and Manasseh. During this period the Hebrews were ruled over by twelve national heroes

9

who served successively as judges. In Scripture the sagas of six major judges (Othaniel, Ehud, Deborah, Gideon, Jephthah and Samson) are recounted at length.

Frequently the Covenant between God and his chosen people – first formulated by Moses – was proclaimed at gatherings in such national shrines as Shechem. Such an emphasis on covenantal obligation reinforced the belief that the Jews were the recipients of God's loving kindness. Now in a more settled existence, the Covenant expanded to include additional legislation, including the provisions needed for an agricultural community. During this period it became increasingly clear to the Jewish nation that the God of the Covenant directed human history: the Exodus and the entry into the Promised Land were viewed as the unfolding of a divine plan.

Under the judges, God was conceived as the supreme monarch. When some tribes suggested to Gideon that he deserved a formal position of power, he declared that it was impossible for the nation to be ruled by both God and a human king. None the less, Saul was subsequently elected as king despite the prophet Samuel's warnings against the dangers of usurping God's rule. In later years the Israelite nation divided into two kingdoms. The northern tribes, led by Ephraim, and the southern tribes, led by Judah, had been united only by their allegiance to King David. But when his successor King Solomon, and his son Rehoboam, violated many of the ancient traditions, the northern tribes revolted. The reason they gave for this rebellion was the injustice of the monarchy, but in fact they sought to recapture the simple ways of the generation that had escaped from Egypt. Then there had been no monarch, and leadership was exercised on the basis of charisma. What the north looked for was allegiance and loyalty to the King of Kings, who had brought them from Egyptian bondage into the Promised Land. It is against this background that the pre-exilic prophets (Elijah, Elisha, Amos, Hosea, Micah and Isaiah) endeavoured to bring the nation back to the true worship of God. Righteousness, they declared, is the standard by which all people are to be judged, especially kings and rulers.

During the first millennium BC the Jews watched their country emerge as a powerful state only to see it sink into spiritual and moral decay. Following the Babylonian conquest in 586 BC the Temple lay in ruins, Jerusalem was demolished, and they despaired of their fate. This was God's punishment for their iniquity, which the prophets had predicted. Yet despite defeat and exile, the nation rose phoenix-like from the ashes of the old kingdoms. In the centuries which followed, the Jewish people continued their religious traditions and communal life. Though they had lost their independence, their devotion to God and his law sustained them through suffering and hardship and inspired them to new heights of creativity. In Babylonia the exiles flourished, keeping their religion alive in the synagogues. These institutions were founded so that Jews could meet together for worship and study; no sacrifices were offered since that was the prerogative of the Jerusalem Temple. When in 538 BC King Cyrus of Persia permitted the Jews to return to their former home, the nation underwent a transformation. The Temple was rebuilt and religious reforms were enacted. This return to the land of their fathers led to national restoration and a renaissance of Jewish life which was to last until the first century AD.

The period following the death of King Herod in 4 BC was a time of intense anti-Roman feeling among the Jewish population in Judea as well as in the diaspora. Eventually such hostility led to war, only to be followed by defeat and the destruction, once again, of the Jerusalem Temple. In AD 70, thousands of Jews were deported. Such devastation, however, did not quell the Jewish hope of ridding the Holy Land of its Roman oppressors. In the second century a messianic rebellion led by Simon Bar Kosiba was crushed by Roman forces, who killed multitudes of Jews and decimated Judea. Yet despite this defeat, the Pharisees carried on the Jewish tradition through teaching and study at Javneh, near Jerusalem.

Rabbinic Judaism

From the first century BC Palestinian rabbinic scholars engaged in the interpretation of Scripture. The most important scholar of the early rabbinic period was Judah ha-Nasi, the head of the Sanhedrin, whose main achievement was the redaction of the *Mishnah* (a compendium of the oral *Torah*) in the second century AD. This volume consisted of the discussions and rulings of sages whose teachings had been transmitted orally. According to the rabbis, the law recorded in the *Mishnah* was given orally to

Moses along with the written law: 'Moses received the *Torah* from Sinai, and handed it down to Joshua, and Joshua to the elders, and elders to the prophets to the men of the Great Assembly'. This view recorded in the *Mishnah* implies that there was an infallible chain of transmission from Moses to the leaders of the nation and eventually to the Pharisees.

The *Mishnah* is an almost entirely legal document, consisting of six sections. The first section ('Seeds') begins with a discussion of benedictions and required prayers and continues with the other tractates dealing with various matters such as the tithes of the harvest to be given to priests, Levites and the poor. The second section ('Set Feasts') contains twelve tractates dealing with the Sabbath, Passover, the Day of Atonement and other festivals as well as shekel dues and the proclamation of the New Year. In the third section ('Women') seven tractates consider matters affecting women, such as betrothal, marriage contracts and divorce. The fourth section ('Damages') contains ten tractates concerning civil law: property rights, legal procedures, compensation for damage, ownership of lost objects, treatment of employees, sale and purchase of land, Jewish courts, punishments and criminal proceedings. In addition a tractate of rabbinic moral maxims ('Sayings of the Fathers') is included in this section. In the fifth section ('Holy Things') there are eleven tractates on sacrificial offerings and other Temple matters. The final section ('Purifications') treats the various types of ritual uncleanliness and methods of legal purification. In addition to the *Mishnah*, the rabbis engaged in the composition of scriptual commentaries. This literature (known as *midrash*) was written over centuries and is divided into works connected directly with the books of the Bible and those dealing with readings for special festivals as well as other topics.

The Sanhedrin, which had been so fundamental in the compilation of the *Mishnah*, met in several cities in Galilee, but later settled in the Roman district of Tiberius. Simultaneously other scholars established their own schools in other parts of the country where they applied the *Mishnah* to everyday life, together with old rabbinic teachings which had not been incorporated in the *Mishnah*. During the third century the Roman Empire encountered numerous difficulties, including inflation, population decline and a lack of technological development to support the army. In addition, rival generals struggled against one another for power, and the government became increasingly inefficient. Throughout this time of upheaval, the Jewish community underwent a similar decline as a result of famine, epidemics and plunder.

At the end of the third century the emperor Diocletian inaugurated reforms that strengthened the empire. In addition, Diocletian introduced measures to repress the spread of Christianity which had become a serious challenge to the official religion of the empire. But Diocletian's successor, Constantine the Great, reversed his predecessor's hostile stance and extended official toleration to Christians. By this stage Christianity had succeeded in gaining a substantial number of adherents among the urban population; eventually Constantine became more involved in Church affairs and just before his death he himself was baptized. The Christianization of the empire continued throughout the century and by the early 400s, Christianity was fully established as the state religion.

By the first half of the fourth century Jewish scholars in Israel had collected together the teachings of generations of rabbis in the academies of Tiberius, Caesarea and Sepphoris. These extended discussions of the *Mishnah* became the Palestinian *Talmud*. The text of this multi-volume work covered four sections of the *Mishnah* ('Seeds', 'Set Feasts', 'Women' and 'Damages') but here and there various tractates were omitted. The views of these Palestinian teachers had an important influence on scholars in Babylonia, though this work never attained the same prominence as that of the Babylonian *Talmud*.

Paralleling the development of rabbinic Judaism in Palestine, Babylonian scholars founded centres of learning. The great third century teacher Rav established an academy at Sura in central Mesopotamia; his contemporary Samuel was head of another Babylonian academy at Nehardea. After Nehardea was destroyed in an invasion in AD 259, the school at Pumbeditha also became a dominant Babylonian academy of Jewish learning. The Babylonian sages carried on and developed the Galilean tradition of disputation, and the fourth century produced two of the most distinguished scholars of the talmudic period, Abbaye and Rava, who both taught at Pumbeditha. With the decline of Jewish institutions in Israel, Babylonia became the most important centre of Jewish scholarship.

By the sixth century Babylonian scholars completed the

redaction of the Babylonian *Talmud* – an editorial task begun by Rav Ashi in the fourth to fifth century at Sura. This massive work parallels the Palestinian *Talmud* and is largely a summary of the rabbinic discussions that took place in the Babylonian academies. Both *Talmuds* are essentially elaborations of the *Mishnah*, though neither commentary contains material on every *Mishnah* passage. The text itself consists largely of summaries of rabbinic discussions: a phrase of the *Mishnah* is interpreted, discrepancies are resolved and redundancies are explained. In this compilation, conflicting opinions of the earlier scholars are contrasted, unusual words are explained and anonymous opinions are identified. Frequently individual teachers cite specific cases to support their views and hypothetical eventualities are examined to reach a solution on the discussion. Debates between outstanding scholars in one generation are often cited, as are differences of opinion between contemporary members of an academy or a teacher and his students. The range of talmudic exploration is much broader than that of the *Mishnah* itself and includes a wide range of rabbinic teachings about such subjects as theology, philosophy and ethics.

Judaism in the Middle Ages

By the sixth century the Jews had become largely a diaspora people. Despite the loss of a homeland, they were unified by a common heritage: law, liturgy and shared traditions bound together the scattered communities stretching from Spain to Persia and Poland to Africa. Though subcultures did form during the Middle Ages which could have divided the Jewish world, Jews remained united in their hope for messianic redemption, the restoration of the Holy Land, and an ingathering of the exiles. Living amongst Christians and Muslims, the Jewish community was reduced to a minority group and their marginal status resulted in repeated persecution. Though there were times of tolerance and creative activity, the threats of exile and death were always present in Jewish consciousness during this period.

Within the Islamic world, Jews along with Christians were recognized as 'Peoples of the Book' and were guaranteed religious toleration, judicial autonomy and exemption from the military. In turn they were required to accept the supremacy of the Islamic state. Such an arrangement was formally codified by the Pact of Omar dating from about 800. According to this treaty, Jews were restricted in a number of spheres: they were not allowed to build new houses of worship, make converts, carry weapons or ride horses. In addition, they were required to wear distinctive clothing and pay a yearly poll tax. Jewish farmers were also obliged to pay a land tax consisting of a portion of their produce. Despite these conditions, Jewish life prospered. In various urban centres many Jews were employed in crafts such as tanning, dyeing, weaving, silk manufacture and metal work; other Jews participated in inter-regional trade and established networks of agents and representatives.

During the first two centuries of Islamic rule under the Ummayad and Abbasid caliphates, Muslim leaders confirmed the authority of traditional Babylonian institutions. When the Arabs conquered Babylonia, they officially recognized the position of the exilarch who for centuries had been the ruler of Babylonian Jewry. By the Abbasid period, the exilarch shared his power with the heads of the rabbinical academies which had for centuries been the major centres of rabbinic learning. The head of each academy was known as the *gaon*, who delivered lectures as well as learned opinions on legal matters.

During the eighth century messianic movements appeared in the Persian Jewish community which led to armed uprisings against Muslim authorities. Such revolts were quickly crushed, but an even more serious threat to traditional Jewish life was posed later in the century by the emergence of an anti-rabbinic sect, the Karaites. This group was founded in Babylonia in the 760s by Anan ben David. The guiding interpretative principle formulated by Anan, 'Search thoroughly in Scripture and do not rely on my opinion', was intended to point to Scripture itself as the source of law. After the death of the founder, new parties within the Karaite movement soon emerged, and by the tenth century Karaite communities were established in Israel, Iraq and Persia. The growth of Karaism provoked the rabbis to attack it as a heretical movement since these various groups rejected rabbinic law and formulated their own legislation.

By the eighth century the Muslim empire began to undergo a process of disintegration; this process was accompanied by a decentralization of rabbinic Judaism. The academies of

Babylonia began to lose their hold on the Jewish scholarly world, and in many places rabbinic schools were established in which rabbinic sources were studied. The growth of these local centres of scholarship enabled individual teachers to exert their influence on Jewish learning independent of the academies of Sura and Pumbeditha. In the Holy Land, Tiberias was the location of an important rabbinical academy as well as the centre of the masoretic scholars who produced the standard text of the Bible. In Egypt Kairouan and Fez became centres of scholarship. But it was in Spain that the Jewish community attained the greatest level of achievement in literature, philosophy, theology and mysticism.

In their campaigns the Muslims did not manage to conquer all of Europe – many countries remained under Christian rule, as did much of the Byzantine empire. In Christian Europe Jewish study took place in a number of important towns such as Mainz and Worms in the Rhineland and Troyes and Sens in northern France. In such an environment the study of the *Talmud* reached great heights: in Germany and northern France scholars known as 'the tosafists' utilized new methods of talmudic interpretation. In addition, Ashkenazic Jews of this period composed religious poetry modelled on the liturgical compositions of fifth- and sixth-century Israel.

Despite such an efflorescence of Jewish life, the expulsion of the Jews from countries in which they lived became a dominant policy of Christian Europe. In 1182 the king of France expelled all Jews from the royal domains near Paris, cancelled nearly all Christian debts to Jewish moneylenders, and confiscated Jewish property. Though the Jews were recalled in 1198, they were burdened with an additional royal tax and in the next century they increasingly became the property of the king. In thirteenth-century England the Jews were continuously taxed and the entire Jewish population was expelled in 1290, as was that in France some years later. At the end of the thirteenth century the German Jewish community suffered violent attack. In the next century Jews were blamed for bringing about the Black Death by poisoning the wells of Europe, and from 1348–9 Jews in France, Switzerland, Germany and Belgium suffered at the hands of their Christian neighbours. In the following two centuries Jewish massacre and expulsion became a frequent occurrence. Prominent Spanish Jewish thinkers of this period were Solomon ibn Gabirol, Bahya ibn Pakuda, Judah Halevi, Moses Maimonides, Hasdai Crescas, and Joseph Albo. During this period the major mystical work of Spanish Jewry, the *Zohar*, was composed by Moses de Leon.

Jewry in the early modern period

By the end of the fourteenth century political instability in Christian Europe led to the massacre of many Jewish communities in Castile and Aragon. Fearing for their lives, thousands of Jews converted to Christianity in 1391. Two decades later Spanish rulers introduced the Castilian laws which segregated Jews from their Christian neighbours. In the following year a public disputation was held in Tortosa about the doctrine of the Messiah; as a result increased pressure was applied to the Jewish population to convert. Those who became apostates (*marranos*) found life much easier, but by the fifteenth century, anti-Jewish sentiment again became a serious problem. In 1480 King Ferdinand and Queen Isabella established the Inquisition to determine whether former Jews practised Judaism in secret. In the late 1480s inquisitors used torture to extract confessions, and in 1492 the entire Jewish community was expelled from Spain. In the next century the Inquisition was established in Portugal.

To escape such persecution many Spanish and Portuguese *marranos* sought refuge in various parts of the Ottoman empire. Some of these Sephardic immigrants prospered and became part of the Ottoman court, such as Dona Gracia and her nephew Joseph Nasi. Prominent among the rabbinic scholars of this period was Joseph ben Ephraim Caro who emigrated from Spain to the Balkans. In the 1520s he commenced a study of Jewish law, *The House of Joseph*, based on previous codes of Jewish law. In addition he composed a shorter work, the *Shulhan Arukh*, which became the authoritative code of law in the Jewish world.

While working on the *Shulhan Arukh*, Caro emigrated to Safed in Israel which had become a major centre of Jewish religious life. In the sixteenth century this small community had grown to a population of over 10,000 Jews. Here talmudic academies were established and small groups engaged in the study of kabbalistic (mystical) literature as they piously awaited the coming of the

Messiah. In this centre of kabbalistic activity one of the greatest mystics of Safed, Moses Cordovero, collected, organized and interpreted the teachings of earlier mystical authors. Later in the sixteenth century kabbalistic speculation was transformed by the greatest mystic of Safed, Isaac Luria.

By the beginning of the seventeenth century Lurianic mysticism had made an important impact on Sephardic Jewry, and messianic expectations had also become a central feature of Jewish life. In this milieu the arrival of self-proclaimed messianic king, Shabbetai Tzevi, brought about a transformation of Jewish life and thought. After living in various cities, he travelled to Gaza where he encountered Nathan Benjamin Levi who believed he was the Messiah. In 1665 his messiahship was proclaimed and Nathan sent letters to Jews in the diaspora asking them to recognize Shabbetai Tzevi as their redeemer. In the following year Shabbetai journeyed to Constantinople, but on the order of the grand vizier he was arrested and put into prison. Eventually he was brought to court and given the choice between conversion and death. In the face of this alternative he converted to Islam. Such an act of apostasy scandalized most of his followers, but others continued to revere him as the Messiah. In the following century the most important Shabbetan sect was led by Jacob Frank who believed himself to be the incarnation of Shabbetai.

During this period Poland had become a great centre of scholarship. In Polish academies scholars collected together the legal interpretations of previous authorities and composed commentaries on the *Shulhan Arukh*. To regulate Jewish life in the country at large Polish Jews established regional federations that administered Jewish affairs. In the midst of this general prosperity, the Polish Jewish community was subject to a series of massacres carried out by the Cossacks of the Ukraine, Crimean Tartars and Ukrainian peasants. In 1648 Bogdan Chmielnicki was elected hetman of the Cossacks and instigated an insurrection against the Polish gentry. As administrators of noblemen's estates, Jews were slaughtered in these revolts.

As the century progressed, Jewish life in Poland became increasingly more insecure due to political instability; none the less the Jewish community increased in size considerably during the eighteenth century. In the 1730s and 1740s Cossacks known as Haidemaks invaded the Ukraine, robbing and murdering Jewish inhabitants, and finally butchering the Jewish community of Uman in 1768. In Lithuania on the other hand, Jewish life flourished and Vilna became an important centre of Jewish learning. Here Elijah ben Solomon Zalman, referred to as the Vilna Gaon, lectured to disciples on a wide range of subjects and composed commentaries on rabbinic sources.

Elsewhere in Europe this period witnessed Jewish persecution and oppression. Despite the positive contact between Italian humanists and Jews, Christian anti-Semitism frequently led to persecution and suffering. In the sixteenth century the Counter-Reformation Church attempted to isolate the Jewish community. The *Talmud* was burned in 1553, and two years later Pope Paul IV reinstated the segregationist edict of the Fourth Lateran Council, forcing Jews to live in ghettos and barring them from most areas of economic life. In addition, *marranos* who took up the Jewish tradition were burned at the stake, and Jews were expelled from most Church domains.

In Germany the growth of Protestantism frequently led to adverse conditions for the Jewish population. Though Martin Luther was initially well disposed to the Jews, he soon came to realize that the Jewish community was intent on remaining true to its faith. As a consequence he composed a virulent attack on the Jews. None the less some Jews, known as Court Jews, attained positions of great importance among the German nobility. A number of these favoured individuals were appointed by the rulers as chief elders of the Jewish community and acted as spokesmen and defenders of German Jewry.

In Holland some Jews had also attained an important influence on trade and finance. By the mid-seventeenth century both *marranos* and Ashkenazi Jews came to Amsterdam and established themselves in various areas of economic activity. By the end of the century there were nearly 10,000 Jews in Amsterdam; there the Jewish community was employed on the stock exchange, in the sugar, tobacco and diamond trades, and in insurance, manufacturing, printing and banking. In this milieu Jewish cultural activity flourished: Jewish writers published works of drama, theology and mystical lore. Though Jews in Holland were not granted full rights as citizens, they nevertheless enjoyed religious freedom, personal protection and the liberty of participating in a wide range of economic affairs.

Jews in the modern world

By the middle of the eighteenth century the Jewish community had suffered numerous waves of persecution and was deeply dispirited by the conversion of the seventeenth-century false messiah Shabbetai Tzevi. In this environment the Hasidic movement – grounded in *kabbalah* (Jewish mysticism) – sought to revitalize Jewish life. The founder of this new sect was Israel ben Eleazer, known as the Baal Shem Tov (*Besht*). Born in southern Poland, he travelled to Medzibozh in Polodia, Russia in the 1730s, where he performed various miracles and instructed his disciples in kabbalistic lore. By the 1740s he attracted a considerable number of disciples who passed on his teaching. After his death, Dov Baer became the leader of his sect and Hasidism spread to southern Poland, the Ukraine and Lithuania. The growth of this movement engendered considerable hostility on the part of rabbinic authorities, and by the end of the century the Jewish religious establishment of Vilna denounced Hasidism to the Russian government.

During the latter part of the century the treatment of Jews in Central Europe greatly improved due to the influence of Christian polemicists who argued that Jewish life should be improved. The Holy Roman Emperor Joseph II embraced such views; he abolished the Jewish badge as well as taxes imposed on Jewish travellers and proclaimed an edict of toleration which granted the Jews numerous rights. As in Germany, reformers in France during the 1770s and 1780s ameliorated the situation of the Jewish population. In 1789 the National Assembly issued a declaration stating that all human beings are born and remain free and equal and that no person should be persecuted for his opinions as long as they do not subvert civil law. In 1791 a resolution was passed which bestowed citizenship rights on all Jews. This change in Jewish status occurred elsewhere in Europe as well – in 1796 the Dutch Jews of the Batviaan republic were granted full citizenship rights, and in 1797 the ghettos of Padua and Rome were abolished.

In 1799 Napoleon became the First Consul of France and five years later he was proclaimed Emperor. Napoleon's Code of Civil Law propounded in 1804 established the right of all individuals to follow any trade and declared equality for all. After 1806 a number of German principalities were united in the

French kingdom of Westphalia, where Jews were granted equal rights. In the same year Napoleon convened an Assembly of Jewish notables to consider a series of religious issues.

In the following year he summoned a Grand Sanhedrin consisting of rabbis and laymen to confirm the views of the Assembly. This body pledged its allegiance to the Emperor and nullified any features of the Jewish traditions that conflicted with the particular requirements of citizenship.

After Napoleon's defeat and abdication, the map of Europe was redrawn by the Congress of Vienna between 1814–15, and in addition the diplomats at the Congress issued a resolution that instructed the German confederation to improve the status of the Jews. Yet despite this decree the German governments disowned the rights of equality that had previously been granted to Jews by the French. In 1830, however, a more liberal attitude prevailed, and various nations advocated a more tolerant approach. The French revolution of 1848 which led to outbreaks in Prussia, Austria, Hungary, Italy and Bohemia forced rulers to grant constitutions which guaranteed freedom of speech, assembly and religion.

Within this environment Jewish emancipation gathered force. At the end of the eighteenth century the Jewish philosopher Moses Mendelssohn advocated the modernization of Jewish life, and to further this advance he translated the Pentateuch into German so that Jews would be able to speak the language of the country in which they lived. Following Mendelssohn's example a number of Prussian followers, known as *maskilim*, fostered a Jewish Enlightenment – the *Haskalah* – which encouraged Jews to abandon medieval forms of life and thought. By the 1820s the centre of this movement shifted to the Austrian Empire, where journals propounding the ideas of the Enlightenment were published. In the 1840s the *Haskalah* spread to Russia where writers made important contributions to Hebrew literature and translated textbooks and European fiction into Hebrew.

Paralleling this development, reformers encouraged the modernization of the Jewish liturgy and the reform of Jewish education. At the beginning of the nineteenth century the Jewish financier and communal leader Israel Jacobson initiated a programme of reform. In 1801 he founded a boarding school for boys in Seesen, Westphalia, and later created other schools throughout the kingdom. In these new foundations general subjects were taught by Christian teachers while a Jewish instructor gave lessons about Judaism. Subsequently, Jacobson built a Reform Temple next to the school and another in Hamburg. Although such changes were denounced by the Orthodox establishment, Reform Judaism spread throughout Europe. In 1844 the first Reform Synod took place in Brunswick; this consultation was followed by another conference in 1845 in Frankfurt. At this gathering one of the more conservative rabbis, Zecharias Frankel, expressed dissatisfaction with progressive reforms to Jewish worship, and resigned from the Assembly, establishing a Jewish theological seminary in Breslau. In 1846 a third Synod took place at Breslau, but the revolution and its aftermath brought about the cessation of these activities until 1868 when another Synod took place at Cassel.

In the United States, Reform Judaism had also become an important feature of Jewish life. The most prominent of the early reformers was Isaac Mayer Wise who came from Bavaria to Albany, New York, in 1846. Later he went to Cincinnati, Ohio, where he published a new Reform prayer book as well as several Jewish newspapers. In addition he attempted to convene a Reform Synod. In 1869 the first Conference of the Central Conference of American Rabbis was held in Philadelphia; this was followed in 1873 by the founding of the Union of American Hebrew Congregations. Two years later the Hebrew Union College was established to train rabbinical students for the Reform congregations. In 1885 a Conference of Reform rabbis met in Pittsburgh, which produced a formal list of principles, the Pittsburgh Platform.

In Eastern Europe conditions were less conducive to emancipation. In 1804 Alexander I specified territory in western Poland as an area in which Jews would be allowed to reside (the Pale of Settlement). After several attempts to expel Jews from the countryside, the Tsar in 1817 initiated a new policy of integrating the Jewish community into the population by founding a society of Israelite Christians which extended legal and financial concessions to baptized Jews. In 1824 the deportation of Jews from villages began. In the same year Alexander I died and was succeeded by Nicholas I who adopted a severe attitude to the Jewish community. In 1827 he initiated a policy of inducting

Jewish boys into the Russian army for a twenty-five year period to increase the number of converts to Christianity. Nicholas I also deported Jews from villages in certain areas. In 1844 the Tsar abolished the *kehillot* (Jewish communal bodies) and put Jewry under the authority of the police as well as municipal government. Between 1850 and 1851 the government attempted to forbid Jewish dress, men's sidecurls, and the ritual shaving of women's hair. After the Crimean War of 1853–6 Alexander II emancipated the serfs, modernized the judiciary and established a system of local self-government. In addition he allowed certain groups to reside outside the Pale of Settlement. As a result Jewish communities appeared in St Petersburg and Moscow. Furthermore a limited number of Jews were allowed to enter the legal profession and participate in local government.

Jews in the twentieth century

After the pogroms of 1881–2 many Jews emigrated to the United States, but a significant number were drawn to Palestine. By the late 1880s the idea of a Jewish homeland had spread throughout Europe. At the first Zionist Congress at Basle in 1887 Theodor Herzl called for a national home based on international law. After establishing the basic institutions of the Zionist movement, Herzl embarked on a range of diplomatic negotiations. At the beginning of the twentieth century a sizeable number of Jews had emigrated to Palestine. After World War One Jews in Palestine organized a National Assembly and an Executive Council. By 1929 the Jewish community numbered 160,000 with 110 agricultural settlements. In the next ten years the population increased to 500,000 with 223 agricultural communities. About a quarter of this population lived in co-operatives. Tel Aviv had 150,000 settlers, Jerusalem 90,000 and Haifa 60,000. Industrialization was initiated by the Palestinian Electric Corporation and developed by the Histadrut. In 1925 the Hebrew University was opened. During this period Palestine was 160 miles long and 70 miles wide; its population was composed of about one million Arabs consisting of peasants and a number of landowners, in addition to the Jewish population. In 1929 the Arab community rioted following a dispute concerning Jewish access to the Western Wall of the ancient Temple.

This conflict caused the British to curtail Jewish immigration as well as the purchase of Arab land.

By the 1920s Labour Zionism had become the dominant force in Palestinian Jewish life; in 1930 various socialist and Labour groups joined together in the Israel Labour Party. Within the Zionist movement a right-wing segment criticized the President of the World Zionist Organization, Chaim Weizmann, who was committed to co-operation with the British. Vladimir Jabotinsky, leader of the Union of Zionist Revisionists, stressed that the central aim of the Zionist movement was the establishment of an independent state in the whole of Palestine. At several Zionist Congresses, the Revisionists founded their own organization and withdrew from the militia of the Haganah to form their own military force. In 1936 the Arabs, supported by Syria, Iraq and Egypt, launched an offensive against Jews, the British, and moderate Arabs. In 1937 a British Royal Commission proposed that Palestine be partitioned into a Jewish and Arab state with a British zone; this recommendation was accepted by Zionists but rejected by the Arabs. Eventually the British government published a White Paper in 1939 which rejected the concept of partition, limited Jewish immigration to 75,000 and decreed that Palestine would become independent in ten years.

As these events unfolded in the Middle East, Jews in Germany were confronted by increasing hostility, amounting to antipathy. Once the Nazis gained control of the government they curtailed civil liberties. In 1935 the Nuremburg Laws made Jews into second class citizens, and all inter-marriage and sexual liaisons between Jews and non-Jews were described as crimes against the state. In 1938 Jewish community leaders were put under control of the Gestapo, and Jews were forced to register their property. On the 9th to the 10th of November of that year, the Nazi party organized an onslaught against the Jewish population in which Jews were killed and Jewish property destroyed. This event, known as *Kristallnacht*, was a prelude to the Holocaust and precipitated the next stage of hostility.

The first stage of the Nazis' plan for European Jewry had already begun with the invasion of Poland. In September 1939 Hitler decided to incorporate much of Poland into Germany, and more than 600,000 Jews were gathered into a large area in Poland. When the Jewish population was ghettoized into what

Hitler referred to as a huge Polish labour camp, a massive work programme was initiated. Jews worked all day, seven days a week, dressed in rags and fed on bread, soup and potatoes. Officially, these workers had no names, only numbers tattooed on their bodies; if one died, a replacement was sought without any inquest into the cause of death.

With the invasion of Russia in 1941 the Nazis used mobile killing battalions of 500–900 men (*Einsatzgruppen*) to destroy Russian Jewry. Throughout the country these units moved into Russian towns, sought out the rabbi or Jewish court and obtained a list of all Jewish inhabitants. The Jews were then rounded up in market places, crowded into trains, buses and trucks and taken to woods where graves had been dug. They were then machine-gunned to death. Other methods were also employed by the Nazis. Mobile gas units were supplied to the *Einsatzgruppen*. Meanwhile these mobile killing operations were being supplanted by the development of fixed centres – the death camps. The six major death camps constituted the major areas of killing. Over 2,000,000 died at Auschwitz; 1,380,000 at Majdanek; 800,000 at Treblinka; 600,000 at Belzec; 340,000 at Chelmno and 250,000 at Sobibor.

Despite acts of resistance against the Nazis such as occurred in 1942 in Warsaw, 6,000,000 Jews died in this onslaught. In Poland more than 90% of Jews were killed (3,300,000). The same percentage of the Jewish population died in the Baltic states, Germany and Austria. More than 70% were murdered in the Bohemian protectorate, Slovakia, Greece and the Netherlands. More than 50% were killed in White Russia, the Ukraine, Belgium, Yugoslavia and Norway.

During the War and afterwards, the British prevented illegal immigrants from entering the Holy Land. Campaigning against the policy, in 1946 the Haganah blew up the King David Hotel in Jerusalem, where part of the British administration was housed. Later in the same year the British Foreign Secretary, Ernest Bevin, handed over the Palestinian problem to the United Nations.

On 29th November 1947 the General Assembly of the United Nations endorsed a plan of partition. Once this proposal was endorsed, the Arabs attacked Jewish settlements. In March 1948 David Ben-Gurion read out the Scroll of Independence of the Jewish state. Immediately a government was formed, the Arabs

25

stepped up their assault. Following the War of Independence, armistice talks were held and later signed with Egypt, the Lebanon, Transjordan and Syria. Later President Gamal Abdel Nasser refused Israeli ships access to the Gulf of Aqaba in 1956 and seized the Suez Canal, and formed a pact with Saudi Arabia and various Arab states. In response Israel launched a strike, conquering Sinai and opening the sea route to Aqaba. In 1967 Nasser began another offensive against Israel which resulted in the Six Day War in which Israel emerged victorious. This was followed by another, the Yom Kippur War in 1973, and in the 1980s by an Israeli offensive against the Palestine Liberation Organization in Southern Lebanon in 1982. Although the invasion of Lebanon provoked discord between Israel and her allies as well as controversy in Israel, the Jewish state has held fast to its aim of providing a refuge for all Jews.

Part One

BELIEFS

1

The Unity of God

In the Hebrew Scriptures, the Israelites experienced God as the Lord of history. The most uncompromising expression of his unity is the *Shema* prayer: 'Hear, O Israel, the Lord, our God, is one Lord' (Deut. 6.4). According to Scripture, the universe owes its existence to the one God, the creator of heaven and earth, and since all human beings are created in his image, all men and women are brothers and sisters. Thus the belief in one God implies for the Jewish faith that there is one humanity and one world. Jewish biblical teaching emphasizes that God alone is to be worshipped. As Isaiah declared:

> I am the Lord, and there is no other,
> besides me there is no God; . . .
> I form light and create darkness,
> I make weal and create woe,
> I am the Lord, who do all these things (Isa. 45.5,7).

Within the Bible the struggle against polytheism was a dominant motif, continuing into the rabbinic period. Combating the dualistic doctrine that there are two gods in heaven, the rabbis commented on Deuteronomy 32.39, ('See now that I, even I, am he, and there is no god beside me'): 'If anyone says that there are two powers in Heaven the retort is given to him: "There is no god with Me" '. In a passage in the *Mekhilta* (*midrash* on Exodus), dualism is rejected since when God said, 'I am the Lord your God' (Exod. 20.2) no one protested. Again the *Mishnah* states that if a person says in his prayers, 'We acknowledge Thee, we acknowledge Thee', implying belief in two gods, he is to be silenced. Although dualistic tendencies are reflected in the doctrines of Satan and Metatron, and in kabbalistic theories about the demonic realm (*Sitra Ahra*), Jewish monotheism became the central tenet of traditional Judaism.

In the early rabbinic period Jewish sages were troubled by the Christian doctrine of the incarnation, which they viewed as dualistic in character. In third century Caesarea for example, R. Abahu commented on the verse, 'God is not man, that he should lie, or a son of man, that he should repent. Has he said, and will he not do it? Or has he spoken, and will he not fulfil it?' (Num. 23.19). According to R. Abahu, the last part of this verse refers to man rather than God. Thus he declared: 'If a man says to you, "I am a god", he is lying; "I am the Son of Man", he will end by being sorry for it; "I am going up to heaven", he will not fulfil what he has said.' Again, in *Exodus Rabbah* (*midrash* on Exodus) R. Abahu states: ' "I am the first" for I have no father; "and I am the last", for I have no brother; "and besides Me there is no God", for I have no son.'

In the Middle Ages the Christian doctrine of the Trinity was frequently attacked by Jewish scholars since it appeared to undermine pure monotheism. In contrast to Christian exegetes who interpreted the *Shema* with its three references to God as denoting the Trinity, Jewish scholars maintained that the *Shema* implies that there is only one God, rather than Three Persons of the Godhead. For medieval Jewish theology the belief in divine unity was a fundamental principle of Judaism. For a number of Jewish theologians the concept of God's unity implies that there can be no multiplicity in his being. Thus the tenth century philosopher Saadiah Gaon insisted in *The Book of Beliefs and Opinions* that the Divine Creator is a single incorporeal Being who created the universe out of nothing. Like the Islamic Mutazilite theologians, he asserted that if God has a plurality of attributes he must be composite in nature. Thus, such terms as 'life', 'omnipotence' and 'omniscience' should be understood as implications of the concept of God as Creator rather than attributes of the Deity. According to Saadiah, the reason why we are forced to describe God by means of these descriptions is because of the limitations of language, but they do not in any way involve plurality in God. In this light Saadiah argued that the anthropomorphic expressions in the Bible must not be taken literally, since this would imply that God is a plurality.

Another thinker of this period, Solomon ben Joseph ibn Gabirol (eleventh century), argued that God and matter are not opposed as two ultimate principles – instead matter is identical with God. It emanates from the essence of the Creator, forming the basis of all subsequent emanations. For ibn Gabirol the universe consists of cosmic existences flowing out of the superabundant light and goodness of the Creator; it is a reflection of God, though God remains in himself and does not enter his creation with his essence. In a poem, 'Religious Crown', ibn Gabirol uses neo-Platonic images to describe God's activity:

Thou art One, the beginning of all computation,
the base of all construction,
Thou art One, and in the mystery of thy
Oneness the wise of heart are astonished,
for they know not what it is.
Thou art One, and thy Oneness neither diminishes
nor increases, neither lacks nor exceeds.
Thou art One, but not as the one that is counted
or owned, for number and chance cannot
reach thee, nor attribute, nor form.

This insistence on God's unity was a theme of the twelfth century philosopher Abraham ben David Halevi ibn Daud, who in *The Exalted Faith* derives God's absolute unity from his necessary existence. For ibn Daud this concept of divine oneness precludes the possibility of any positive attributes of God. Similarly Moses Maimonides in the same century argued in the *Guide for the Perplexed* that no positive attributes can be predicated of God since the Divine is an absolute unity. Thus when God is described positively in the Bible, such ascriptions refer to his activity. The only true attributes are negative ones; they lead to a knowledge of God because in negation no plurality is involved. Each negative attribute excludes from God's essence some imperfection.

In the Middle Ages kabbalistic belief in divine unity was also a central doctrine. The early kabbalists of Provence and Spain referred to the Divine Infinite as *Ayn Sof* – the absolute perfection in which there is no distinction or plurality. The *Ayn Sof* does not reveal itself; it is beyond all thought. In kabbalistic thought, creation is bound up with the manifestation of the hidden God and his outward movement. According to the *Zohar*, a mystical work of the time, the *sefirot* (divine emanations) come successively from above to below, each one revealing a stage in the process. The common order of the *sefirot* and the names most generally used are: (1) supreme crown; (2) wisdom; (3) intelligence; (4) greatness; (5) power; (6) beauty;

(7) endurance; (8) majesty; (9) foundation; (10) kingdom. These ten *sefirot* together demonstrate how an infinite, undivided and unknowable God is the cause of all the modes of existence in the finite plane.

In their totality the *sefirot* are frequently represented as a cosmic tree of emanation. It grows from its roots – the first *sefirah* – and spreads downwards in the direction of the lower worlds to the *sefirot* which constitute its trunk and its main branches. Another depiction of the *sefirot* is in the form of a man: the first *sefirah* represents the head; the next three *sefirot* the cavities of the brain; the fourth and fifth *sefirot* the arms; the sixth the torso; the seventh and eighth the legs; the ninth the sexual organ; and the tenth the all-embracing totality of this image. In kabbalistic literature this heavenly man is also divided into two parts – the left column is made up of the female *sefirot* and the right column of the male. Another arrangement presents the *sefirot* as ten concentric circles, a depiction related to medieval cosmology in which the universe is understood as made up of ten spheres.

For the kabbalists the *sefirot* are dynamically structured; through them divine energy flows from its source and separates into individual channels, reuniting in the lowest *sefirah*. These *sefirot* were also understood as divine substances as well as containers of the divine essence; often they are portrayed as flames of fire. Yet despite their individuality, they are unified with the *Ayn Sof* in the moment of creation. According to the *Zohar*, all existences are emanations from the Deity – he is revealed in all things because he is immanent in them: 'He is separated from all things, and is at the same time not separated from all things. There is nothing which is not in Him . . . In assuming a shape, He has given existence to all things. He has made ten lights spring from his midst.' To reconcile this process of emanation with the doctrine of *creatio ex nihilo*, some kabbalists argued that the *Ayn Sof* should be seen as *ayin* (nothingness); thus the manifestation of the divine through the *sefirot* is a self-creation out of divine nothingness. Other kabbalists however maintained that creation does not occur within the Godhead. It takes place at a lower level where created beings are formed independent of God's essence.

The elaboration of these mystical ideas took place in the sixteenth century through the teachings of Isaac Luria. Of primary importance in the Lurianic system is the mystery of creation. In the literature of early kabbalists, creation was understood as a positive act; the will to create was awakened within the Godhead and this resulted in a long process of emanation. For Luria, however, creation was a negative event: the *Ayn Sof* had to bring into being an empty space in which creation could occur since divine light was everywhere leaving no room for creation to take place. This was accomplished by the process of *tzimtzum* – the contraction of the Godhead into itself. Thus the first act was not positive, but rather one that demanded withdrawal. God had to go into exile from the empty space so that the process of creation could be initiated. *Tzimtzum* therefore postulates divine exile as the first step of creation.

After this act of withdrawal a line of light flowed from the Godhead into empty space and took on the shape of the *sefirot* in the form of *Adam Kadmon* (primeval man). In this process divine lights created the vessels – the external shapes of the *sefirot* – which gave specific characteristics to each divine emanation. Yet these vessels were not strong enough to contain such pure light and they shattered. This breaking of the vessels brought disaster and upheaval to the emerging emanations: the lower vessels broke down and fell, the three highest emanations were damaged and the empty space was divided into two parts.

In explaining the purpose of the *tzimtzum*, Luria pointed out that the *Ayn Sof* before creation was not completely unified – there were elements in it that were potentially different from the rest of the Godhead. The *tzimtzum* separated these different elements from one another. After this contraction occurred a residue was left behind like water clinging to a bucket after being emptied. This residue included different elements that were part of the Godhead, and after the withdrawal, they were emptied into the empty space. Thus the separation of different elements from the Godhead was accomplished. The reason for the emanation of the divine powers was the attempt to integrate these now separate elements into the scheme of creation and thereby transform them into co-operative forces. Their task was to create the vessels of the *sefirot* into which the divine lights would flow. But the breaking of the vessels was a rebellion of these different elements, a refusal to participate in the process of creation. For Luria evil is opposed to existence; therefore it is not able to exist by its own power. Instead it has to derive spiritual force from the divine light. This is accomplished by keeping captive the sparks of the divine light that fell with them when the vessels were broken and subsequently gave sustenance to the satanic domain. Divine attempts to bring unity to all existence now have to focus on the struggle to overcome these evil forces.

The Lurianic concept of *tzimtzum* was subsequently embraced by Habad Hasidism, founded by Schneur Zalman of Lyday in the eighteenth century. According to Shneur Zalman, the doctrine of God's unity implies that there is only one God; in other words God is all. From his point of view there are no creatures, only God himself. The multiplicity of objects we observe, as well as we ourselves, are therefore the result of the screening of divine light. This *tzimtzum* does not in fact actually occur; rather the divine light is progressively concealed so that creatures experience existence from their standpoint rather than the divine perspective. On this monistic scheme the multiplicity of things is included in God's unity. It is God alone who embraces all and is in all. Here the doctrine of God's unity is taken to its utmost limit. Although such mystical notions have not been adopted by the mainstream branches of Jewry, the doctrine of God's unity is today accepted within Orthodoxy as well as other branches of the Jewish faith as fundamental to Judaism.

2

Transcendence and Immanence

For Jews, God is conceived as the transcendent creator of the universe. Thus in Genesis 1.1-2 he is described as forming heaven and earth:

> In the beginning God created the heavens and the earth. The earth was without form and void, and darkness was upon the face of the deep; and the Spirit of God was moving over the face of the waters.

Throughout Scripture this theme of divine transcendence is repeatedly affirmed. Thus the prophet Isaiah proclaims:

> Have you not known? Have you not heard?
> Has it not been told you from the beginning?
> Have you not understood from the foundations of the earth?
> It is he who sits above the circle of the earth,
> and its inhabitants are like grasshoppers;
> who stretches out the heavens like a curtain
> and spreads them like a tent to dwell in (Isa. 40.21-2).

Later in the same book Isaiah declares that God is beyond human comprehension:

> For my thoughts are not your thoughts
> neither are your ways my ways, says the Lord.
> For as the heavens are higher than the earth,
> so are my ways higher than your ways
> and my thoughts than your thoughts (Isa. 55.8–9).

In the book of Job the same idea is repeated – God's purposes transcend human understanding:

> Can you find out the deep things of God?
> Can you find out the limit of the Almighty?
> It is higher than heaven – what can you do?
> Deeper than Sheol – what can you know?

Its measure is longer than the earth, and broader than the sea (Job 11.7–9).

According to the author of Ecclesiastes, God is in heaven whereas human beings are confined to earth. Thus the wise person should recognize the limitations of his knowledge:

Be not rash with your mouth, nor let your heart be hasty to utter a word before God, for God is in heaven, and you upon earth; therefore let your words be few (Eccles. 5.2).

Despite this view of God's remoteness from his creation, he is also viewed as actively involved in the cosmos. In the Bible his omnipresence is repeatedly stressed. Thus the Psalmist rhetorically asks:

Whither shall I go from thy Spirit?
Or whither shall I flee from thy presence?
If I ascend to heaven, thou art there!
If I make my bed in Sheol, thou art there!
If I take the wings of the morning
and dwell in the uttermost parts of the sea,
even there thy hand shall lead me (Ps. 139.7–12).

In the rabbinic period Jewish scholars formulated the doctrine of the *Shekhinah* to denote the divine presence. As the indwelling presence of God, the *Shekhinah* is compared to light. Thus the *midrash* paraphrases Numbers 6.25 ('The Lord make his face to shine upon you, and be gracious to you'): 'May he give thee of the light of the *Shekhinah*' (divine presence). In another *midrash* the 'shining' of the *Shekhinah* in the Tent of Meeting is compared to a cave by the sea. When the sea rushes in to fill the cave, it suffers no diminution of its waters. Likewise the divine presence filled the Tent of Meeting, but simultaneously filled the world. In the third century the Babylonian scholar Rab said: 'In the world to come there is no eating nor drinking nor propagation nor business nor jealousy nor hatred nor competition, but the righteous sit with their crowns on their heads and enjoy the brightness of the *Shekhinah*.' Again, the *Talmud* states: 'Come and see how beloved Israel is before God; for wherever they went into exile the *Shekhinah* went with them; in Babylon, the *Shekhinah* was with them and in the future, when Israel will be redeemed, the *Shekhinah* will be with them.'

In the medieval period the doctrine of the *Shekhinah* was further elaborated by Jewish scholars. According to Saadiah Gaon (ninth to tenth century) the *Shekhinah* is identical with the glory of God, which serves as an intermediary between God and man during the prophetic encounter. For Saadiah the 'Glory of God' is a biblical term whereas the *Shekhinah* is a rabbinic concept which refers to the created splendour of light which acts as an intermediary between God and human beings. At times this manifestation takes on human form. Thus when Moses asked to see God's glory, he was shown the *Shekhinah*. Similarly when the prophets in their vision saw God in human form, what they actually perceived was the *Shekhinah*. Such a view avoids compromising God's unity and incorporeality.

Following Saadiah, Judah Halevi (eleventh to twelfth century) argues in the *Kuzari* that it is the *Shekhinah* rather than God himself who appears to prophets. However, unlike Saadiah he does not describe the *Shekhinah* as a created light. Rather he identifies the *Shekhinah* with the divine influence. For Halevi the *Shekhinah* initially dwelt in the Tabernacle; subsequently it was manifest in the Temple. With the cessation of prophecy it ceased to appear, but will return with the Messiah. In his discussion Halevi distinguishes between the visible *Shekhinah* which dwelt in the Temple and appeared to the prophets, and the invisible *Shekhinah* which is 'with every born Israelite of virtuous life, pure heart, and upright mind.'

In his *Guide*, Maimonides (twelfth century) embraces Saadiah's belief that the *Shekhinah* is a created light, identified with glory. In addition, he associates the *Shekhinah* with prophecy. According to Maimonides prophecy is an overflow from God which passes through the mediation of the active intellect and then to the faculty of imagination. It requires perfection in theoretical wisdom, morality and development of the imagination. On the basis of this conception, Maimonides asserted that human beings can be divided into three classes according to the development of their reasoning capabilities. First there are those whose rational faculties are highly developed and receive influences from the active intellect, but whose imagination is defective. These are wise men and philosophers. The second group consists of those where the imagination alone is in good condition, but the intellect is defective – these are statesmen, lawgivers and politicians.

Thirdly there are the prophets – those whose imagination is consistently perfect and whose active intellect is all developed.

In kabbalistic teaching the *Shekhinah* also played an important role. In early kabbalistic thought the *Shekhinah* is identified as the feminine principle in the world of the *sefirot*. Later the *Shekhinah* was understood as the last in the hierarchy of the *sefirot*, representing the feminine principle. Like the moon, this *sefirah* has no light of her own, but instead receives the divine light from the other *sefirot*. The symbolism describing the *Shekhinah* refers to her relationship with the other *sefirot* (such as her acceptance of divine light, her relationship to them as an inferior aspect of themselves, and her coming close to the masculine element in the divine sphere). In addition, other symbols depict the *Shekhinah* as the battleground between the divine powers of good and evil.

As the divine power closest to the created world, she is the medium through which the divine light passes. Further, in kabbalistic thought the *Shekhinah* is the divine principle of the Jewish people. Everything that happens to Israel is reflected upon the *Shekhinah* which grows stronger or is weakened with every meritorious act or sinful act of each Jew and of the people as a whole. Finally the *Shekhinah* is viewed as the goal of the mystic who attempts to achieve communion with the divine powers.

In the early modern period the traditional belief in God's transcendence and immanence was attacked by the seventeenth century heretical Jewish philosopher Benedict Spinoza. In *Tractatus Theological-Politicus* Spinoza propounds a metaphysical system based on a pantheistic conception of nature. Beginning with the belief in an infinite, unlimited, self-caused Substance which he conceives as God or nature, Spinoza maintains that Substance possesses a theroretical infinity of attributes, only two of which – extension and thought – are apprehended by human beings. God or nature can also be seen as a whole made up of finite, individual entities. In this way God exists in all things as their universal essence; they exist in God as modifications.

With the rise of science in the eighteenth century, the traditional belief in divine immanence became more difficult to sustain. None the less Jewish thinkers continued to insist on the validity of the biblical and rabbinic view of God's involvement with the universe. Pre-eminent among those who championed the traditional view was Schneur Zalman (eighteenth century), the founder of the Habad movement of Hasidism. In the *Tanya* he writes:

Here lies the answer to the heretics and here is uncovered the root of their error, in which they deny God's providence over particular things and the miracles and wonders recorded in Scripture. Their false imagination leads them into error, for they compare the work of the Lord, Creator of heaven and earth, to the works of man and his artifices. These stupid folk compare the work of heaven and earth to the vessel which comes from the hands of a craftsman. Once the vessel has been fashioned it requires its maker no longer. Even when the maker has completed his task and goes about his own business, the vessel retains the form and appearance it had when fashioned. Their eyes are too blind to notice the important distinction between the works of man and his artifices – in which 'something' is made from 'something', the form alone being changed from a piece of silver into an ornament – and the creation of heaven and earth, which is the creation of 'something' out of 'nothing'. . . . It follows *a fortiori* that with regard to creation *ex nihilo* . . . it is certain that the creature would revert to the state of nothingness and negation, God forfend, if the Creator's power over it were removed. It is essential, therefore, for the power of the Worker to be in his work constantly if that work is to be kept in existence.

Such an argument has been echoed across the modern Jewish religious spectrum. Religious believers from all groups within the Jewish fold have continued to affirm the biblical and rabbinic doctrine of God's transcendence and immanence. Although some thinkers have argued that God limited his own intervention in the world by allowing human beings to exercise free will, there has been a firm rejection of deistic ideas in which the Deity is perceived as an absentee God. Instead Jews have universally affirmed that the transcendent God is immanent in the universe he has created. The song of the Hasidic master, R. Levi Yitzhak of Berditchev (eighteenth to nineteenth century) is characteristic of Jewish belief through the ages to the present:

Where I wander – You!
Where I ponder – You!
Only you, You again, always You!
You! You! You!
When I am gladdened – You!
When I am saddened – You!
Only You, You again, always You!
You! You! You!

3

Eternity

Throughout Scripture God is described as having neither beginning nor end. Thus the Psalmist declared:

Before the mountains were brought forth,
or ever thou hadst formed the earth and the world,
from everlasting to everlasting thou art God (Ps. 90.2).

Again the prophet Isaiah proclaimed:

Thus says the Lord, the King of Israel,
and his Redeemer, the Lord of hosts:
'I am the first and I am the last;
besides me there is no god' (Isa. 44.6).

In the Bible the term *olam* is most frequently used to denote the concept of God's eternity. In Genesis 21.33 he is described as the Eternal God; he lives for ever (Deut. 32.40), and reigns for ever (Exod. 15.18; Ps. 10.16). He is the living God and everlasting King (Jer. 10.10); his counsel endures for ever (Ps. 33.11) as does his mercy (Ps. 106.1). For the biblical writers, God's eternal existence is different from the rest of creation – he exists permanently without beginning or end.

This biblical teaching was elaborated by the rabbis. According to the *Talmud* there is an unbridgeable gap between God and man: 'Come and see! The measure of the Holy One, blessed be He, is unlike the measure of flesh and blood. The things fashioned by a creature of flesh and blood outlast him; the Holy One, blessed be He, outlasts the things he has fashioned.' In midrashic literature God's eternal reign is similarly affirmed. Thus, according to a *midrash*, when Pharaoh was ordered by Moses and Aaron in the name of God to let the people go, Pharaoh declared that God's name is not found in his list of gods. In reply Moses and Aaron declared: 'O fool! The dead can be sought among the living but how can the living be sought among the dead. Our God lives, but those you mention are

41

dead. Our God is "the living God, and everlasting King" ' (Jer. 10.10). In response Pharaoh asked whether this God is young or old, how old he is, how many cities he has conquered, how many provinces he has subdued, and how long he has been king. In reply they proclaimed: 'The power and might of our God fill the world. He was before the world and was created and he will be when all the world comes to an end and he has created thee and gave thee the spirit of life.'

Again in the *Talmud* it is reported that when Rabban Johanan ben Zakkai (first century AD) was about to die, he wept. When his pupils asked why he cried, he said:

> If I were being taken before a king of flesh and blood who is here today and tomorrow in the grave, whose anger does not last for ever, who cannot imprison me for ever, who cannot kill me for ever even if he sentences me to death, and whom I can persuade and bribe to reconsider his judgment, even so I would weep. Now that I am being taken before the supreme King of kings, the Holy One, blessed be He, who lives and endures for ever and ever, whose anger, if he is angry with me, is everlasting, who if he imprisons me, the imprisonment is for ever, who if he puts me to death, puts me to death for ever, and whom I cannot persuade or bribe . . . shall I not weep?

Although the rabbis were convinced that God would endure for ever, they discouraged speculation about the nature of eternity. Such reluctance is reflected in the *Mishnah's* dictum: 'Whoever reflects on four things, it were better for him that he had not come into the world: What is above? What is beneath? What is before? What is after?' Yet despite such teaching, in the Middle Ages Jewish theologians debated this issue. In the *Guide* Maimonides (twelfth century) argues that time itself was part of creation. Therefore when God is described as existing before the creation of the universe, the notion of time should not be understood in its normal sense:

> In the beginning God alone existed and nothing else; neither angels nor spheres, nor the things that are contained within the spheres existed. He then produced from nothing all existing things such as they are, by his will and desire. Even time itself is among the things created; for time depends on

motion, i.e. on an accident in things which move, and the things upon whose motion time depends are themselves created beings, which have passed from non-existence into existence. We say that God *existed* before the creation of the Universe, although the verb *existed* appears to imply the notion of time; we also believe that he existed in an infinite space of time before the Universe was created; but in these cases we do not mean time in its true sense. We only use the term to signify something analogous or similar to time . . . We consider time a thing created; it comes into existence in the same manner as other accidents, and the substances which form the substratum for the accidents. For this reason, viz., because time belongs to the things created, it cannot be said that God produced the Universe in the beginning.

This concept of time as part of creation was later developed by the fifteenth century Jewish philosopher Joseph Albo. In his *Ikkarim* he maintains that the concepts of priority and perpetuity can only be applied to God in a negative sense. That is, when God is described as being 'before' or 'after' some period, this only means he was not non-existent before or after that time. However, these terms indicating a time span cannot be applied to God himself. Following Maimonides, Albo asserted that there are two types of time: measured time which depends on motion, and time in the abstract. This second type of time has no origin – this is the infinite space of time before the universe was created. Although it is difficult to conceive of God existing in such a duration, it is likewise difficult to imagine God outside space. For this reason, Albo argues, the rabbis state that one should not ask what is above, what is below, what is before, and what is behind.

According to other Jewish thinkers God is outside time altogether – he is in the 'Eternal Now'. Such a view is paralleled in Christian thought. Thus the sixth century Christian Neo-Platonic theologian Boethius wrote in *The Consolation of Philosophy*:

Since God lives in the eternal present, His knowledge transcends all movement of time and abides in the simplicity of its immediate present. It encompasses the infinite sweep of past and future, and regards all things in its simple comprehension as if they were not taking place. Thus, if you think about the foreknowledge by which God distinguishes all things, you will rightly consider it to be not a foreknowledge of future events but knowledge of a never changing present.

In the eleventh century St Anselm similarly states in *Proslogion*: 'Thou wast not, then, yesterday, nor wilt Thou be tomorrow; but yesterday and today and tomorrow Thou art; or rather, neither yesterday and today and tomorrow Thou art; but simply, Thou art, outside all time.'

Within the Jewish tradition similar views were expressed. Thus the thirteenth century theologian Bahya ibn Asher ibn Halawa in his commentary on the Pentateuch discussed the verse, 'The Lord will reign for ever and ever (Exod. 15.18): 'All times, past and future, are in the present so far as God is concerned, for he was before time and is not encompassed by it.' Likewise the sixteenth century scholar Moses Almosnino commented on 'For now I know' (Gen. 22.12). According to Almosnino, God is in the 'Eternal Now' and he uses this notion to explain how God's foreknowledge is not incompatible with human free will. In the eighteenth century the Hasidic teacher Nahman of Bratslav wrote in *Likkute Maharan, Tinyana*:

> God, as is well-known, is above all time. This is a truly marvellous notion, utterly incomprehensible, impossible for the human mind to grasp. You must appreciate, however, that basically time is the product of ignorance, that is to say, time only appears real to us because our intellect is so puny. The greater the mind the smaller and less significant does time become for it. Take, for instance, a dream, in which the mind is dormant and the imaginative faculty takes over. In the dream it is possible for a seventy year span to pass by in a quarter of an hour . . . On awakening, the dreamer senses that the whole seventy year period of the dream occupied in a reality only a fraction of time. This is because man's intellectual capacity has been restored to him in his waking life and so far as his mind is concerned the whole seventy year period of the dream is no more than a quarter of an hour. . . . There is a Mind so elevated that for It the whole of time is counted as naught, for so great is that Mind that for It the whole time span is as nothing whatever. Just as, so far as we are concerned, the seventy years which pass by in the dream are

no more than a quarter of an hour in reality, as we have seen, so it is with regard to that Mind, which is so far above anything we know as mind for It time has no existence at all.

According to this view God is outside time – he does not live in the present, have a past, or look forward to the future. He lives in the Eternal Now. Such a notion is very difficult to understand since it is totally outside the sphere of our experience. According to this view God is experiencing every moment in the past and future history of the created world simultaneously and eternally. What for us are fleeting moments rushing by, bringing one experience after another, are a huge static tapestry for God, of which he sees every part continually. An analogous experience is that of a cinema. When we go to a film, we see shown on the screen the experiences of other people. Almost invariably they are portrayed in the order in which they occurred. But if after the film we go into the room where the film was projected, we would be able to look at the film roll itself (composed of a series of small pictures). When we look at it, we can perhaps have some experience of God's timelessness: we see all these photographs simultaneously which we had previously experienced in a temporal sequence. Such an experience is akin to God's eternal timelessness.

This conception of God's eternity – that he is outside time – and the alternative view that God exists in infinite duration before creation, constitute the two central Jewish interpretations of the Deity's relation to time. Yet for most Jews God's eternal existence is an impenetrable mystery. None the less the doctrine of God's eternity is a major feature of the Jewish faith. Through the centuries Jews have been convinced that God was, is, and for ever will be. Hence in Maimonides' formulation of the thirteen central principles of the Jewish faith, the belief that God is eternal is the fourth tenet: 'This means,' he writes, 'that the unity whom we have described is first in the absolute sense. No existent thing outside Him is primary in relation to him. The proofs of this in the Scriptures are numerous. This fourth principle is indicated by the phrase: "The eternal God is a refuge" (Deut. 33.27)'. In the *Ani Maamin* prayer the fourth principle is formulated as follows: 'I believe with perfect faith that the Creator, blessed be his name, is the first and the last.' And at the conclusion of synagogue services in all branches of

Judaism the faithful voice their commitment that God is eternal in time in the *Adon Olam* prayer:

> He is the Lord of the universe,
> Who reigned ere any creature yet was formed,
> At the time when all things shall have had an end,
> He alone, the dreaded one, shall reign:
> Who was, who is, and who will be in glory.

4

Omnipotence and Omniscience

From biblical times the belief in God's omnipotence has been a central feature of Judaism. Thus in Genesis when Sarah expressed astonishment at the suggestion she should have a child at the age of ninety, she was criticized: 'The Lord said to Abraham, "Why did Sarah laugh, and say 'Shall I indeed bear a child now that I am old?' Is anything too hard for the Lord?" ' (Gen. 18.13–14). Similarly in the book of Jeremiah when the city was threatened by the Chaldeans, God declared: 'Behold, I am the Lord the God of all flesh: is anything too hard for me?' (Jer. 32.27). On such a view there is nothing God cannot do: what appears impossible is within his power.

For the biblical writers as well as the rabbis, this conviction was an essential feature of their faith. However in the Middle Ages, Jewish thinkers wrestled with the concept of divine omnipotence. Pre-eminent among their concerns was the question whether God can do absolutely everything. According to Saadiah Gaon (ninth to tenth century) in his *Beliefs and Opinions*, the soul will not praise God for causing five to be more than ten without further addition, nor for being able to put the world through the hollow of a signet ring without making the world narrower and the ring wider, nor for bringing back the day which has passed in its original state. These would be absurd acts: 'Of course', he writes, 'certain heretics ask us about such matters, and we do indeed answer them that God is able to do everything. This thing, however, that they ask of him is not anything because it is absurd, and the absurd is nothing. It is therefore, as though they were to ask: "Is God capable of doing what is nothing?" '.

Subsequently Moses Maimonides (twelfth century) in his *Guide* explored the same issue. According to Maimonides, although God is all-powerful, there are certain actions that he cannot perform because they are logically impossible:

That which is impossible has a permanent and constant property, which is not the result of some agent, and cannot in any way change, and consequently we do not ascribe to God the power of doing what is impossible . . . it is impossible to produce a square with a diagonal equal to one of its sides, or a solid angle that includes four right angles, or similar things. . . . We have thus shown that according to each one of the different theories there are things which are impossible, whose existence cannot be admitted, and whose creation is excluded from the power of God.

In the thirteenth century Ezra ben Solomon similarly writes in his commentary on the Song of Songs:

The fact that God is unable to bring about what is logically absurd, e.g., creating a square the diagonal of which is equal in length to one of its sides, or asserting and denying the same proportion, does not indicate any deficiency in God's power. Just as this does not indicate any deficiency in his power, so the fact that God cannot cause an emanation of something from nothing does not indicate that God is deficient in any way. This, also, would be logically absurd.

Such theological reflection was paralleled within Christianity. In the *Summa Theologica* Thomas Aquinas (thirteenth century) cautions against assuming that God can do everything:

When you say that God has the power for everything, you are most correctly interpreted as meaning this: that since power is relative to what is possible, divine power can do everything that is possible, and on this account is God called omnipotent . . . . Now it is incompatible with the meaning of absolute possibility that anything involving the contradiction of simultaneously being and not being should be conceived as divine omnipotence . . . . Whatever does not involve a contradiction is in that realm of the possible with respect to which God is called omnipotent. Whatever involves a contradiction is not held by omnipotence, for it just cannot possibly make sense of being possible.

Such medieval reflections were not intended to impose restrictions on God's power; rather these theologians were preoccupied with defining those acts which are logically incoherent. Since they are inherently absurd, they argued, it is impossible to believe that God could perform them. In the twentieth century Jewish theologians have not been preoccupied by such problems. Instead, a number of Jewish thinkers have advanced the doctrine of a limited or finite God. Following Christian writers such as Charles Hartshorne, Jewish writers such as Levi Olan have conceived of God as limited by his own nature. This has been propounded to account for the existence of evil: if God is limited in power, he should not be held responsible for human suffering. God does not desire such a state of affairs – he would eradicate moral and physical evil if he could, but it is not within his power to do so. On this account God should be seen as a partner with human beings in the quest to create a better world. Within Judaism such a conception of a limited God has not gained many adherents: instead most religious believers have continued to accept the traditional doctrine of an all-powerful God who has created the universe and continues to direct its destiny without any limitation.

Paralleling the doctrine of God's omnipotence, Jews throughout the ages have affirmed that God is all-knowing. In the Bible the Psalmist declares:

> The Lord looks down from heaven,
> he sees all the sons of men . . .
> he who fashions the hearts of them all,
> and observes all their deeds. (Ps. 33.13,15)

Again in Psalm 139 we read:

> Thou knowest when I sit down and when I rise up;
> thou discernest my thoughts from afar.
> Thou searchest out my path and my lying down,
> and art acquainted with all my ways. (Ps. 139.2–3)

Following the biblical view, rabbinic Judaism asserted that God's knowledge is not limited by space and time. Rather, nothing is hidden from him. Further, the rabbis declared that God's foreknowledge of events does not deprive human beings of free will. Thus in the *Mishnah*, Akiva (first to second century AD) declares: 'All is foreseen, but freedom of choice is given'.

In his *Guide* Maimonides claims that God knows all things before they occur. None the less human beings are unable to comprehend the nature of God's knowledge because it is of a different order from that of human beings. On this account it is similarly not possible to understand how divine foreknowledge is compatible with human freedom. Other medieval thinkers however were unconvinced by such an explanation. In his *The Wars of the Lord*, the fourteenth century philosopher Gersonides argues that God only knows things in general. The world is thus constituted so that a range of possibilities is open to human beings. Since human beings are able to exercise free will, these are possibilities, rather than certainties (which they would be if God knew them in advance). Thus although God knows all it is possible to know, his knowledge is not all-embracing. He does not know how individuals will respond to the possibilities open to them since they are only possibilities. According to Gersonides, such a view does not undermine God's providential plan. Even though God does not know all future events, he is cognisant of the outcome of the whole process. In the same century the Jewish theologian Hasdai Crescas, however, held a radically different position in his *The Light of the Lord*. For Crescas human beings only appear to be free, but in reality all their deeds are determined by virtue of God's foreknowledge. Thus rather than attempting to reconcile free will and omniscience, he asserts that God's knowledge is absolute and free will is an illusion.

In the modern period the devout have been less concerned about such philosophical issues. Instead there has been a universal reaffirmation of the traditional belief that God knows past, present and future and that human beings have freedom of choice. Thus in his explanation of the Jewish faith, *The Jewish Religion*, the twentieth-century Jewish writer, Michael Friedlander, declares with regard to divine foreknowledge:

His knowledge is not limited, like the knowledge of mortal beings, by space and time. The entire past and future lies unrolled before his eyes, and nothing is hidden from him. Although we may form a faint idea of the knowledge of God by considering that faculty of man that enables him within a limited space of time, to look backward and forward, and to unroll before him the past and the future, as if the events that have happened and those that will come to pass were going on in the present moment, yet the true nature of God's knowledge no man can conceive. 'God considereth all the deeds of man', without depriving him of his free will; he may in this respect be compared to a person who observes and notices the actions and the conduct of his fellow-men, without interfering with them. It is the will of God that man should have free will and should be responsible for his actions; and his foresight does not necessarily include predetermination. In some cases the fate of nations or of individual men is predetermined; we may even say that the ultimate fate or development of mankind is part of the design of the Creation. But as the actual design in the Creation is concealed from man's searching eye, so is also the extent of the predetermination a mystery to him. To solve this problem is beyond the intellectual powers of short-sighted mortals; it is one of 'the hidden things that belong to the Lord our God'.

5

Creation

According to Genesis 1.1–4 God created the universe:

> In the beginning God created the heaven and the earth.
> The earth was without form and void,
> and darkness was upon the face of the deep;
> and the Spirit of God was moving over the face of the waters.
> And God said, 'Let there be light': and there was light.
> And God saw that the light was good.

This belief has become a central feature of the synagogue service – in the synagogue hymn before the reading from the Psalms, for example, God is depicted as the creator of everything:

> Blessed be he who spake, and the world existed:
> Blessed be he;
> Blessed be he who was the Master of the world in the beginning.

In another synagogue hymn the same view is expressed:

> Thou wast the same before the world was created;
> Thou hast been the same since the world hath been created.

In the *Ani Maamin* prayer, the first principle of Jewish faith is formulated as:

> I believe with perfect faith that
> the Creator, blessed be his name, is
> the Author and Guide of everything
> that has been created, and that He alone
> has made, does make, and will make all things.

In rabbinic literature scholars speculated about the manner of the creative process. In *Genesis Rabbah* (*midrash* on Genesis) for example, the idea of the world as a pattern in the mind of God is expressed in relation to the belief that God looked into the *Torah* and created the world. Here the *Torah* is conceived as a type of

52

primordial blueprint. With respect to the order of creation the School of Shammai stated: 'The heavens were created first and then the earth' (following Genesis 1.1). The School of Hillel, in contrast, argued that the heaven and the earth were created simultaneously. In the same text a philosopher said to Rabban Gamaliel: 'Your God is a great craftsman, but he found good materials to help him in the work of creation, namely *tohu* and *vohu*, darkness, spirit, water and the deep.' Rabban Gamaliel (first century AD), however, cited other verses which illustrate that these materials were created by God. In the third century R. Johanan argued that God took two coils, one of fire and the other of snow, wove them into each other, and created the world. According to another rabbinic source, all things were formed at the same time on the first day of creation, but appeared at the other six days just as figs are gathered simultaneously in one basket but each selected individually. Again, in *Genesis Rabbah* the sages stress that God created several worlds, but destroyed them before creating this one. The goal of creation is summed up in the rabbinic claim that whatever the Holy One, blessed be he, created in his world, he created for his glory.

In the Middle Ages a number of Jewish theologians believed that God created the universe *ex nihilo*. The kabbalists, however, interpreted the doctrine of *ex nihilo* in a special sense. God, they maintained, should be understood as the Divine Nothing because as he is in and of himself, nothing can be predicated. The Divine is beyond human understanding. Creation *ex nihilo* thus refers to the creation of the universe out of God, the Divine Nothing. This occurred, they argued, through a series of divine emanations. For the kabbalists the first verses of Genesis allude to the processes within the Godhead prior to the creation of the universe. In Lurianic kabbalah the notion of God creating and destroying worlds before the creation of this world is viewed as referring to spiritual worlds. Thus *tohu* (void) in Genesis denotes the stage of God's self-revelation known as *olam ha-tohu* (world of the void) which precedes *olam ha-tikkun* (world of perfection). In later kabbalistic thought the fourteenth century kabbalist Kalonymous Kalman of Cracow in his *Maor Va-Shemesh* maintains that the void in Genesis is the primordial void remaining after God's withdrawal to make room for the universe. On this reading, God's decree, 'Let there be light'

(Gen. 1.3), means that God caused his light to be emanated into the void in order to provide sustaining power required for the worlds which were later to be formed.

Regarding the question whether in the process of creating the cosmos, God also created intelligent beings on other planets, the Bible offers no information. Although rabbinic sources attest to the creation of other worlds, they similarly contain no reference to the existence of other sentient creatures. In the nineteenth century, however, Phineas Elijah ben Meir Hurwitz of Vilna discussed this issue. On the basis of Isaiah 45.18 ('For thus says the Lord who created the heavens (he is God!), who formed the earth and made it, he established it; he did not create it a chaos, he formed it to be inhabited': "I am the Lord; and there is no other" ') he maintained that there are creatures on other planets than earth. In this connection he refers to the passage in the *Talmud* in which *Meroz* (Judg. 5.23) is a star. Since it is cursed, Hurwitz concludes that it is inhabited. He alleges that creatures on other planets may have intelligence, yet he does not think they would have free will since only human beings have such capacity. 'Consequently', he writes, 'there is only room for *Torah* and worship in this world, for neither *Torah* nor worship has any meaning where there is no free will.'

The belief in extraterrestial beings raises problems for both Judaism and Christianity. In his *The Fall and Rise of Man*, the modern writer Jerome Eckstein explores the religious implications of such a possibility:

Let our imagination roam, and let us speculate about the possible conflicts between future discoveries of space exploration and our old religious beliefs, if these religious beliefs are understood as offering knowledge of the kind given by science. Suppose a strangely figured race of creatures with the approximate intelligence of humans and a culture and ethics radically different from ours was discovered on some distant star, would this not pose serious problems to the dogmatic and authoritarian interpretations of the Judeo-Christian religions? Would these creatures, who obviously were not descended from Adam and Eve, be tainted with original sin? Would they too have souls? Would they be in need of grace and salvation? Did Jesus absorb their sins? Would they be in need of the Messiah? Would they be subject to all the laws and traditions of these earth-centred religions? Would they be eligible to life in the hereafter?

From the Christian side, C. S. Lewis in *The Seeing Eye* points out that such creatures might be wholly good; in this case they would not need to be redeemed. However, if such creatures were both good and evil, they might have been given some other form of redemption. Alternatively, such creatures might actually need redemption – according to Lewis, this would be a task for Christian missionaries. The final possibility is that these creatures would be utterly demonic. If this were the case, Christians would need to readjust their assumption about devils, who previously were conceived as incorporeal in nature.

Within the Jewish community, W. Gunther Plaut in *Judaism and the Scientific Spirit* asks:

Will the possibility that there are intelligent creatures on other planets impose any strain on our religious beliefs? . . . The modern Jew will answer this question with a firm 'No'. An earlier generation, rooted in beliefs in an earth-centred universe, might have had some theological difficulties, but we have them no longer . . . . Just as a father may love many children with equal love, so surely may our Father on high spread his pinions over the vastness of creation.

An alternative Jewish view has been advanced by Norman Lamm in *The Religious Implication of Extraterrestrial Life*. There are, he believes, three major challenges confronting Judaism. The existence of extraterrestrial beings undermines the conviction that human beings are the ultimate purpose of God's creation. The second challenge relates to the generation of life. If life is generated by natural processes on other planets, how is one to understand the doctrine of God as Creator? The final challenge concerns the temptation to view God in non-personal terms given this new vision of the universe. Lamm believes that Judaism is able to resolve these difficulties. He concludes: 'We may yet learn that, as rational, sentient, and self-conscious creatures, "we are not alone". But then again we never felt before nor need we feel today or in the future that we are alone, "For Thou art with me" '.

In his *A Jewish Theology*, Louis Jacobs points out that the challenges Lamm mentions are not the crucial ones. The most serious difficulty is the question of the uniqueness of the *Torah*: 'Lamm's arguments,' he writes, 'centre around what the *Torah* means in the light of the new possible situation. But if this possibility is real, the far more difficult and radical question to be faced is that there are whole words for which the *Torah*, given to humans, can have no meaning. In asking what Judaism has to say about extraterrestrial life, Lamm begs the question whether Judaism has any relevance in this context.'

Regarding creatures other than human beings, Maimonides (twelfth century) in his *Guide* argued that it is a mistake to believe that the sole purpose of all creation is for the benefit of human beings. Yet on such an account how is one to explain the suffering of animals? In his *Kuzari*, Judah Halevi (eleventh to twelfth century) declares that if the wisdom of the Creator is truly wise, then human beings must accept in faith that nature is not contrary to the ways of an all-benevolent Creator. As far as the human treatment of animals is concerned, the tradition is strictly opposed to inflicting pain on animals unless it is for the purpose of satisfying urgent human needs. Turning to angels, they are referred to frequently in the Bible and rabbinic sources: they are immortal and have no evil inclination. Often they serve as God's messengers and at times they offer moral objections to God's conduct of the world.

In the Middle Ages a number of Jewish theologians interpreted such figures in spiritual and rationalistic terms. According to Maimonides they are creatures who possess form without matter – they are pure spirits. When the prophets depict angels as fire or as possessing wings, they are simply using figurative language. The higher the angel, the greater his perception of God. With regard to demons, the *Talmud* contains numerous accounts of their activities. Even though some Jewish philosophers such as Maimonides disputed such beliefs, the belief in the demonic realm was an important feature of Jewish folk belief through the ages.

In the modern period, however, Jews have largely abandoned belief in angels and demons, yet the conviction that God created the universe still remains a central feature of the faith. The belief that God is the source of all continues to animate religious sensibilities. Maimonides' formulation of this principle in the beginning of his *Code* expresses what has remained the central feature of the Jewish religious system: 'The foundation of all foundations and the pillar of wisdom is to know that there is a First Being. He it is who brought all things into being and all the beings in heaven and earth and in between only enjoy existence by virtue of his true being.'

6

Providence

In the Bible the notion that God controls and guides the universe is an essential belief. The Hebrew term for such divine action is *hashgahah*, derived from Psalm 33.14: 'From where he sits enthroned he looks forth (*hishgiah*) on all the inhabitants of the earth.' Such a view implies that the dispensation of a wise and benevolent providence is found everywhere – all events are ultimately foreordained by God. According to the biblical tradition, there are two types of providence: (1) general providence – God's provision for the world in general, and (2) special providence – God's care for each individual. In Scripture God's general providence was manifest in his freeing the ancient Israelites from Egyptian bondage and guiding them to the Promised Land. The belief in the unfolding of his plan for salvation is a further illustration of such providential care for his creatures. Linked to this concern for all is God's providential concern for every person. In the words of Jeremiah: 'I know, O Lord, that the way of man is not in himself, that it is not in man who walks to direct his steps' (Jer. 10.23).

Subsequently the doctrine of divine providence was developed in rabbinic literature. The *Mishnah* declares: 'Everything is foreseen.' In the Talmud we read: 'No man suffers so much as the injury of a finger when it has been decreed in heaven.' Such a conviction became a central feature of the *Rosh Hashanah* (New Year) service. According to the New Year liturgy, God, the judge of the world, provides for the destiny of individuals as well as nations on the basis of their actions.

In the medieval period Jewish theologians were preoccupied with this doctrine. In his *Guide* Maimonides (twelfth century) defends both general and special providence. The latter, he argues, extends only to human beings and is in proportion to a person's intellect and moral character. Such a view implies that God is concerned about each non-human species, but not with every individual. Only humans come under divine care as they rise in intellectual and moral stature. Hasdai Crescas (fourteenth to fifteenth century), however, maintains that God created human beings out of his love for them – thus his providential care is not related to their personal characteristics. All persons enjoy God's special providence.

The kabbalists were also concerned with this subject. In his *Shomer Emunim*, for example, the eighteenth century scholar Joseph Ergas explains that there are various types of providence:

> Nothing occurs by accident, without intention and divine providence, as it is written: 'Then will I also walk with you in chance' (Lev. 21.24). You see that even the state of 'chance' is attributed to God, for all proceeds from him by reason of special providence.

Nonetheless, Ergas limited special providence to human beings:

> However, the guardian angel has no power to provide for the special providence of non-human species; for example, whether this ox will live or die, whether this ant will be trodden on or saved, whether this spider will catch this fly and so forth. There is no special providence of this kind for animals, to say nothing of plants and minerals, since the purpose for which they were created is attained by means of the species alone, and there is no need for providence to be extended to individuals of the species. Consequently, all events which happen to individuals of these species are by pure chance and not by divine decree, except . . . where it is relevant for the divine providence regarding mankind.

Such views caused offence to a number of Hasidic teachers – divine providence, they insisted, is exercised over all things. Thus Phineas of Koretz (eighteenth century) in his *Peer LaYesharim* states: 'A man should believe that even a piece of straw that lies on the ground does so at the decree of God. He decrees that it should lie there with one end facing this way and the other end the other way.' Again Hayim of Sanz in his *Divre Hayim* to *Mikketz* contends: 'It is impossible for any creature to enjoy existence without the Creator of all worlds sustaining it and keeping it in being, and it is all through divine providence. Although Maimonides has a different opinion in this matter the truth is that not even a bird is snared without providence from above.'

In the Middle Ages Jewish theologians also wrestled with dilemmas concerning God's foreknowledge as it relates to human freedom. If God knows everything which will come to pass, how can human beings be free? As we have seen, Maimonides mentioned that human beings are free despite God's knowledge of future events. This is possible, he asserted, because God's knowledge is not our knowledge. In his *Code* he writes:

> You may ask: God knows all that will happen. Before someone becomes a good or a bad man God either knows that this will happen or he does not know it. If he knows that the person will be good is it impossible for that person to be bad. You must know that the solution to this problem is larger than the earth and wider than the sea . . . . God does not 'know' with a knowledge that is apart from him, like human beings . . . . God's knowledge and his self are one and the same though no human being is capable of clearly comprehending this matter – it is beyond human capacity to comprehend or discover the Creator's knowledge. It follows that we are incapable of comprehending how God knows all creatures and all deeds. But this we do know beyond any doubt, that man's deeds are in his own hands, God neither compelling him nor determining that he should behave in a certain way.

Other scholars, such as the twelfth century Jewish theologian Abraham Ibn Daud, disagreed. For Ibn Daud God's foreknowledge is not determinative or causative. Thus human beings are able to act freely: 'His knowledge is not in the nature of a compelling decree but can be compared to the knowledge of the astrologers who know, by virtue of some other power, how a certain person will behave.'

Some later scholars such as Yom Tobh Lippman Heller (sixteenth to seventeenth century) in his *Tos.* Yom Tobh appealed to the concept of the Eternal Now to resolve this problem:

> When a man sees someone else doing something the fact that he sees it exercises no compulsion on the thing that is done. In exactly the same way the fact that God sees man doing the

act exercises no compulsion over him to do it. For before God
there is no early and late since he is not governed by time.

In the modern world such theological issues have ceased to
preoccupy Jewish thinkers. Rather, the rise of science has
challenged the traditional understanding of God's providential
activity. In place of the religious interpretation of the universe as
controlled by the Diety, scientific investigation has revealed that
nature is governed by complex laws. Thus it is no longer
possible for most Jews to accept the biblical and rabbinic
conception of divine activity. As a result, many Jews have
simply abandoned the belief in providence. Others however
envisage God as working through natural causes: as Creator of
all, he established the laws which regulate the natural order.
Regarding special providence, many Jews would want to say
that God is concerned with each individual even though he does
not miraculously intervene in the course of human history.
Divine providential concern should hence be understood as a
mode of interaction in which God affects the consciousness of
the individual without curtailing his free will. Knowing the
innermost secrets of every human heart, he introduces into the
conscious awareness of individuals aims consonant with his
will. Viewed in this way, special providence involves a dynamic
relationship between the human and the divine. Such a
reinterpretation of the traditional doctrine of providence has
enabled many contemporary Jews to affirm the ancient formulation of the *Ani Maamin* prayer: 'I believe with perfect faith that
the Creator, blessed be his name, is the author and guide of
everything that has been created, and that he alone has made,
does make, and will make all things.'

7

Goodness

According to Scripture God is the all-good ruler of the universe. Thus in the Psalms he is described as good and upright (Ps. 25.8); his name is good (Ps. 52.11; 54.8); he is good and ready to forgive (Ps. 86.5); he is good and does good (Ps. 118.68); he is good to all (Ps. 145.9). In rabbinic literature the same view prevails: God is the supremely beneficent creator who guides all things to their ultimate destiny. In the unfolding of his plan he has chosen Israel as his messenger to all peoples – as creator and redeemer, he is the father to all. Such affirmations about God's goodness have given rise to intense speculation about the mystery of evil. In Scripture the authors of Job and Ecclesiastes explored the question why the righteous suffer, and this quest continued into the rabbinic period. Yet it was not until the Middle Ages that Jewish thinkers began to wrestle with the philosophical perplexities connected with the existence of evil.

In the twelfth century, for example, Abraham Ibn Daud argued that both human reason and the Jewish tradition teach that God cannot be the cause of evil. Reason demonstrates that this is so because God is wholly good; it would be self-contradictory for him to be the source of evil. Because God does not have a composite nature, it is logically impossible for him to bring about both good and evil. But why then does evil exist? Poverty, for example, is the absence of wealth; darkness the absence of light, and folly the absence of understanding. It is a mistake to think that God creates any of these things just as it would be an error to assume that God made no elephants in Spain. Such a lack of elephants is not divinely willed. Similarly evil is not divinely created. It occurs when goodness is not present. The absence of good is not inherently evil; instead imperfections in the world exist so that God can benefit a multitude of creatures of different forms.

In his *Guide*, Maimonides (twelfth century) argued along similar lines. All evils, he asserts, are privations. For this reason

God is not responsible for evil – he is liable only for the privation of good.

This attempt to resolve the problem of evil is paralleled in early Christian thought. In the fifth century Augustine asked: 'For what is that which we call evil but the absence of good?' Continuing this argument, he asserts:

> In the bodies of animals, disease and wounds mean nothing but the absence of health; for when a cure is effected, that does not mean that the evils which were present – namely, the diseases and wounds – go away from the body and swell elsewhere: they altogether cease to exist; for the wound or disease is not a substance, but a defect in the fleshy substance –the flesh itself being a substance, and therefore something good of which those evils – that is, privations of the good which we call health – are accidents.

By defining evil as a privation of good, Augustine like Ibn Daud and Maimonides was anxious to demonstrate how apparent evil could exist in a universe created by a wholly good and omnipotent God. Since evil does not in fact exist, it is incorrect to assume that God is reponsible for its occurrence. For Augustine, evil 'is nothing but the corruption of natural measure, form or order. What is called an evil nature is a corrupt nature. If it were not corrupt it would be good. But when it is corrupted, so far as it remains a natural thing, it is good. It is bad only so far as it is corrupted.' Thus everything that exists is good, and those things which are now less good or no longer good at all have merely fallen away from their original state.

For the kabbalists, the existence of evil constituted a central problem for the Jewish faith. According to one tradition evil has no objective reality. Human beings are unable to receive all of the influx from the *sefirot*, and it is this inability which is the origin of evil. Created beings are therefore estranged from the source of emanation and this results in the illusion that evil exists. Another view depicts the *sefirah* of power as 'an attribute whose name is evil'. On the basis of such a teaching Isaac the Blind (twelfth to thirteenth century) concluded that there must be a positive root of evil and death. During the process of differentiation of forces below the *sefirot* evil became concretized. This interpretation led to the doctrine that the source of evil was the supra-abundant growth of judgement – this was due to the separation and substitution of the attribute of judgement from its union with compassion. Pure judgement produced from within itself 'the other side' (*Sitra Ahra*). The *Sitra Ahra* consists of the domain of emanations and demonic powers. Though it originated from one of God's attributes, it is not part of the divine realm.

In the *Zohar* there is a detailed hierarchical structure of this emanation in which the *Sitra Ahra* is depicted as having ten *sefirot* of its own. The evil in the universe, the *Zohar* explains, has its origins in the leftovers of worlds that were destroyed. Another view in the *Zohar* is that the Tree of Life and the Tree of Knowledge were harmoniously bound together until Adam separated them, thereby bringing evil into the world. This event is referred to as 'the cutting of the shoots' and is the prototype of sins in the Bible. Evil thus originated through human action. Both these views concerning the origin of evil were reconciled in another passage where it is asserted that the disposition towards evil derives from the cosmic evil which is in the realm of the *Sitra Ahra*.

According to the *Zohar*, evil is like the bark of a tree of emanation; it is a husk or shell in which lower dimensions of existing things are encased. As the *Zohar* explains: 'When King Solomon went into the nut garden, he took a nutshell and drew an analogy from its layers to these spirits which inspire sensual desires in human beings, as it is written, "and the delights of the sons of men are from male and female demons" ' (Ecclus. 2.8). This verse also indicates that the pleasures in which men indulge in the time of sleep give birth to multitudes of demons. In this context evil is understood as a waste product of an organic process – it is compared to bad blood, foul water, dross after gold has been refined and the dregs of wine. Yet despite this depiction, the *Zohar* asserts that there is holiness even in the *Sitra Ahra*, regardless of whether it is conceived as a result of the emanation of the last *sefirah* or a consequence of man's sin. The domains of good and evil are intermingled and it is man's duty to separate them.

In explaining this picture of the divine creation, kabbalists adopted a neo-Platonic conception of a ladder of spiritual reality composed of four worlds in descending order. First is the domain of *Atzilut* (emanation) consisting of the ten *sefirot* which form *Adam Kadmon* (primordial man). The second world is the realm of *Beriyah* (creation) which is made up of the throne of glory and the seven heavenly palaces. In the third world *Yetsirah* (formation) most of the angels dwell, presided over by the angel *Metatron*. This is the scene of the seven heavenly halls guarded by angels to which *Merkavah* mystics attempt to gain admission. In the fourth world of *Asiyah* (making) are the lower order of angels – the *ophanim* who combat evil and receive prayers. This is the spiritual archetype of the material cosmos, heaven, and the earthly world. *Asiyah* is both the last link in the divine chain of being and the domain where the *Sitra Ahra* is manifest; in this realm the forces of good struggle with the demons.

In modern times philosophical theories about the existence of evil have ceased to attract attention within the Jewish community. Similarly, most Jews have ignored the mystic theories in the *Zohar* and their later development by Isaac Luria. Instead, a number of Jewish writers have grappled with the question whether it is possible to believe in God's goodness after the Holocaust. In *The Face of God after Auschwitz*, Ignaz Maybaum contends that Jews died in the concentration camps for the sins of humanity, as God's suffering servant. For Maybaum Jews suffer in order to bring about the rule of God over the world and its peoples – their God-appointed mission is to serve the course of historical progress and bring human beings into a new era.

An alternative approach to the Holocaust is to see in the death camps a manifestation of God's will that his chosen people survive. Such a view has been expressed in various writings by Emil Fackenheim who asserts that God revealed himself to Israel out of the furnaces and through the ashes of the victims of Auschwitz. Through the Holocaust, he believes, God issued an additional 614th commandment to the traditional 613:

> Jews are forbidden to hand Hitler posthumous victories. They are commanded to survive as Jews, lest the Jewish people perish. They are commanded to remember the victims of Auschwitz lest their memory perish. They are forbidden to despair of man and his world, and to escape into either cynicism or otherworldliness, lest they co-operate in delivering the world over to the forces of Auschwitz. Finally, they are forbidden to despair of the God of Israel, lest Judaism perish.

Another interpretation of the Holocaust involves the rejection of any kind of explanation; instead, the events of the Holocaust are seen as part of God's inscrutable plan. In *Faith After the Holocaust*, Eliezer Berkovits maintains that the modern Jewish response to the destruction of six million Jews should be modelled on Job's example. We must believe in God, he maintains, because Job believed. If there is no answer to the quest for any understanding of God's silence in the face of Nazi genocide, 'it is better to be without it than in the sham of . . . the humbug of a disbelief encouraged by people who have eaten their fill at the tables of a satiated society.' At Auschwitz God was hidden, yet according to Berkovits, in his hiddenness he was actually present.

A radically different assessment of the religious implications of the Holocaust is formulated in *After Auschwitz* by Richard Rubenstein who argues that it is no longer possible to believe in an all-good God. According to Rubenstein, Auschwitz is the utter and decisive refutation of the traditional affirmation of a providential God who acts in history and watches over the Jewish people whom he has selected from all nations. Although there are Jews who would agree with Rubenstein's assessment, most Jewish believers continue to affirm the traditional belief in a wholly good God. Despite the horrors of the concentration camps, they remain convinced that he rules the world in goodness, justice and truth.

8

Revelation

According to tradition the entire Bible was communicated by God to the Jewish people. In Maimonides' formulation of the thirteen principles of Jewish faith, this belief is the eighth tenet:

> The *Torah* was revealed from heaven. This implies our belief that the whole of the *Torah* found in our hands this day is the *Torah* that was handed down by Moses, and that it is all of divine origin. By this I mean that the whole of the *Torah* came unto him from before God in a manner which is metaphorically called 'speaking'; but the real nature of that communication is unknown to everybody except to Moses (peace to him!) to whom it came.

In rabbinic literature a distinction is drawn between the revelation of the Pentateuch (*Torah* in the narrow sense) and the prophetic writings. This is frequently expressed by saying that the *Torah* was given directly by God, whereas the prophetic books were given by means of prophecy. The remaining books of the Bible (Hagiographa) were conveyed by means of the holy spirit rather than through prophecy. None the less all these writings constitute the canon of Scripture. The Hebrew term referring to the Bible as a whole is *Tanakh*. This word is made up of the first letters of the three divisions of Scripture: *Torah* (Pentateuch); *Neviim* (Prophets); and *Ketuvim* (Writings). This is the Written *Torah* (*Torah She-Bi-Ketav*).

According to the rabbis, the expositions and elaborations of the Written Law were also revealed by God to Moses on Mount Sinai; subsequently they were passed from generation to generation, and through this process additional legislation was incorporated. This process was referred to as 'The Oral *Torah*' (*Torah She-Be-Al Peh*). Thus traditional Judaism affirms that God's revelation is two-fold and binding for all time. Committed to this belief, Jews pray in the synagogue that God will guide them to do his will as recorded in their sacred literature:

O our Father, merciful Father, ever compassionate, have mercy upon us: O put it into our hearts to understand and to discern, to mark, learn and teach, to heed, to do and to fulfil in love all the words of instruction in thy *Torah*. Enlighten our eyes in thy *Torah*, and let our hearts cling to thy commandments, and make us single-hearted to love and fear thy name, so that we be never put to shame.

In the Middle Ages this traditional belief was continually affirmed. Like Maimonides (twelfth century), Nahmanides (thirteenth century) in his Commentary to the Pentateuch argued that Moses wrote the Five Books of Moses at God's dictation. It is likely, he observed, that Moses wrote Genesis and part of Exodus when he descended from Mount Sinai. At the end of the forty years in the wilderness he completed the rest of the Pentateuch. Nahmanides observes that this view follows the rabbinic tradition that the *Torah* was given scroll by scroll. For Nahmanides, Moses was like a scribe who copied an older work. Underlying this conception is the mystical idea of a primordial *Torah* which contains the words describing events long before they happened. This entire record was in heaven before the creation of the world. In addition, Nahmanides maintains that the secrets of the *Torah* were revealed to Moses and are referred to in the *Torah* by the use of special letters, the numerical values of words and letters, and the adornment of Hebrew characters.

Paralleling Nahmanides' mystical interpretation of the *Torah*, the *Zohar* asserts that the *Torah* contains mysteries beyond human comprehension. As the *Zohar* explains:

Said R. Simeon: 'Alas for the man who regards the *Torah* as a book of mere tales and everyday matters! If that were so, even we could compose a *Torah* dealing with everyday affairs, and of even greater excellence. Nay, even the princes of the world possess books of greater worth which we could use as a model for composing such *Torah*. The *Torah*, however, contains in all its words supernal truths and sublime mysteries . . . . Thus, had the *Torah* not clothed herself in garments of this world, the world could not endure it. The stories of the *Torah* are thus only her outer garments, and whoever looks upon that garment as being the *Torah* itself, woe to that man – such a one has no portion in the next world.'

In the modern period, however, it has become increasingly difficult to sustain the traditional concept of divine revelation in the light of scholarly investigation and discovery. As early as the sixteenth century, scholars pointed out that the Five Books of Moses appear to be composed of different sources. In the middle of the nineteenth century sustained investigation by two German scholars, Karl Heinrich Graf and Julius Wellhausen, concluded that the Five Books of Moses are composed of four main documents which once existed separately but were later combined by a series of editors or redactors. The first document, 'J', dating from the ninth century BC, attributes the most anthropomorphic character to God, referred to by the four Hebrew letters YHWH. The second source, 'E', stemming from the eighth century BC, is less anthropomorphic and utilizes the divine name *Elohim*. In the seventh century BC the 'D' source was written, concentrating on religious purity and the priesthood. Finally the 'P' source from the fifth century BC, which has a more transcendental view of God, emphasizes the importance of the sacrificial cult.

By utilizing this framework, Graf and Wellhausen maintained that it is possible to account for the manifold problems and discrepancies in the biblical text. The Graf-Wellhausen hypothesis was subsequently modified by other scholars. Some preferred not to speak of separate sources, but of circles of tradition. On this view, J,E,D, and P represent oral traditions rather than written documents. Further, these scholars stress that the separate traditions themselves contain early material; thus it is a mistake to think they originated in their entirety at particular periods. Other scholars reject the theory of separate sources altogether; they argue that oral traditions were modified throughout the history of ancient Israel and only eventually were compiled into a single narrative. Yet despite these different theories there is a general recognition among modern biblical critics (including non-Orthodox Jews) that the Pentateuch was not written by Moses; rather, it is seen as a collection of traditions originating at different times in ancient Israel.

In addition to biblical criticism, textual studies of ancient manuscripts highlight the improbability of the traditional view of Scripture. According to tradition, the Hebrew text of the Five Books of Moses used in synagogues today (the Masoretic text) is the same as that given to Moses. Yet it is widely accepted among scholars that the script of contemporary *Torah* scrolls is not the same as that which was current in ancient Israel from the time of the monarchy until the sixth century BC. It was only later, possibly under Aramaic influence, that the square script was adopted as the standard for Hebrew writing. Furthermore, the fact that the ancient translations of the Hebrew Bible into languages such as Syriac and Greek contain variant readings from the Masoretic text suggests that the Hebrew text of the Pentateuch now in use is not entirely free from error.

A final aspect of modern studies which bears on the question of Mosaic authorship concerns the influence of the ancient Near East on the Bible. According to Orthodoxy the Five Books of Moses were essentially created out of nothing. But there are strong parallels in the Bible to laws, stories and myths found throughout the ancient Near East. It is unlikely that this is simply a coincidence – the similarities offer compelling evidence that the Five Books of Moses emerged in a specific social and cultural context. The authors of the biblical period shared much the same world view as their neighbours and no doubt transformed this framework to fit their own religious notions. In this light, most modern biblical scholars would find it impossible to reconcile the traditional conception of Mosaic authorship of the Five Books of Moses with the findings of modern biblical scholarship and scientific discovery.

For the Orthodox such investigations are irrelevant. Orthodox Judaism remains committed to the view that the Written as well as the Oral *Torah* were imparted by God to Moses on Mount Sinai. This act of revelation serves as the basis for the entire legal system as well as doctrinal beliefs about God. Yet despite such an adherence to tradition, many modern Orthodox Jews pay only lip-service to such a conviction. The gap between traditional belief and contemporary views of the *Torah* is even greater in the non-Orthodox branches of Judaism. Here there is a general acceptance of the findings of biblical scholarship – the Five Books of Moses are perceived as divinely inspired but at the same time the product of human reflection. Thus the Pentateuch is viewed as a unified text – combining centuries of tradition – in which a variety of individual sources were woven together by a number of editors. Such a non-fundamentalist approach, which takes account of recent scholarly developments in the field of biblical studies, rules out the traditional belief in the infallibility of Scripture and thereby provides a rationale for changing the law. The same applies to the Oral tradition. Non-Orthodox Jews similarly regard the chain of rabbinic teaching as the product of human reflection rather than the unfolding of the divine will. This shift in orientation has brought about considerable confusion within the ranks of Conservative, Reconstructionist and Reform Judaism. If the law needs to be altered, what criteria should be implemented in deciding which laws should be retained, discarded or changed? By what criteria is one to decide which elements of the *Torah* were revealed to Moses? The lack of satisfactory answers to these questions points to the religious chaos that exists in the various branches of non-Orthodox Judaism.

9

Torah and Mitzvah

According to tradition God revealed 613 commandments
(*mitzvot*) to Moses on Mount Sinai: they are recorded in the Five
Books of Moses. These prescriptions, which are to be observed
as part of God's covenant with Israel, are classified in two major
categories: (1) statutes concerned with ritual performances
characterized as obligations between human beings and God;
and (2) judgements consisting of ritual laws that would have
been adopted by society even if they had not been decreed by
God (such as laws regarding murder and theft). These 613
commandments consist of 365 negative (prohibited) and 248
positive (duties to be performed) prescriptions.

Traditional Judaism maintains that Moses received the Oral
Torah in addition to the Written Law. This was passed down
from generation to generation and was the subject of rabbinic
debate. The first authoritative compilation of the Oral Law was
the *Mishnah* composed by Judah Ha-Nasi in the second century
AD. This work is the most important book of law after the Bible;
its purpose was to supply teachers and judges with an authoritative guide to the Jewish legal tradition. In subsequent
centuries sages continued to discuss the content of Jewish law;
their deliberations are recorded in the Palestinian and
Babylonian *Talmuds*. Both *Talmuds* incorporate the *Mishnah* and
later rabbinic discussions known as the *Gamara*. The *Gamara* text
preserves the proceedings of the academics in both Palestine
and Babylonia, where scholars assembled to study the *Mishnah*.
The central purpose of these deliberations was to elucidate the
Mishnah text.

After the compilation of the *Talmuds* (sixth century AD),
outstanding rabbinic authorities continued the development of
Jewish law by issuing answers to specific questions. These
responses (known as 'responsa') touched on all aspects of
Jewish law and insured a standardization of practice. In time,
various scholars felt the need to produce codes of Jewish law so

that all members of the community would have access to the legal tradition. In the eleventh century, Isaac Alfasi produced a work that became the standard code for Sephardic Jewry. Two centuries later, Asher ben Jehiel wrote a code that became the code for Ashkenazi Jews. Moses Maimonides in the twelfth century also wrote an important code that had a wide influence, as did the code by Jacob ben Asher (thirteenth to fourteenth century), the son of Asher ben Jehiel. In the sixteenth century Joseph Caro published the *Shulhan Arukh*, which together with glosses by Moses Isserles has served as the standard code of Jewish law for Orthodox Jewry until the present day.

In kabbalistic thought the observance of the *mitzvot* takes on cosmic significance. For the mystic, deeds of *tikkun* (cosmic repair) sustain the world, activate nature to praise God, and bring about the coupling of the tenth and the sixth *sefirot*. Such repair is accomplished by keeping the commandments which were conceived as vessels for establishing contact with the Godhead and for enduring divine mercy. Such a religious life provided the kabbalist with a means of integrating into the divine hierarchy of creation – the *kabbalah* was able to guide the soul back to its infinite source.

The supreme rank attainable by the soul at the end of its sojourn is the mystical cleaving to God. The early kabbalists of Provence defined such cleaving as the ultimate goal. According to Isaac the Blind (twelfth to thirteenth century): 'The principal task of the mystics and of they who contemplate on his name is, "And you shall cleave to him" (Deut. 13.4), and this is a central principle of the *Torah* and of prayer, and of blessings, to harmonize one's thought above, to conjoin God in his letters and to link the ten *sefirot* to him.' For Nahmanides (thirteenth century), such cleaving is a state of mind in which one constantly remembers God and his love, 'to the point that when (a person) speaks with someone else, his heart is not with them at all but is still before God . . . . Whoever cleaves in this way to his Creator becomes eligible to receive the Holy Spirit.' According to Nahmanides, the pious are able to attain such a spiritual state. Mystical cleaving does not completely eliminate the distance between God and human beings – it denotes instead a state of beatitude and intimate union between the soul and its source.

Within Lurianic *kabbalah*, these notions were elaborated.

According to Isaac Luria (sixteenth century), when the vessels were shattered, the cosmos was divided into two parts – the kingdom of evil in the lower part and the realm of divine light in the upper part. For Luria evil was seen as opposed to existence; therefore it was not able to exist by its own power. Instead it had to derive spiritual force from the divine light. This was accomplished by keeping captive the sparks of the divine light that fell with them when the vessels were broken and subsequently gave sustenance to the satanic domain. Divine attempts to bring unity to all existence now had to focus on the struggle to overcome the evil forces. This was first achieved by a continuing process of divine emanation which at first created the *sefirot*, the sky, the earth, the Garden of Eden and human beings. Human beings were intended to serve as the battleground for this conflict between good and evil. In this regard Adam reflected symbolically the dualism in the cosmos – he possesses a sacred soul while his body represents the evil forces. God's intention was that Adam defeat the evil within himself and bring about Satan's downfall. But when Adam failed, a catastrophe occurred parallel to the breaking of the vessels; instead of divine sparks being saved and uplifted, many new divine lights fell and evil became stronger.

Rather than relying on the action of one person, God then chose the people of Israel to vanquish evil and raise up the captive sparks. The *Torah* was given to symbolize the Jews' acceptance of this allotted task. When the ancient Israelites undertook to keep the law, redemption seemed imminent. Yet the people of Israel then created the golden calf, a sin parallel to Adam's disobedience. Again, divine sparks fell and the forces of evil were renewed. For Luria, history is a record of attempts by the powers of good to rescue these sparks and unite the divine and earthly spheres. Luria and his disciples believed they were living in the final stages of this last attempt to overcome evil, in which the coming of the Messiah would signify the end of the struggle.

Related to the contraction of God, the breaking of the vessels and the exiled sparks, was Luria's conception of *tikkun*. For Lurianic mystics, this concept refers to the mending of what was broken during the shattering of the vessels. After the catastrophe in the divine realm, the process of restoration began and every disaster was seen as a setback in this process. In this battle, keeping God's commandments was understood as contributing to repair – the divine sparks which fell down can be redeemed by ethical and religious deeds. According to Luria, a spark is attached to all prayers and moral acts; if the Jew keeps the ethical and religious law these sparks are redeemed and lifted up. When the process is complete evil will disappear, but every time a Jew sins a spark is captured and plunges into the satanic abyss. Every deed or misdeed thus has cosmic significance in the system of Lurianic *kabbalah*.

In the modern world such traditional and mystical ideas have lost their force except among the Hasidim. Today Orthodoxy claims the largest number of adherents. Yet the majority of those who profess allegiance to Orthodox Judaism do not live by the code of Jewish law. Instead each individual Jew feels free to write his own *Shulhan Arukh*. This is also so within the other branches of Judaism. For most Jews the legal tradition has lost its hold on Jewish consciousness – the bulk of rituals and observances appear anachronistic and burdensome. In previous centuries this was not the case; despite the divisions within the Jewish world all Jews accepted the binding authority of the law contained in the *Torah*. The 613 commandments were universally viewed as given by God to Moses on Mount Sinai and understood as binding for all time. Thus food regulations, stipulations regarding ritual purity, the moral code as well as other *mitzvot* served as the framework for an authentic Jewish way of life.

Throughout Jewish history the validity of the written *Torah* was never questioned. In contemporary society, however, most Jews of all religious positions have ceased to regard the legal heritage in this light. Instead individual Jews, including those of the Orthodox persuasion, feel at liberty to choose which *mitzvot* have a personal spiritual significance. Such an anarchic approach to the legal tradition highlights the fact that Jewish law no longer serves as a cohesive force for contemporary Jewry. In short, many modern Jews no longer believe in the doctrine of *Torah* from Sinai, which previously served as a cardinal principle of the Jewish faith. Instead they subscribe only to a limited number of legal precepts which for one reason or another they find meaningful. Such a lack of uniformity of Jewish practice means that there is a vast gulf between the requirements of legal observance and the actual lifestyle of the majority of Jews, both in Israel and the diaspora.

10

Sin and Repentance

In the Bible, sin is understood as a transgression of God's decree. In biblical Hebrew the word *het* means 'to miss' or 'to fail'. Here sin is understood as a failing, a lack of perfection in carrying out one's duty. The term *peshah* means a 'breach'; it indicates a broken relationship between man and God. The word *avon* expresses the idea of crookedness. Thus according to biblical terminology, sin is characterized by failure, waywardness, and illicit action. A sinner is one who has not fulfilled his obligations to God.

According to rabbinic Judaism, sins can be classified according to their gravity as indicated by the punishments prescribed by biblical law: the more serious the punishment, the more serious the offence. A distinction is also drawn in rabbinic texts between sins against other human beings (*bain adam la-havero*) and offences against God alone (*bain adam la-Makom*). Sins against God can be atoned for by repentance, prayer, and giving charity. In cases of offence against others, however, such acts require restitution and placation as a condition of atonement.

Rabbinic literature teaches that there are two tendencies in every person: the good inclination (*yetzer ha-tov*), and the evil inclination (*yetzer ha-ra*). The former urges individuals to do what is right, whereas the latter encourages sinful acts. At all times, a person is to be on guard against assaults of the *yetzer ha-ra*. It is not possible to hide one's sins from God since the Omnipresent knows all things. In the words of the *Mishnah*, 'Know that is above thee – an eye that sees, an ear that hears, and all the deeds are written in a book.' Thus, God is aware of all sinful deeds, yet through repentance and prayer it is possible to achieve reconciliation with him.

In rabbinic sources the *yetzer ha-ra* is often identified with the sex drive (which embraces human physical appetites in general as well as aggressive desires). Frequently it is portrayed as the force which impels human beings to satisfy their longings.

76

Although it is described as the evil inclination, it is essential to life itself. Thus the *midrash* remarks that if it were not for the *yetzer ha-ra*, no one would build a house, marry, have children, or engage in trade. For this reason Scripture states: 'And God saw everything that he had made and behold, it was very good' (Gen. 1.31). Here 'good' refers to the good inclination; very good to the evil inclination. In this light the *Talmud* relates that the men of the Great Synagogue (Ezra and his colleagues) wanted to kill the *yetzer ha-ra*, but the evil inclination (who is here personified) warned them that this would result in the destruction of the world. As a result, he was imprisoned, and they subsequently put out his eyes so that he would not be able to entice men to incest.

According to the rabbis, human beings are engaged in a continual struggle against the *yetzer ha-ra*. In this quest the *Torah* serves as the fundamental defence. Hence the *Talmud* declares that the *Torah* is the antidote to the poison of the *yetzer ha-ra*. The implication of this passage is that when human beings submit to the discipline provided by the *Torah*, they are liberated from the influence of the *yetzer ha-ra*. The rabbis state that this is like a king who struck his son and subsequently urged him to keep a plaster on his wound. When the wound is protected in this way the prince can eat and drink without coming to harm. But if he removes the plaster, the wound will grow worse if the prince indulges his appetites. For the rabbis the *Torah* is the plaster which protects the king's son.

Rabbinic literature also teaches that this struggle against the *yetzer ha-ra* is unending. All that one can do is to subdue it through self-control – no person can destroy it. Arguably, such a view parallels the Christian concept of original sin, yet unlike Christian exegetes, the rabbis interpreted Genesis 2—3 as simply indicating how death became part of human destiny. According to the rabbis death was the direct result of Adam's disobedience. Although they did not teach a doctrine of original sin on this basis, they did accept that 'the wickedness of man was great in the earth, and that every imagination of the thoughts of his heart was only evil continually' (Gen. 6.5). They explain this by positing the existence of the evil inclination within every person.

In the Bible the concept of repentance is of fundamental importance. Throughout the prophetic books sinners are admonished to give up their evil ways and return to God. Thus 2 Kings declares: 'Yet the Lord warned Israel and Judah by the hand of every prophet, and of every seer, saying: "Turn from your evil ways, and keep my commandments and my statutes, in accordance with all the law which I commanded your fathers, and which I sent to you by my servants the prophets" ' (2 Kings 17.13). According to Jewish teaching, atonement can only be attained after a process of repentance involving the recognition of sin. It requires remorse, restitution, and a determination not to commit a similar offence. Both the Bible and rabbinic sources emphasize that God does not want the death of the sinner, but desires that he return from his evil ways. Unlike in Christianity, God does not instigate this process through prevenient grace; rather, atonement depends on the sinner's sincere act of repentance. Only at this stage does God grant forgiveness and pardon.

With regard to unwitting offences against ritual law, a sin offering was required in the biblical period as a sacramental act that restores the relationship between God and the transgressor. Following the destruction of the second Temple in AD 70, prayer took the place of sacrifice. In addition, fasting, kindly acts, and the giving of charity were also viewed as means of atonement. In the Jewish yearly cycle, a ten day period (Ten Days of Penitence) is set aside, commencing with *Rosh Hashanah* (New Year) and ending with *Yom Kippur* (Day of Atonement), which is devoted to prayer and fasting. An echo of the ancient scapegoat ritual is observed by some traditional Jews on the Day of Atonement, whereby an individual's sins are expiated by the death of a white fowl. The Day of Atonement, however, only brings forgiveness for sins committed against God; for sins against others, atonement is granted only after the sinner has made final restitution and sought forgiveness from the offended party.

In the Middle Ages Maimonides' (twelfth century) discussion of repentance in the *Mishneh Torah* summarizes the rabbinic view. According to Maimonides, when a person sins wittingly or unwittingly and repents of his wrongdoing, he is obliged to confess his sins to God. Now that the Temple is no longer standing, he asserts, repentance itself atones for all sins. True repentance takes place if the sinner has the opportunity of sinning, but refrains from doing so because he has repented.

The sinner must confess verbally, and it is praiseworthy for him to do so in public: 'Whoever is too proud to confess his sins to others,' he asserts, 'but keeps them to himself, is not a true penitent.' This however does not apply to offences against God where a declaration of sinfulness should be made to him alone. With regard to offences against others, the sinner must make restitution and beg for forgiveness.

Here Maimonides maintains that repentance is effected by a resolve to give up the transgression by confession and restitution – mortification plays no role in this process. Other medieval writers differed regarding the necessity of ascetic actions. In his *Shaare Teshuvah*, for example, Jonah ben Abraham Gerondi (thirteenth century) lists twenty factors of sincere repentance, some of which involve self-mortification: (1) remorse; (2) relinquishing sin; (3) pain for the sin; (4) affliction of the body through fasting and weeping; (5) fear of the consequences of the sinful act and of repeating it; (6) shame; (7) submission to God; (8) gentleness in future actions; (9) overcoming physical lust through asceticism; (10) the use of the organ with which the sinner transgressed to do good; (11) self-observation; (12) reflection on the suitable appropriate punishment; (13) treating minor sins as major; (14) confession; (15) prayer; (16) compensating the victim; (17) almsgiving; (18) consciousness of sin; (19) refraining from repeating the transgression; (20) leading others away from sinfulness.

In another medieval work Isaac Alfasi (eleventh to twelfth century) outlines twenty-four things which act as a barrier to repentance: (1) slander and gossip; (2) anger; (3) evil thoughts; (4) association with evil people; (5) partaking of food so as to deprive the host of his share; (6) looking lustfully at women; (7) partaking of the spoils of robbery; (8) sinning with the intention to repent at a later stage; (9) attaining fame at others' expense; (10) separating oneself from the community; (11) holding parents in disgrace; (12) holding teachers in disgrace; (13) cursing the public; (14) preventing the public from performing good acts; (15) leading a neighbour astray; (16) using a pledge obtained from the poor; (17) taking bribes to pervert justice; (18) keeping a lost article that one has found; (19) refraining from preventing one's son from doing evil; (20) eating the spoil of widows and orphans; (21) disagreeing with sages; (22) suspecting the innocent; (23) hating rebuke; (24) mocking Jewish practices.

In the modern period, such speculation about the nature of repentance as well as obstacles toward true remorse have given way to the more simple view that human beings are responsible for their actions and must repent of their sins. For Jews of all religious persuasions, such action is fundamental to the faith. Although non-Orthodox Judaism does not accept biblical and rabbinic precepts as binding, it nevertheless affirms that all Jews are required to search their ways and make atonement for transgression. The Day of Atonement is designed to remind the Jewish people of this divinely sanctioned task.

11

The Chosen People

The concept of Israel as God's chosen people has been a constant feature of Jewish thought from biblical times to the present. In the Bible the Hebrew root *'bhr'* (to choose) denotes the belief that God selected the Jewish nation from all the other peoples. As the Book of Deuteronomy declares, 'For you are a people holy to the Lord your God: the Lord your God has chosen you to be a people for his own possession out of all the peoples that are on the face of the earth' (Deut. 7.6). According to Scripture this act was motivated by divine love: 'It was not because you were more in number than any other people that the Lord set his love upon you and chose you, for you were the fewest of all peoples; but it is because the Lord loves you' (Deut. 7.7–8). Such love for Israel was later echoed in the synagogue liturgy, especially in the prayer for holy days, which begins: 'Thou hast chosen us from all peoples; thou has loved us and found pleasure in us and hast exalted us above all tongues; thou hast sanctified us by thy commandments and brought us near unto thy service, O king, and hast called us by thy great and holy name.'

Through its election Israel has been given an historic mission to bear divine truth to humanity. Thus, before God proclaimed the Ten Commandments on Mount Sinai, he admonished the people to carry out this appointed task:

> You have seen what I did to the Egyptians, and how I bore you on eagles' wings, and brought you to myself. Now therefore, if you will obey my voice, and keep my covenant, you shall be my own possession among all peoples; for all the earth is mine, and you shall be to me a kingdom of priests and a holy nation (Exod. 19.4–6).

God's choice of Israel thus carries with it numerous responsibilities. As Genesis proclaims: 'For I have chosen him, that he may charge his children and his household after him to keep the way of the Lord by doing righteousness and justice' (Gen 18.19).

Divine choice demands reciprocal response. Israel is obligated to keep God's statutes and observe his laws. In doing so, the nation will be able to persuade the nations of the world that there is only one universal God. Israel is to be a prophet to the nations, in that it will bring them to salvation. Yet despite this obligation, the Bible asserts that God will not abandon his chosen people even if they violate the covenant. The wayward nation will be punished, but God will not reject them: 'Yet for all that, when they are in the land of their enemies, I will not spurn them, neither will I abhor them so as to destroy them utterly and break my covenant with them: for I am the Lord their God' (Lev. 26.44).

In rabbinic sources the biblical doctrine of the chosen people is a constant theme. While upholding the belief that God chose the Jews from all peoples, the rabbis argued that their election was due to an acceptance of the *Torah*. This conviction was based on Scripture: 'If you will hearken to my voice, indeed, and keep my covenant, then you shall be my own treasure from among all the peoples' (Exod. 19.5). According to the rabbis the *Torah* was offered first to other nations of the world, but they all rejected it because its precepts conflicted with their way of life. Only Israel accepted it. According to one tradition this occurred only because God suspended a mountain over the Jewish people, threatening to destroy the nation if they refused: 'If you accept the *Torah* it will be well with you, but if not, here you will find your grave.' The dominant view, however, was that the Israelites accepted God's law enthusiastically. For this reason Scripture states that the Jewish people declared: 'All that the Lord has spoken we will do' (Exod. 24.7), showing a willingness to obey God's decrees without knowledge of its contents.

Rabbinic Judaism asserts that there is a special relationship between the children of Israel and God based on love – this is the basis of the allegorical interpretations in rabbinic sources of the Song of Songs, and is also expressed in the *Talmud* by such sayings as: 'How beloved is Israel before the Holy One, blessed be He; for wherever they were exiled the *Shekhinah* (divine presence) was with them.' Rabbinic literature also emphasizes that God's election of the Jewish people is due to the character of the nation and of the patriarchs in particular; according to the *Talmud*, mercy and forgiveness are characteristic of Abraham and his descendants.

In the Middle Ages the Jewish claim to be God's chosen people was disputed by the Church which saw itself as the true Israel. In response such philosophers as Judah Halevi (eleventh to twelfth century) maintained the entire Jewish people was endowed with a special religious sense. According to Halevi, this faculty was first given to Adam, and then passed on through a line of representatives to all the Jewish people. In consequence, the Jewish people was able to enter into communion with God. Further, because of this divine influence, the election of Israel implies dependence on special providence which sustains the people of Israel, while the remainder of the human race is subject to the general workings of the laws of nature and general providence.

Like Halevi, other Jewish philosophers of the period emphasize Israel's special role in God's plan of salvation. In *Book of Beliefs and Opinions*, Saadiah Gaon (ninth to tenth century) discusses God's promise that the Jewish nation would continue to exist as long as the heavens and the earth. Only Israel, Saadiah insists, is assured of redemption and will be included in the resurrection of the dead. According to Abraham ibn Daud, only Israel is privileged to receive prophecy. For Maimonides, the Jewish faith is the one true revelation which will never be superseded by another divine encounter. Among these Jewish thinkers the doctrine of election was stressed largely as a reaction to oppression by the non-Jewish world. Forced to withdraw into the imposed confines of the ghetto, Jews sought consolation from the belief that despite their sufferings they are God's special people whom he loves above all others.

The concept of Israel's chosenness is also a major theme of medieval kabbalistic thought. According to the *kabbalah*, the Jewish people on earth has its counterpart in the *Shekhinah* in the *sefirotic* realm – the *sefirah Malkhut* is known as the 'community of Israel' which serves as the archetype of the Israelite people on earth. For the kabbalists, Israel's exile mirrors the cosmic disharmony in which the *Shekhinah* is cast into exile from the Godhead. The drama of Israel's exile and its ultimate restoration reflects the dynamic of the upper worlds. In later *Habad* mysticism the Jew has two souls: the animal soul and the divine soul. This divine soul is possessed only by Jews, and even the animal soul of Israel is derived from a source which is an admixture of good and evil. The animal souls of Gentiles on the other hand derive from an unclean source. For this reason no Gentile is capable of acting in a completely good fashion.

During the Enlightenment the Jewish community underwent a major transformation – no longer was the community confined to a ghetto existence. This alteration in Jewish existence challenged the concept of Jewish uniqueness. At the end of the eighteenth century the Jewish philosopher Moses Mendelssohn argued that the intellectual content of Judaism is identical with the religion of reason. In response to the question, 'Why should one remain a Jew?', he responded that Jewry has been singled out by the revelation on Mount Sinai. For this reason it was compelled to carry out a divinely appointed mission to the peoples of the earth.

Subsequently this conception has remained a central teaching of the various branches of the Jewish religious community. Within Reform Judaism for example the notion of Jewish mission was developed, stressing the special message of God which is to be passed on to all the nations. None the less, within non-Orthodox Judaism a number of writers have expressed considerable unease about the claim that the Jews constitute a divinely chosen people. The rejection of this traditional doctrine derives from universalistic and humanist tendencies; unlike traditionalists, progressive Jews believe that Jews are inherently no different from the rest of humanity. Although the Jewish community has a unique history, they believe, this does not imply that God has selected the nation as his very own. Instead, the God of Israel is also the Lord of history who loves all people and guides the destiny of humanity to its ultimate conclusion.

12

The Promised Land

Throughout history the Jewish people have longed for a land of their own. In Genesis God called Abraham to travel to Canaan where he promised to make him a great nation: 'Go from your country and your kindred and your father's house to the land that I will show you. And I will make of you a great nation' (Gen. 12.1–2). This same declaration was repeated to his grandson Jacob who, after wrestling with God's messenger, was renamed Israel (meaning 'he who struggles with God'). After Jacob's son Joseph became vizier in Egypt, the Israelite clan settled in Egypt for several hundred years. Eventually Moses led them out of Egyptian bondage, and the people settled in the Promised Land. There they established a monarchy, but due to the corruption of the nation, God punished his chosen people through the instrument of the foreign powers who devastated the northern kingdom in the eighth century BC and the southern kingdom two centuries later.

Though the Temple lay in ruins and Jerusalem was destroyed, Jews who had been exiled to Babylonia had not lost their faith in God. Sustained by their belief that God would deliver them from exile, a number of Jews sought permission to return to their former home. In 538 BC King Cyrus of Persia allowed them to leave. Under the leadership of Joshua and Zerubbabel, restoration of the Temple began. After the destruction of the First Temple, the nation had strayed from the religious faith of their ancestors. To combat such laxity, the prophet Nehemiah asserted that the community must purify itself; in this effort he was joined by the priest Ezra. Although religious reforms were carried out, the people continued to abandon the *Torah*, and the Temple was destroyed a second time in the first century AD by the Romans.

After Jerusalem and the Second Temple were devastated, the Jews were bereft of a homeland. The glories of ancient Israel had come to an end, and the Jews were destined to live among the nations. In their despair the nation longed for a messianic figure of the House of David who would lead them back to Zion. Basing their beliefs on prophecies in Scripture, they foresaw a period of redemption in which earthly life would be transformed and all nations would bow down to the one true God. Such a vision animated rabbinic reflection about God's providential plan for his chosen people. According to rabbinic speculation, this process would involve the coming of a messianic figure, Messiah ben Joseph, who would serve as the forerunner of the second Messiah. The second Messiah would bring back all the exiles to Zion and complete earthly existence. Eventually at the end of the messianic era, all human beings would be judged: the righteous would enter into heaven whereas the wicked would be condemned to eternal punishment. This eschatological vision served as a means of overcoming the nation's trauma at suffering the loss of its sacred home and institutions.

In the early rabbinic period some Jews believed that Jesus would usher in the period of messianic redemption. Although mainstream Judaism rejected such claims, the Jewish community continued to long for deliverance, and in AD 132 the military leader, Simon bar Kosiba, was acclaimed by many Jews as the Davidic Messiah. When the rebellion he led was crushed, Jews put forward the year of redemption until the fifth century. In about the middle of this century another messianic pretender, Moses from Crete, declared he would lead Jewish inhabitants from the island back to their homeland. After this plan failed, Jews continued to hope for a future return and their aspirations are recorded in a number of midrashic collections.

In the ninth century the Jewish theologian Saadiah Gaon attempted to determine the date of the final redemption on the basis of scriptural texts. In addition, during this period a number of pseudo-Messiahs appeared, and the traveller Eldad Ha-Dani brought news from Africa of the ten lost tribes which further stimulated messianic longing. Such messianic speculation continued into the medieval period. Many Jews viewed the year of the First Crusade (1096) as a year of deliverance: when Jews were slaughtered during this period, their suffering was viewed as the birth pangs of the Messiah. In later years the same yearning for a return to Zion was expressed by Jews who continued to be persecuted by the Christian population.

Medieval Jews, like their ancestors, yearned for release from the bondage of exile, and in their misery looked to God's promises of messianic fulfilment as the means of deliverance.

The early modern period witnessed this same aspiration for messianic redemption. During the sixteenth and seventeenth centuries various messianic treatises were produced, and in the next century the tradition of messianic calculation was continued by numerous rabbinic scholars. During this century several false Messiahs also appeared, claiming to bring about a new age. In the middle of the seventeenth century the Cossack rebellion that devastated Polish Jewry heightened Jewish yearning for deliverance, and in 1665 the arrival of Shabbetai Tzevi electrified the Jewish world. Claiming to be the Messiah, he attracted a large circle of followers; however his conversion to Islam evoked widespread despair.

With the apostasy of Shabbatai Tzevi, the Jewish preoccupation with messianic calculation diminished: many Jews became disillusioned with messianic anticipation and belief in the Messiah receded in significance. Instead many Jews looked to the Enlightenment as their salvation. Yet despite this shift in orientation, a number of religious Jews continued to believe in the coming of the Messiah and linked this yearning to an advocacy of Zionism. Paralleling these religious aspirations to establish a Jewish settlement in the Holy Land prior to the coming of the Messiah, modern secular Zionists encouraged such a development in order to solve the problem of anti-Semitism. In *The Jewish State* the foremost Zionist leader Theodor Herzl argued that the only solution to Judeophobia is for the Jewish people to reconstitute themselves in their own country.

The Zionist movement, however, was met with considerable opposition within the Jewish community. Ultra-Orthodox critics of Zionism believed the creation of a Jewish state was a betrayal of traditional Judaism. It is forbidden, they asserted, to accelerate the coming of the Messiah through human effort. At the opposite end of the spectrum Reform Judaism attacked Zionism as misguided utopianism. According to these progressives, only emancipation could serve as a solution to the Jewish problem – Zionism is a reactionary delusion. In place of a national homeland, they promoted assimilation as a remedy to anti-Jewish sentiment.

Nevertheless, the Zionist cause gained increasing acceptance in the Jewish world. The first steps towards creating a Jewish homeland were taken at the end of the nineteenth century with the first Zionist Congress. Subsequently, Zionists attempted to persuade the British governement to permit the creation of a Jewish home in Palestine. Although Britain eventually approved of such a plan, the British government insisted that the rights of the Arab population be protected. After World War One British representatives attempted to oversee this policy but were met with considerable opposition by militant Zionists. In 1939 a White Paper was published which set limits on the number of Jewish emigrants who could be allowed into Palestine. The Jewish populace rejected this policy and inaugurated a campaign of terror against the British. After World War Two the creation of a Jewish state was approved by the United Nations. Despite such an official endorsement, this plan was rejected by the Arabs. In subsequent years Arabs and Jews have engaged in a series of conflicts. Arab-Israeli antagonism thus continues to undermine the Jewish quest for a homeland in the land of their ancestors.

This saga of Jewish aspiration for a homeland reveals the utopian aspects of the nation's yearning. Through four millennia, Jewry was guided by the belief that it was possible to create God's kingdom on earth. In ancient Israel, the state was to be a theocracy. Continually the prophets reminded the nation of its divine obligations. With the destruction of Jerusalem and the Temple, the desire for a Jewish home was transformed into an eschatological vision of messianic redemption in Zion. The Jews were to return triumphantly with the Messiah at their head. As time passed, this dream faded, yet the longing for a Jewish home did not diminish. Increasingly Jewry came to believe that this eternal quest could be realized only through the labours of the Zionists. The early Zionists were infused with hope and enthusiasm. Their task was to create a Jewish society which would be a light to the nations. Now that the state of Israel has become a reality, a number of Jewish writers have stressed that the Jewish nation should not lose sight of the moral and spiritual dimensions of the Jewish tradition. As the Jewish people stand on the threshold of the third millennium, they argue, the nation must attempt to reconcile the political, social and economic concerns of everyday life with an idealistic vision of God's kingdom on earth.

13

Prayer

According to the Jewish tradition, human beings are able to communicate with God individually or collectively; in response, God answers the prayers which are addressed to him. In Scripture he is portrayed as a personal Deity who created human beings in his image; as a consequence, they are able to attain this exalted position. In the Bible the word most frequently used for such communication is *'tefillah'* – it is derived from the Hebrew root which means to think, entreat, or judge. In its reflexive verbal form it has the sense of judging oneself.

The Bible itself lists more than eighty examples of both formalized and impromptu worship. Initially no special prayers were required for regular prayer, but later worship services became institutionalized through sacrifices and offerings. In biblical times sacrifice was made to God to obtain his favour or atone for sin. The Canaanites sacrificed human beings (2 Kings 3.27), but the story of the binding of Isaac (Gen 22.1–19) teaches God's displeasure with this type of sacrificial act. In ancient Israel three types of sacrifice were offered in the Temple: animal sacrifice (*zerah*), made as a burnt offering for sin, meal offerings (*minhah*), and libations. The rituals and practices prescribed for the Temple sacrifice are set down in Leviticus chapters 2 and 23 and Numbers chapters 28 and 29.

The *Mishnah* states that priests serving in the Second Temple participated in a short liturgy comprising the *Shema* (Deut. 6.4), the Ten Commandments (Exod. 20.3–17) and the priestly blessing (Num. 6.24–6). During this period the entire congregation began to pray at fixed times, and an order of prayers has been attributed to the men of the Great Assembly. Regular services were held four times daily by the delegations of representatives from the twenty-four districts of the country. These services were referred to as: *shaharit* (morning), *musaf* (additional), *minhah* (afternoon), and *neilat shearim* (evening).

Several orders of prayers coexisted until Gamaliel II produced a regularized standard after the destruction of the Second Temple (AD 70). Prayers then officially replaced the sacrifices that could no longer be made. This new ritual, referred to as 'service of the heart' was conducted in the synagogue. The core of the liturgy included the prayer formula 'Blessed are You, O God . . .', the *Shema*, and the *Amidah* (also known as *tefillah*) consisting of nineteen benedictions. On special occasions (such as the Sabbath and festivals), an additional *Amidah* was included. Ideally prayers were recited by a *minyan* (quorum of ten men). However if such a number did not exist, certain prayers had to be omitted including the *kaddish*, *kedushah* and the reading of the Law. The *alenu* prayer, originating from the New Year liturgy, and the *kaddish* were the two concluding prayers of all services.

During the worship service portions of the Pentateuch and the Prophets were recited, and this became normal practice by the time of the *Mishnah*. By the end of the talmudic period the prayer service was supplemented by liturgical hymns (*piyyutim*). These compositions were produced in Palestine as well as Babylonia from geonic times until the twelfth century. The Palestinian rite itself was distinguished by a triennial cycle of readings of the Pentateuch, a recension of the benedictions of the *Amidah*, and an introductory blessing before the recitation of the *Shema*. The Babylonian rite was first recorded in *Sedar Rav* by Amram Gaon in the ninth century – this work serves as the official ordering of prayers with their legal requirements. Such an act of setting down liturgical arrangements led to the dissolution of the ban against committing prayers to writing, and in the tenth century the first authoritative prayer book (*siddur*) was edited by Saadiah Gaon.

Among Jewish mystics mystical cleaving to God (*devekut*) in prayer is of fundamental importance. For the early kabbalists of Provence *devekut* was the goal of the mystic way. According to Isaac the Blind: 'The principal task of the mystics and of they who contemplate on his name is, "And you shall serve him and cleave to him" (Deut. 13.4), and this is a central principle of the *Torah* and of prayer, and of blessings, to harmonize one's thought above, to conjoin God in his letters and to link the ten *sefirot* to him.' For the philosopher Nahmanides (thirteenth century) *devekut* is a state of mind in which one constantly remembers God and his love, 'to the point that when (a person) speaks with someone else, his heart is not with them at all but is still before God . . . whoever cleaves in this way to his Creator becomes eligible to receive the Holy Spirit.' According to Nahmanides, the true *hasid* is able to attain such a spiritual state. *Devekut* does not completely eliminate the distance between God and man – it denotes instead a state of beatitude and intimate union between the soul and its source.

In ascending the higher worlds, the path of prayer paralleled the observance of God's commandments. Yet unlike the *mitzvot*, prayer is independent of action and can become a process of meditation. Mystical prayer, accompanied by meditative *kavvanot* (intention) focusing on each prayer's kabbalistic content, was a feature of the various systems of *kabbalah*. For the kabbalist, prayer is seen as the ascent of man into the higher realm where the soul can integrate with the higher spheres. By using the traditional liturgy in a symbolic fashion, prayer repeats the hidden processes of the cosmos. At the time of prayer, the hierarchy of the upper realms is revealed as one of the names of God. Such disclosure is what constitutes the mystical activity of the individual in prayer, as the kabbalist concentrates on the name that belongs to the omain through which his prayer is passing. The *kavvanah* involved in mystic prayer is seen as a necessary element in the mystery of heavenly unification which brought the divine down to the lowest realm and tied the *sefirot* to each other and the *Ayn Sof*. As the *Zohar* explains: 'Both upper and lower worlds are blessed through the man who performs his prayer in a union of action and word, and thus effects a unification.'

In the nineteenth century *Hasidim* incorporated kabbalistic ideas in their understanding of prayer. According to *hasidic* thought, the kabbalistic type of *kavvanot* brings about an emotional involvement and attachment to God. In Hasidism, prayer is understood as a mystical encounter with the Divine in which the human heart is elevated towards its ultimate source. Frequently the act of prayer was viewed as the most important religious activity. Thus R. Shneur Zalman of Lyady, the founder of Habad Hasidism, wrote in the eighteenth century: 'For although the forms of the prayers and the duty of praying three times a day are rabbinic, the idea of prayer is the foundation of the whole *Torah*. This means that man knows God, recognizing his greatness and his splendour with a serene and whole mind, and an understanding heart'. In Habad Hasidism prayer involves the contemplation of the kabbalistic scheme in which God's infinite light proceeds through the entire chain of being. The devout should reflect on this until their hearts are moved in rapture.

The advent of the Enlightenment in the same century brought about major changes in Jewish life. In 1801 the Jewish communal leader Israel Jacobson initiated a programme of reform: the consistory under his leadership introduced reforms to the Jewish worship service including singing, hymns and addresses as well as prayers in German. In 1810 he built the first Reform Temple. In his address at the dedication ceremony, he stated: 'Our ritual is still weighed down with religious customs which must be rightly offensive to reason as well as to our Christian friends. It desecrates the holiness of our religion and dishonours the reasonable man to place a value upon such customs.'

Subsequently other temples were established in which innovations were made to the liturgy, including prayers and sermons in German as well as choral singing and organ music. The central aim of these early reformers was to adapt Jewish worship to contemporary aesthetic standards. For these innovators, the informality of the traditional service seemed foreign and undignified, and they therefore insisted on greater decorum, more unison in prayer, a choir, hymns and musical responses, as well as alterations in prayers and the length of the service. When Reform Judaism spread to the United States, such reformers continued to promote liturgical change based on both aesthetic and theological criteria, resulting in the publication of a variety of prayer books. Within the Conservative and Reconstructionist movements, prayer books have adhered more closely to the traditional *siddur* although they have similarly departed from traditional Judaism in various respects. Thus within the various branches of Judaism prayer continues to serve as a focal point of the faith.

14

The Love of God

Within the Jewish tradition, the love of God is of central importance. Thus Deuteronomy declares: 'You shall love the Lord your God with all your heart and with all your soul and with all your might' (Deut. 6.5). In the *Mishnah* this verse is quoted to demonstrate that human beings must love God not only for the good that befalls them, but for evil as well. This explanation is based on an interpretation of three expressions in this verse: 'with all your heart' means with both the good and evil inclinations; 'with all your soul' means even if God takes away our soul through martyrdom; 'with all your might' means with all your wealth. According to the *Mishnah*, the injunction to love God involves being faithful even if this requires the loss of one's wealth or one's life.

The *midrash* also comments on this biblical text. Concerning the phrase, 'You shall love the Lord your God', the *Sifre* (*midrash* on Exodus) states:

> Do it out of love. Scripture distinguishes between one who does it out of love and one who does it out of fear. Out of love, his reward is doubled and again doubled. Scripture says: 'You shall fear the Lord your God: you shall serve him and cleave to him' (Deut. 10.20). A man who fears his neighbour will leave him when his demands become too troublesome, but you do it out of love. For love and fear are never found together except in relation to God.

Here the *Sifre* maintains that love and fear are incompatible in human relations, but not with regard to the love of God. The *Sifre* also points out that loving God involves convincing others to love God just as Abraham did when he brought unbelievers under the wings of the *Shekhinah*. Commenting on the verse, 'And these words which I command you this day shall be upon your heart' (Deut. 6.6), the *Sifre* explains: 'Why is this said? Because it is said: "You shall love the Lord your God with all your heart", and I do not know in what way God is to be loved, therefore it says: "Take these to heart and in this way you will come to recognize God and cleave to his ways".' Here loving God is understood as cleaving to his commandments.

In these rabbinic sources, loving God is perceived as living according to his decrees. Among medieval Jewish thinkers, however, stress was placed on mystical love. Thus in his *Beliefs and Opinions* Saadiah Gaon (ninth to tenth century) asks how it is possible to have knowledge of God, much less love him, since we have not perceived him with our senses. In response he asserts that certain statements are believed as true even though they cannot be proved on empirical grounds. According to Saadiah, it is possible to acquire knowledge of God through rational speculation and the miracles afforded by Scripture. Hence truth about God is able to mingle with the human spirit. For this reason the prophet Isaiah states: 'My soul yearns for thee in the night, my spirit within me earnestly seeks thee' (Isa. 26.9). As a result, the soul is filled with love. In this connection Saadiah quotes Deuteronomy 6.5: 'You shall love the Lord your God with all your heart. . .'. The soul of God's servants, he explains, will remember him at all times; as a result the devout will have complete faith and trust in him. He will be grateful for all the good he receives and will steadfastly endure any hardship.

Again in *Duties of the Heart* Bahya ibn Pakudah (eleventh century) sees the love of God as the final goal – this is the aim of all virtues. However, the only way is through fear of him. For Bahya such fear involves the abstinence from worldly desires:

> For it is impossible for the love of God to find a place in our hearts together with love of the world. But when because of his discernment and comprehension the heart of the believer is emptied of the love of the world and free of its desires, then the love of God will find lodgement in his heart and become fixed there in direct proportion to his desire for it.

According to Bahya the love of God is the soul's longing for the Creator. When human beings contemplate God's power and greatness, they bow before his majesty until God stills this fear. Individuals who love God in this fashion have no other interest than serving him. With complete faith and trust they accept all sufferings. In this regard Bahya quotes the saint who used to proclaim at night: 'My God! Thou hast made me hungry and left me naked. Thou hast caused me to dwell in night's darkness and hast shown me thy power and might. Yet even if thou wouldst burn me in fire I would continue only to love thee and rejoice in thee.' Having depicted such love for God, Bahya asks whether human beings are capable of attaining such heights. In response he stresses that only a few individuals are capable of sacrificing their wealth or lives for God's sake. In the history of Israel only prophets and martyrs have been able to reach such a pure state of love, devoid of self-interest.

In his *Code of Law* Maimonides (twelfth century) discusses the love of God in relation to the nature of the universe:

> It is a religious obligation to love and fear this glorious and tremendous God, and it is said: 'You shall love the Lord your God' (Deut. 6.5); and it is said: 'You shall fear the Lord your God' (Deut. 6.13). How does a man come to love and fear God? No sooner does man reflect on his deeds and on his great and marvellous creatures, seeing in them his incomparable and limitless wisdom, than he is moved to love and to praise and to glorify and he has an intense desire to know the great Name . . . . When man reflects on these matters and recognizes all creatures – angels, the spheres and other humans – and when he observes the wisdom of the Holy One, Blessed be He, as manifested in all creatures, his love for God increases so that his soul thirsts and his flesh longs to love God. Blessed be He.

According to Maimonides, one who truly loves God serves him not out of an ulterior motive but disinterestedly. When a person loves God, he automatically carries out the divine commandments: this state is like being lovesick, unable to get the person he loves out of his mind, pining constantly when he stands, sits, eats or drinks. Like Bahya, Maimonides asserts that not everyone is able to attain such a state of pure love. Rather, God can be loved only in proportion to the knowledge one has of him. 'Where there is little knowledge', he writes, 'there is little love; where there is much knowledge there is much love. Consequently, a man must devote himself to the understanding of those sciences and arts which make God known to him in accordance with his capacity to understand and to comprehend.'

In kabbalistic literature the love of God plays a major role. Concerning the verse, 'You shall love the Lord your God', the *Zohar* states that human beings are here commanded to cleave unto God with selfless devotion:

> It is necessary for man to be attached to God with a most elevated love, that all man's worship of the Holy One, blessed be he, should be with love; for no form of worship can be compared to the love of the Holy One, blessed be he . . . . Come and see, nothing is so precious to the Holy One, blessed be he, as the one who loves him with a pure love . . . . The man who loves the Holy One, blessed be he, is surrounded by loving-kindness to all, having no regard for his own person and property.

In the writings of later kabbalists the theme of the love of God was further elaborated. Thus, the sixteenth century writer Elijah de Vidas in his *Reshite Hokhmah* argues that it is impossible for human beings to love a disembodied spirit. Here the love of God must refer to something which is embodied. Since God as *Ayn Sof* (the Infinite) has no body, human love of the divine must be understood as love of the *Shekhinah* (God's presence). For de Vidas, the *Shekhinah* is in no way apart from God; rather, God manifests himself through the *Shekhinah* in order to provide human beings with something tangible they can grasp so as to rise above worldly desires. In this connection de Vidas relates that he has heard numerous tales about sages who had no physical sensations while they studied the *Torah*, so lost were they in divine contemplation. This is comparable, he writes, to a man who so loves a woman that he is insensitive to anything else. To illustrate this idea he cites a story told by the seventeenth century scholar Isaac of Acre:

> A man sitting near a bathhouse saw a princess emerge and was overcome by her beauty. When she heard him singing, she rebuked him saying: 'This can only be in the cemetery, not here', implying that only in death are class distinctions abolished. The man however misunderstood and assumed she would come to him in the cemetery. Patiently he waited for her every day, unable to think of anything else. Eventually he was so absorbed with thoughts of the princess that he became a holy hermit.

'From this tale', de Vidas writes, 'we can learn that the man who loves the *Torah* so passionately that he thinks of nothing else in the world by day and by night will undoubtedly attain to a marvellous degree of soul, without him requiring any mortification of the flesh or fasting. For attachment to God depends on nothing other than the love of *Torah*, to the extent that he loves the *Torah* as a man loves the woman he passionately desires.'

Subsequently among Hasidic Jews, joy in God's service was conceived as central to the love of God; in addition, it was at times understood in the form of martyrdom. Thus the eighteenth century writer Elimelech of Lizensk wrote:

Whenever a man has leisure from his studies he should imagine a terrible fire burning in front of him into which he is ready to allow himself to be cast rather than be false to Israel's God, 'breaking his nature' for God's sake. He should have in mind this thought of readiness to suffer martyrdom when reading the *Shema* and the first benediction of the *Shemoneh Esreh*, and he should imagine that he is cruelly tortured without yielding. This thought should also be in his mind during eating, drinking, and the marital act. He should say to himself, in fact, as soon as he experiences the physical pleasure, that he would take far greater delight in being tortured to death for God's sake.

15

The Fear of God

In Scripture there are numerous references to the fear of God. Often allusions to the love and fear of God are intermingled: they express a particularly intense relationship with the Divine. Frequently the fear of God refers to piety and moral worth. Thus in the Book of Job, Job is described as 'blameless and upright, one who feared God and turned away from evil' (Job 1.1). In rabbinic literature the Hebrew terminology for such awesome reverence is *yirat shamayim* (the fear of heaven).

Among medieval theologians a distinction is drawn between *yirat ha-onesh* (fear of punishment), and *yirat ha-romemut* (fear in the presence of the exalted majesty of God). Concerning these two types of fear, Abraham Ibn Daud (twelfth century) argued in *Emunah Ramah*:

> 'You shall fear the Lord your God' (Deut. 10.20). However, the reference is to the fear produced by his greatness, not to the fear of harm. There is a difference between these two types of fear. A man may be afraid of an honourable prophet who would certainly not harm him, and he may be afraid of a hyena and a snake. The first type is fear at the greatness of the one feared, shame in his presence, and recognition on the part of the one who fears of his imperfections in relation to the one feared. As Job said: 'Behold, I am of small account; what shall I answer thee?' (Job 40.4). And Ezra said: 'O my God, I am ashamed and blush to lift up my face to thee' (Ezra 9.6) . . . . Fear of God should be of this kind, not of the kind of fear we have for kings whom we are afraid will do harm to us.

In *Duties of the Heart* Bahya Ibn Pakudah (eleventh century) draws a similar distinction. Only *yirat ha-romemut* can lead to the pure love of God. A person who attains this degree of reverence will neither fear nor love anything other than the Creator. In this regard Bahya refers to a saint who found a God-fearing man sleeping in the desert. He asked: 'Are you not afraid of lions that you sleep in such a place?' In reply the God-fearer said: 'I am ashamed that God should see that I am afraid of anything apart from him.'

In mystical sources this distinction is also maintained. Thus the *Zohar* asserts:

> There are three types of fear: two of these have no proper foundation but the third is the main foundation of fear. A man may fear God in order that his sons may live and not die or because he is afraid of some punishment to be visited upon his person or his wealth, and because of it he is in constant fear. But it follows that such a man's fear has no proper foundation. There is another man who fears God because he is terrified of punishment in the next world, in dread of Hell. Both these types of fear do not belong to the main foundation of fear and to its root meaning. But the fear which does have a proper foundation is when a man fears his master because he is the great and mighty ruler, the foundation and root of all worlds, and all before him are accounted as naught.

According to this passage the highest type of fear is fear of God himself since such fear has its foundation solely in him rather than something else.

In his *Ikkarim*, Joseph Albo (fifteenth century) defines fear as 'the receding of the soul and the gathering of all her powers into herself, when she imagines some fear-inspiring thing.' Yet there is another type of fear in which the soul is awe-struck not because of any fear of harm, but because of her unworthiness in the face of majesty. For Albo this higher fear is elevating:

> For if man reflects and considers that God sees his open and as well as his hidden acts, and compares his imperfections and poverty of understanding with the sublimity and dignity of God, he will stand in awe before him and will be ashamed to transgress his commandments and not to do his will.

Because human beings are usually unable to reach this state, the *Torah* establishes punishments to coerce obedience to God's will. Both types of fear are therefore necessary: the lower to subdue man's wayward nature, and the higher as an authentic response to God's greatness and power.

In *Reshite Hokhmah*, Elijah de Vidas (sixteenth century) argues that the fear of God is the gate through which every servant of the Lord must pass: it is a necessary condition for loving God and doing his will. Basing his views on kabbalistic doctrine, de Vidas maintains that since human beings are created after the pattern of the upper world, all acts have a cosmic effect. Good deeds cause the divine grace to flow through all worlds, whereas evil deeds arrest this flow and bring about a flaw in the domain of the *sefirot*: the fear of sin thus has cosmic significance. Further, de Vidas contends that human sin prevents the transgressor's entry into Paradise. Mortals should therefore be apprehensive about their fate, and in particular the horrors of hell which await evildoers – for de Vidas this more elementary fear serves as a spur for those of a less refined nature.

In the eighteenth century the Italian kabbalist R. Moses Hayim Luzzatto in *The Path of the Upright* maintains that the fear of sin should be identified with the higher type of fear (*yirah ha-romemut*) rather than with the fear of punishment. The latter means fear of transgressing a divine precept because of physical or spiritual punishment. Such fear is only suitable for the ignorant and for women. Men of learning, however, are able to reach a higher type of fear which consists in refraining from sin through the recognition of God's glory. Such fear is difficult to attain since it requires knowledge of God and the worthlessness of the human being. Only through deep contemplation can the pious achieve such a state. Only Moses was able to reach this higher fear of God easily because he was attached to God: other human beings are held back because of their physical nature. None the less, all saintly individuals must attempt to achieve this state. According to Luzzatto, this is attainable only after much contemplation:

> When a man sits, walks, lies down or rises up, he should ponder on God's omnipresence, and upon our confronting God at all times, until these truths become deeply rooted in his mind. Then will he fear God in truth. Thus David prayed: 'Teach me, thy way, O Lord, that I may walk in thy truth; unite my heart to fear thy name' (Ps. 86.11).

Among the Hasidim the fear of God is viewed as complementary to the love of God. Basing his views on kabbalistic notions, Zevi Elimelech Spira (nineteenth century) in his *Bene Yisakhar*, argues that effort is required to reach this state:

The disciples of the Baal Shem Tov write in the name of their master that human effort is only required in order to attain to the state of worship out of fear, whereas God himself sends man the love of him since the male pursues the female; and you know that fear is the category of the female and love that of the male.

Again, Levi Yitzhak of Berditchev (eighteenth century) in *Kedushat Levi* draws a distinction between the lower fear of sin, and the higher fear where he is overawed by God's majesty. In this state he has no self-awareness. Yet, he continues, this higher fear can only be attained as a product of the lower fear. In the Lithuanian *musar* movement of the nineteenth century, however, the fear of punishment occupies a more central place: it is viewed as essential for those who struggle to reach perfection. According to Isaac Blazer (nineteenth century) the higher fear is the ultimate aim, but it is impossible to attain it without serious reflection on the fear of punishment. Only serious contemplation of severe punishment can penetrate the human heart so that this deeper understanding can be gained.

In modern times there has been less speculation about different types of fear of God. This is in part due to the fact that the belief in punishment in the hereafter has been discarded by a large number of Jews. Such a shift has occurred because punishment as retaliation in a vindictive sense is generally rejected. As Louis Jacobs notes in *A Jewish Theology*: 'The value of punishment as a deterrent and for the protection of society is widely recognised. But all the stress today is on the reformatory aspects of punishment. Against such a background the whole question of reward and punishment in the theological sphere is approached in a more questioning spirit.' For most Jews the rabbinic view of hell is seen as morally repugnant, and as a consequence Jewish theologians have stressed that it is a delusion to believe that a God of love could have created a place of eternal punishment. Thus in his commentary on the Prayer Book, the former Chief Rabbi Joseph Herman Hertz categorically declares, 'Judaism rejects the doctrine of eternal damnation.' And in *Jewish Theology* the Reform rabbi Kaufman Kohler argues that the question whether the tortures of Hell are reconcilable with divine mercy 'is for us superfluous and superseded.'

In this light earlier discussions about the distinction between lower and higher types of fear have ceased to be relevant: as the fear of future punishment has lost its hold on Jewish conscious-ness, divine retribution seems no longer credible. None the less, the higher type of fear which is evoked by an awareness of one's insignificance in the face of God's majesty still remains a feature of Jewish spirituality. As in the past, Jewish writers continue to view such fear as an essential preliminary to the love of God.

16

The Via Negativa

Despite the frequent anthropomorphic descriptions of God in Scripture, there are a number of instances which caution against describing God in such a fashion. Thus Deuteronomy states: 'Therefore take good heed to yourselves. Since you saw no form on the day that the Lord spoke to you at Horeb out of the midst of the fire' (Deut. 4.15). Again Exodus 33.20–3 declares:

> And he said, 'You cannot see my face; for man shall not see me, and live.' And the Lord said, 'Behold there is a place by me where you shalt stand upon the rock; and while my glory passes I will put you in a cleft of the rock, and I will cover you with my hand until I have passed by; then I will take away my hand, and you shall see my back; but my face shall not be seen.'

In rabbinic literature there are similar passages which suggest that human beings should refrain from attempting to describe God. Thus the Palestinian teacher Abin said: 'When Jacob of the village of Neboria was in Tyre, he interpreted the verse "For thee, silence is praise, O God" to mean that silence is the ultimate praise of God. It can be compared to a jewel without price: however high you appraise it, you still undervalue it.'

In another talmudic passage a story is told of the prayer reader who was rebuked by Hanina (first century). This individual praised God by listing as many of his attributes as he could. When he finished, Hanina asked if he had exhausted the praises of God. Hanina then said that even the three attributes 'The Great', 'The Valiant' and 'The Tremendous' could not legitimately be used to describe God were it not for the fact that Moses used them and they subsequently became part of the Jewish liturgy. This text concludes with a parable: if a king who possessed millions of gold pieces is praised for having millions of silver pieces such praise disparages his wealth rather than glorifies it.

The later development of the theory of the *via negativa* owes much to the writings of the neo-Platonists such as the Christian theologian Pseudo-Dionysius (sixth century) who speaks of God as 'It':

> Concerning this hidden Super-Essential Godhead we must not dare, as I have said, to speak, or even to form any conception thereof, except those things which are divinely revealed to us from the Holy Scriptures. For as It has lovingly taught us in the Scriptures concerning Itself, the understanding and contemplation of Its actual nature is not accessible to any being; for such knowledge is super-essentially exalted above them all. And many of the Sacred Writers thou wilt find who have declared that It is not only invisible and incomprehensible, but also unsearchable and past finding out, since there is no trace of any that have penetrated the hidden depths of Its infinitude.

Such notions appealed to a number of Jewish thinkers, particularly in the Middle Ages. In his *Duties of the Heart*, for example, Bahya Ibn Pakudah (eleventh century) argues that the concept of God's unity involves the negation from God of all human and infinite limitations. According to Bahya, if we wish to ascertain the nature of anything, we must ask two fundamental questions: (1) if it is; and (2) what it is. Of God, however, it is possible to ask only if he is. And once having established his existence, it is not possible to go on to inquire about his nature, since it is beyond human understanding.

Given this point of view, how is one to make sense of the descriptions of God in Scripture and the Jewish liturgy? For Bahya there are three main attributes which should be understood in a negative sense: God's existence, unity and eternity. Even when these three attributes are expressed positively, they are in fact understood negatively. Hence, to say that God exists, implies that he is not non-existent. When one asserts that he is one, this means that there is no multiplicity in him. And finally, when he is depicted as eternal, this signifies that he is not bound by time. God's nature is thus inscrutable; none the less, we do have knowledge about him. Concerning other positive attributes (such as his goodness), these can be understood in a positive sense because unlike the other three attributes, they deal with God's acts rather than his essence.

In the *Guide for the Perplexed*, Maimonides also focuses on the concept of negative attributes. As we have seen, Maimonides believes that the ascription to God of positive attributes is a form of idolatry because it suggests that his attributes are coexistent with him. To say that God is one, Maimonides contends, is simply a way of negating all plurality from his being. Even when one asserts that God exists, one is simply affirming that his non-existence is impossible. Positive attributes are only admissible if they are understood as referring to God's acts. Attributes which refer to his nature, however, are only permissible if they are applied negatively. Moreover, the attributes which refer to God's actions imply only the acts themselves – they do not refer to the emotions from which these actions are generated when performed by human beings.

Following Maimonides, Joseph Albo (fourteenth to fifteenth century) in *Ikkarim* contends that God's attributes, referring to God's nature, can only be used in a negative sense. On the other hand, attributes which refer to God's acts can be used positively as long as they do not imply change in God:

> But even the attributes of this class, those taken from God's acts, must be taken in the sense involving perfection, not in the sense involving defect. Thus, although these attributes cause emotion in us and make us change from one of the contraries to the other, they do not necessitate any change or emotions in God, for his ways are not our ways, nor are his thoughts our thoughts.

Like these theologians, the kabbalists advocated a theory of negation in describing God. According to kabbalistic doctrine, there is a distinction between God as he is in and of himself, and as he manifests himself. In kabbalistic thought God reveals himself through the ten *sefirot*, but lying behind this emanation is the *Ayn Sof*. In espousing this doctrine, kabbalists emphasized the impersonal nature of *Ayn Sof*. Thus, Asariel of Gerona (thirteenth century) stated: 'Know that *Ayn Sof* cannot be thought of, much less spoken of, even though there is a hint of It in all things, for there is nothing else apart from It. Consequently, It can be contained neither by letter nor name nor writing nor anything.' Similarly the *Zohar* maintains that the *Ayn Sof* is incomprehensible. Even the higher realms of God's manifestation represented by God's will, wisdom and understanding (*keter, hokhmah, and binah*) are portrayed in negative terms: God's will represented by *keter* is referred to as *Ayin* (nothingness); divine wisdom represented by *hokhmah* is beyond all questioning; of *binah* one can ask what it is, but one should not expect a reply. Later in the eighteenth century, the Gaon of Vilna declared that, strickly speaking, it is not even possible to give the name *Ayn Sof* to the *Ayn Sof*.

17

The Messiah

The term 'Messiah' is an adaptation of the Hebrew *Ha-Mashiah* (the Anointed), a term frequently used in Scripture. Initially in the Book of Samuel the view was expressed that the Lord had chosen David and his descendants to reign over Israel to the end of time (2 Sam. 7; 23.1,3,5). In addition it was held that this figure had been granted dominion over all nations. Thus 2 Samuel 22.50–1 declares:

> For this I will extol thee, O Lord, among the nations,
> and sing praises to thy name.
> Great triumphs he gives to his king,
> and shows steadfast love to his anointed,
> to David, and his descendants for ever.

Here David is 'the anointed' in the sense that he was consecrated for a divine purpose. However it was not only Israelites who would become God's emissaries. Second Isaiah, for example, described the Persian Cyrus as the Lord's anointed (Isa. 45.1). This early biblical doctrine thus presupposes that David's position would endure throughout his lifetime and would be inherited by a series of successors (including non-Israelites) who would carry out God's will.

With the fall of the Davidic empire after Solomon's death, there arose the view that the house of David would eventually rule over the two divided kingdoms as well as neighbouring peoples. Such an expectation paved the way for the vision of a transformation of earthly life. During the Second Temple period, the idea of eschatological salvation became an animating force in Jewish life. During this time there was intense speculation about the nature of the Messiah. In the Book of Zechariah, for example, two messianic figures – the high priest and the messianic king – are depicted. Later, in the Dead Sea sect, these two figures also played an important role and were joined by a third personage, the prophet of the last days. These three messianic roles correspond to the three major functions of a future Jewish state where kingship, priesthood and prophecy will exist side by side.

Yet despite such a proliferation of messianic figures, it was the Davidic Messiah who came to dominate Jewish thought. In the Sibyline oracles he is portrayed in utopian terms. According to tradition, this king-Messiah will put an end to all wars on earth, make a covenant with the righteous and slay the wicked. The Psalms of Solomon extol the messianic king who will rebuild the land and draw all nations to Zion. Such a conception served as the basis for subsequent rabbinic reflection about messianic redemption, the ingathering of exiles, and salvation in the world to come.

As time passed the rabbis elaborated the themes found in the Bible and Jewish literature of the Second Temple period. In the *midrashim* and the *Talmud* they formulated an elaborate eschatological scheme divided into various stages. Some scholars emphasized that the prevalence of iniquity would be a prelude to the messianic age. Yet despite such dire predictions, the rabbis believed that the prophet Elijah would return prior to the coming of the Messiah to resolve all earthly problems. An illustration of this belief is found in the Talmud where the Aramaic word *teku* is used whenever a religious question cannot be resolved. Literally the word means 'let it remain undecided', but the term was interpreted as a phrase meaning: 'The Tishbite (Elijah) will resolve difficulties and problems'. As the fore-runner of the Messiah, Elijah will announce his coming from the top of Mount Carmel: it will be the king-messiah of Israel who will bring about the end of history and the advent of God's kingdom on earth.

In their depictions of the Messiah, the rabbis formulated the doctrine of another Messiah, the son of Joseph, who would precede the king-Messiah, the Messiah ben David. According to legend this Messiah would engage in battle with Gog and Magog, the enemies of Israel, and be slain; only after this would the Messiah ben David arrive in his glory. With the coming of this second Messiah, the dispersion of Israel will cease and all exiles will return from the four corners of the earth to the Holy Land with God at their head. Clouds of glory shall spread over them, and they will come singing with joy on their lips.

In rabbinic literature, as we saw in chapter 12, there is

frequent speculation about the Days of the Messiah. In their descriptions of the messianic age, the rabbis stressed that the Days of the Messiah will be totally unlike the present world. On the length of this epoch, the rabbis differed. Rabbi Eliezer (first to second century), for instance, stated 'The Days of the Messiah will be forty years'; Dosa (first to second century) said 'Four hundred years'; Rabbi Jose the Galilean (second century) declared 'Three hundred and sixty-five years'. In another rabbinic passage, it was taught that the world will endure six thousand years: two thousand in chaos; two thousand under the Law; and two thousand during the messianic age. Despite such disagreements, there was a general acceptance among the sages that at the end of this era a final judgement will come upon all humankind. Those who are judged righteous will enter into heaven (*Gan Eden*) whereas the wicked will be condemned to hell (*Gehinnom*).

The destruction of the Temple and the city of Jerusalem in the first century AD intensified Jewish longing for the coming of the Messiah who would bring about the restoration of the kingdom. In this milieu, a Jewish sect emerged during the years following Herod's death, which believed that Jesus, a carpenter from Galilee, would usher in the era of messianic redemption. Attracting adherents from among the most marginalized sectors of Jewish society, Jesus soon aroused hostility and was put to death. None the less his disciples believed that he had risen from the dead and would return to reign in glory.

Although mainstream Judaism rejected such claims, the Jewish community continued to long for divine deliverance, and in AD 132 a messianic revolt was led by Simon bar Kosiba. This rebellion was inspired by the conviction that God would empower the Jews and the year of deliverance was put forward until the fifth century. In about 448 a messianic figure named Moses appeared in Crete, declaring he would lead the Jews across the sea to Judea. After his plan failed, Jews continued to engage in messianic speculation and their reflections are recorded in a number of midrashic works of the next few centuries. In the ninth century the scholar Saadiah Gaon calculated the date of final redemption on the basis of biblical texts. During these centuries of heightened messianic awareness, a number of pseudo-Messiahs (Abu Isa al-Isphani (eighth century), Serene (eighth century), and Yudghan (eighth century)) appeared on the scene.

During the time of the Crusades, Jewish aspirations for the coming of the Messiah intensified. Initially the date of the First Crusade (1096) was viewed as the year of messianic deliverance. When the massacres of this year occurred, the Jewish community envisaged this tragedy as the birth pangs of the Messiah. In the next two centuries a number of Jewish writers attempted to determine the date of deliverance on the basis of verses in the Book of Daniel. Also during this period several would-be Messiahs appeared in the Jewish world. Previously such figures came from Asia Minor, Babylonia and Persia, but with the shift of Jewry to Mediterranean countries pseudo-Messiahs also emerged in western Europe. The most important false Messiah of this period was David Alroy (twelfth century) who, even after his death, was viewed by his followers as the Redeemer of Israel. In subsequent centuries messianic calculators continued to speculate about the year of deliverance and return of the exiles to the Holy Land on the basis of scriptural texts. Frequently they relied on kabbalistic forms of exegesis in their computations. Mystical works of this era such as the *Zohar* also contained speculations about the advent of the Messiah. In the thirteenth century another messianic figure, Abraham Abulafia, appeared on the scene: although he attracted a wide circle of followers, he also aroused considerable hostility from the scholarly community.

During the fourteenth and fifteenth centuries the Jewish community continued to anticipate the coming of the Messiah despite his failure to appear in 1348 and 1403 as predicted. These centuries witnessed the production of messianic treatises, and various scholars speculated about the year of his arrival. This tradition of messianic speculation was continued in the sixteenth century by numerous sages, and at this time several false Messiahs appeared on the Jewish scene such as David Reuveni (sixteenth century) and Solomon Molko (sixteenth century). Undaunted by the failure of these would-be Messiahs, messianic calculators of the seventeenth century persisted in their investigations. Eventually the Cossack Rebellion of 1648 which devastated Polish Jewry heightened the belief that the coming of the Messiah was close at hand. In 1665 the arrival of the self-proclaimed messianic king, Shabbatai Tzevi, was announced by his disciple Nathan of Gaza. Throughout the world, Jewry was electrified. Yet when Shabbatai converted to

Islam rather than face death, his apostasy evoked widespread disillusionment.

With the conversion to Islam of Shabbatai Tzevi in the seventeenth century, the Jewish preoccupation with messianic calculation diminished: the longing for the Messiah who would lead the Jewish people to the Holy Land and bring about the end of history seemed a distant hope. Instead, eighteenth and early nineteenth century Jewry hailed the breaking down of the ghetto walls and the elimination of social barriers between Jews and Christians. In this milieu the belief in the kingdom of God inaugurated by the Messiah-king receded in importance; in its place the clarion call for liberty, equality and fraternity signified the dawning of a golden age for the Jewish people.

Within Reform Judaism in particular, the doctrine of messianic redemption was radically modified in the light of these developments. In the nineteenth century Reform Jews tended to interpret the new liberation in the Western world as the first step towards the realization of the messianic dream. For these reformers messianic redemption was understood in this-worldly terms. No longer, according to this view, is it necessary for Jews to pray for a restoration in *Eretz Israel* (the Land of Israel); rather Jews should view their own countries as Zion and their political leaders as bringing about the messianic age. Secular Zionists, on the other hand, saw the return to Israel as the legitimate conclusion to be drawn from the realities of Jewish life in Western countries, thereby viewing the state of Israel as a substitute for the Messiah himself. Thus, as Louis Jacobs explains in his *Principles of the Jewish Faith*: 'Most modern Jews prefer to interpret the messianic hope in naturalistic terms, abandoning the belief in a personal Messiah, the restoration of the sacrificial system, and to a greater or lesser degree, the idea of direct divine intervention.'

There has thus been a major transformation of Jewish thought in the modern world. In the past Jews longed for the advent of a personal Messiah who would bring about the messianic age and the ultimate fulfilment of human history. Although this doctrine continues to be upheld by a number of devout Orthodox believers, it has been eclipsed by a more secular outlook on the part of most Jews.

18

The Hereafter

Though there is no explicit reference to the hereafter in the Old Testament, a number of expressions are used to refer to the realm of the dead. In Psalms 28.1 and 88.5 *bor* refers to a pit. In Psalm 6.5 as well as in Job 28.22 and 30.23, *mavet* is used in a similar sense. In Psalm 22.15 the expression *afar mavet* refers to the dust of death; in Exodus 15.12 and Jonah 2.6 the earth (*eretz*) is described as swallowing up the dead, and in Ezekiel 31.14 the expression *eretz tachtit* refers to the nether parts of the earth where the dead dwell. Finally, the word *sheol* is frequently used to refer to the dwelling of the dead in the nether world. In addition, the words *ge ben hinnom*, *ge hinnom* and *ge* are used to refer to a cursed valley associated with fire and death where, according to Jeremiah, children were sacrificed as burnt offerings to Moloch and Baal. In later rabbinic literature the word ordinarily used for hell (*Gehinnom*) is derived from these names.

Though these passages point to a biblical conception of an afterlife, there is no indication of a clearly defined concept; it was only later in the Greco-Roman world that such a notion began to take shape. The idea of a future world in which the righteous would be compensated for the ills they suffered in this life was prompted by a failure to justify the ways of God by any other means. According to biblical theodicy individuals were promised rewards for obeying God's law and punishments were threatened for disobedience. As time passed, however, it became clear that life did not operate in accordance with such a tidy scheme. In response to this dilemma the rabbis developed a doctrine of reward and punishment in the hereafter. Such a belief helped Jews to cope with suffering in this life, and it also explained, if not the presence of evil in the world, then at least the value of creation despite the world's ills.

Given that there is no explicit belief in eternal salvation in the Bible, the rabbis of the post-biblical period were faced with the difficulty of proving that the doctrine of resurrection of the dead is contained in Scripture. To do this they employed methods of exegesis based on the assumption that every word in the Pentateuch was transmitted by God to Moses. Thus, for example, Eleazar, the son of R. Jose (second century), claimed to have refuted the sectarians who maintained that resurrection is not a biblical doctrine:

> I said to them: 'You have falsified your Torah . . . For you maintain that resurrection is not a biblical doctrine, but is written (in Numbers 15.31ff), "Because he has despised the word of the Lord, and has broken his commandment, that person shall be utterly cut off; his iniquity shall be upon him." Now seeing that he shall be utterly cut off in this world, when shall his iniquity be upon him? Surely in the next world.'

According to rabbinic Judaism, the world to come is divided into several stages. First, there is the time of messianic redemption. According to the *Talmud* the messianic age (*yemot hamashiah*) is to take place on earth after a period of decline and calamity, and will result in a complete fulfilment of every human wish. Peace will reign throughout nature; Jerusalem will be rebuilt; and at the close of this era, the dead will be resurrected and rejoined with their souls, and a final judgement will come upon all mankind. Those who are judged righteous will enter into heaven (*Gan Eden*) which is portrayed in various ways in rabbinic literature. One of the earliest descriptions of *Gan Eden* is found in the *midrash Konen*:

> The *Gan Eden* at the east measures 800,000 years (at ten miles per day or 3,650 miles per year). There are five chambers for various classes of the righteous. The first is built of cedar, with a ceiling of transparent crystal. This is the habitation of non-Jews who become true and devoted converts to Judaism. They are headed by Obadiah the prophet and Onkelos the proselyte, who teach them the Law. The second is built of cedar, with a ceiling of fine silver. This is the habitation of the penitents, headed by Manasseh, King of Israel, who teaches the Law. The third chamber is built of silver and gold, ornamented with pearls. It is very spacious, and contains the best of heaven and of earth, with spices, fragrance, and sweet

odours. . . . The fourth chamber is made of olive-wood and is inhabited by those who have suffered for the sake of their religion . . . The fifth chamber is built of precious stones, gold and silver, surrounded by myrrh and aloes . . . This chamber is inhabited by the Messiah of David, Elijah, and the Messiah of Ephraim.

Conversely, those who are judged wicked are condemned to eternal punishment. In one of the most elaborate descriptions of this place of punishment, Moses is depicted as guided by an angel through hell:

When Moses and the Angel of Hell entered Hell together, they saw men being tortured by the Angels of Destruction. Some sinners were suspended by their eyelids, some by their ears, some by their hands, and some by their tongues . . . In another place . . . Moses saw sinners suspended by their heads downward and their bodies covered with long black worms. These sinners were punished in this way because they swore falsely, profaned the Sabbath and the Holy Days, despised the sages, called their neighbours by unseemly nicknames, wronged the orphan and the widow and bore false witness.

On the basis of this scheme of eternal salvation and damnation –which was at the heart of rabbinic theology throughout the centuries – it might be expected that modern Jewish theologians would attempt to explain contemporary Jewish history in the context of traditional eschatology. This, however, has not happened: instead many Jewish writers have set aside doctrines concerning messianic redemption, resurrection, final judgement and reward for the righteous and punishment for the wicked. This shift in emphasis is in part due to the fact that the views expressed in the narrative sections of the *midrashim* and the *Talmud* are not binding. While all Jews are obliged to accept the divine origin of the Law, this is not so with regard to theological concepts and theories expounded by the rabbis. Thus it is possible for a Jew to be religious and pious without accepting all the central beliefs of mainstream Judaism. Indeed, throughout Jewish history there has been widespread confusion as to what these beliefs are.

The doctrine of the resurrection of the dead has in modern

times been largely replaced in both Orthodox and non-Orthodox Judaism by the belief in the immortality of the soul. The original belief in resurrection was an eschatological hope bound up with the rebirth of the nation in the Days of the Messiah, but as this messianic concept faded into the background so also did this doctrine. For most Jews the physical resurrection is simply inconceivable in the light of a scientific understanding of the world. The late Chief Rabbi, Dr Joseph Herman Hertz, for example, argued that what really matters is the doctrine of the immortality of the soul. Thus he wrote:

> Many and various are the folk beliefs and poetical fancies in the rabbinical writings concerning Heaven, *Gan Eden* and Hell, *Gehinnom*. Our most authoritative religious guides, however, proclaim that no eye hath seen, nor can mortal fathom, what awaiteth us in the Hereafter; but that even the tarnished soul will not forever be denied spiritual bliss.

In the Reform community a similar attitude prevails. A well-known statement of the beliefs of Reform Judaism contends that Reform Jews,

> reassert the doctrine of Judaism that the soul is immortal, grounding this belief on the divine nature of the human spirit, which forever finds bliss in righteousnes and misery in wickedness. We reject as ideas not rooted in Judaism the belief in bodily resurrection and in *Gehenna* and *Eden* as eternal punishment or reward.

Traditional rabbinic eschatology has thus lost its force for a large number of Jews in the modern world, and in consequence there has been a gradual this-worldly emphasis in Jewish thought. Significantly, this has been accompanied by a powerful attachment to the state of Israel. For many Jews the founding of the Jewish state is the central focus of their religious and cultural identity. Jews throughout the world have deep admiration for the astonishing achievements of Israelis in reclaiming the desert and building a viable society, and great respect for the heroism of Israel's soldiers and statesmen. As a result it is not uncommon for Jews to equate Jewishness with Zionism, and to see Judaism as fundamentally nationalistic in character. The wheel has therefore turned full circle from the faint allusions to immortality in the biblical period which led to an elaborate development of the concept of the hereafter in rabbinic Judaism. Whereas the rabbis put the belief in an afterlife at the centre of their religious system, modern Jewish thinkers have abandoned such an other-worldly outlook. Although a number of contemporary Jews still continue to believe in some form of immortality, this is far removed from the elaborate doctrine of the hereafter as formulated in traditional rabbinic sources.

19

Judaism and Other Faiths

In the biblical period there was friction between Israel and other religions. Pagan deities are described in the Bible in the most negative fashion; they are *elilim* – non-entities, loathsome, and abominable. The worship of God is the way of faith; other religions are false. Yet despite such condemnation of pagan worship, the prophets did not plead for other nations to give up their gods. According to Deuteronomy, God permits the nations to serve their own deities: 'Things which the Lord your God has allotted to all the peoples under the whole heaven' (Deut. 4.19). Indeed, it is even suggested that when non-Jews worship their gods, they are actually worshipping the God of Israel. According to Malachi, 'from the rising of the sun to its setting my name is great among the nations; and in every place incense is offered to my name, and a pure offering, for my name is great among the nations' (Mal. 1.11).

The rabbis continued the struggle against idolatry. The tractate *Avodah Zarah* in the *Talmud* is devoted to the laws regarding the worship of other gods in the Greek and Roman religion as well as in Zoroastrianism, Christianity and Gnostic dualism. Nevertheless, rabbinic Judaism maintained that salvation is open to non-Jews as well as Jews as long as they observe the seven precepts of the sons of Noah. These are classified as follows: (1) not to worship idols; (2) not to commit murder; (3) not to commit adultery and incest; (4) not to eat a limb torn from a living animal; (5) not to blaspheme; (6) not to steal; (7) to have an adequate system of law and justice.

In the medieval period in Europe the two rival faiths to Judaism were Christianity and Islam. The general view of Jewish thinkers in the Middle Ages was that Islam was not to be classified as idolatry, but there was considerable debate regarding Christianity. Despite this uncertainty about the status of the Christian faith, it was not unusual to find some Jewish writers who regarded the teachings of Christians and Muslims as contributing to the spiritual life. Bahya ibn Pakudah (eleventh century), for example, relied on Sufi teachers and defended his right to use them as teachers of religion. Nevertheless, as religious faiths, Islam and Christianity were unanimously regarded as false; there is simply no mention of Far Eastern religions in rabbinic sources.

By the time of the Enlightenment it was widely held among Jews that Christians and Muslims were in no way to be included in the harsh condemnation of heathens in classical sources. The general view was that these denunciations applied only to the ancient pagans and to contemporary idolators. Thus, Phineas Elijah Hurwitz (eighteenth century) writes that Jeremiah's injunction 'Pour out thy wrath upon the nations that know thee not' (Jer. 10.25) refers to nations that do not know God, like the men of India and Japan who worship fire and water and who are called 'heathen'. The legal authorities of this period all view Eastern religions in this way. This is the position, for example, of Ezekiel Landau (eighteenth century) concerning a priest who married a Hindu woman according to Hindu rite, but later divorced her and repented of his actions. Jewish law rules that a priest who has once worshipped idols is not permitted to bless the people even after his repentance. But in this case Landau permitted him to bless the people because his participation in a marriage service did not in and of itself constitute idolatrous worship. The clear assumption lying behind this decision is that the Hindu faith should be understood as idolatrous.

From the earliest times, then, the Jewish community had a selectively tolerant attitude to other religions. Jews did not attempt to convert non-Jews even though they regarded their own faith as the touchstone of truth. Nevertheless, they viewed all other religions as false except in so far as they agreed with Judaism. No doubt this was the reason why rabbinic authorities did not view Islam as idolatry whereas they maintained that polytheistic religions such as Zoroastrianism, Gnosticism and Hinduism were idolatrous. From this vantage point Judaism is at the centre of the universe of faiths, whereas all other belief systems encircle it only at those points where there is common ground.

According to this traditional model, Judaism is at the centre because it is absolutely true. Its source is God: at Mount Sinai God revealed to Moses his holy *Torah*. It is this bedrock of certainty which is the mainstay of the Jewish faith. Sinaitic revelation is seen as a unique divine act which provides a secure foundation for the religious traditions of Israel. It is from the Pentateuchal account that we learn of God's true nature, his dealings with his chosen people, and the promise of the world to come. In this fashion the written *Torah* as well as the rabbinic interpretation of Scripture serves as the yardstick for evaluating the truth claims of other religions.

The significant feature of this model is that it excludes the possibility of God revealing himself to others. It assumes that throughout the history of the world, people have mistakenly believed that they have had an encounter with the Divine, but in fact God only made himself known to the Jews. This accounts for the wide diversity and contradictory character of religious beliefs among the religions of the world. As to those religions which have ideas similar to those found in Judaism, this concurrence is not due to God's intervention. Rather, the adherents of these religions would have arrived – possibly through the aid of human reason – at religious conceptions which happen to be true and therefore conform to what is found in the Jewish faith.

Though such a model is consonant with the attitude of many Jews in the past, a number of modern Jewish writers argue that it suffers from serious theological defects. If God is the providential Lord of history, they maintain, it is difficult to understand why he would have hidden his presence and withheld his revelation from humanity – except for the Jews. To allow people from the beginning of human history to be weighed down by false notions of divine reality is hardly what we would expect from a loving, compassionate and caring God. While it is true that traditional Judaism holds that in the hereafter all the nations of the earth will come to know God's true nature, this does not explain why he would have refrained from disclosing himself to the mass of humanity in this life on earth.

According to these Jewish thinkers, what is much more likely is that in the past God revealed himself not only to the Jews but to others as well. On this view, Judaism would still be at the centre of the universe of faiths, encircled by other religions. But the significant difference between this second model and the previous one concerns the role of revelation. Here, non-Jewish religions would be regarded as true, not simply because adherents happened to have similar ideas to what is found in Judaism, but because of a real encounter with the Divine. Judaism would on this view be regarded as ultimately true; its doctrines would serve as a basis for testing the validity of all alleged revelations.

The advantage of this model is that it not only takes seriously God's love, but it also comes to terms with the human spiritual quest. While preserving the centrality of the Jewish faith, it gives credence to the claims of the followers of other religions who believe they have experienced the Divine. Yet other even more progressive Jewish thinkers argue that it is questionable whether this picture of the universe of faith goes far enough. Even this liberal approach, they believe, does not do full justice to God's nature as a loving father who truly cares for all his children. On this second model, it is the Jewish people who really matter. They are the ones who have received the full and ultimate disclosure of his revelation; other faiths have only a partial and incomplete view and are pale reflections by comparison. What is missing from this vision of the world's religions is an adequate recognition of God's providential love and concern for all humanity.

Influenced by Christian religious pluralists such as John Hick, these progressive Jewish writers maintain that in each and every generation and to all peoples of the world, God has disclosed himself in numerous ways. Thus, neither in Judaism, nor for that matter in any other religion, has God revealed himself absolutely and completely. Instead, God's revelation was made manifest to different peoples in varied forms. In each case the revelations, and the traditions to which they gave rise, were conditioned by such factors as history, language and culture. For these reasons the form of the revelation has been characteristically different in every case. Such a conception of God's activity serves as the basis of a third model of Judaism and the universe of faiths. Here God, rather than the Jewish tradition, is at the centre. Judaism, like other faiths, encircles him intersecting only at those points at which the nature of divine reality is reflected.

According to these Jewish religious pluralists, this vision of Judaism in the context of the world religions is more coherent with the Jewish understanding of God; further, it paves the way for interfaith encounter at the deepest levels. Already Jews work together with members of other faiths on common projects of fellowship and charity. Yet, they contend, if Jews could free themselves from an absolutist Judeocentric position, the way would be open for interfaith dialogue of the most profound kind. With the Divine at the centre of the universe of faiths, Jewish dialogue with other religious traditions would assume an altogether different and beneficial character. From its biblical origins, Judaism adopted a generally tolerant attitude to other religious traditions; what is possible today is for this spirit of tolerance to deepen and serve as a foundation for a common religious quest.

Part Two

PRACTICES

20

The Community

Through the centuries Jews have been organized as a distinct group. In ancient Israel they were a Hebrew clan; subsequently, as they changed from a nomadic to an agricultural existence, they settled in towns. In consequence their leadership became urbanized: elders were responsible for administering justice, and towns were organized in territorial or tribal units. During the Babylonian exile the emergence of Jewish institutions established the pattern for later communal development throughout the diaspora. As early as the second century BC Jews in Alexandria formed their own corporation with a council (*gerousia*) which conducted its affairs in conformity with Jewish law, built synagogues, and sent taxes collected for the Temple to Jerusalem. Throughout the Roman Empire, Jews were judged by their own courts according to Jewish law – this system established the basis for legal autonomy that characterized Jewish life for the next two millennia.

With the destruction of the Second Temple in AD 70, Jewish life underwent a major transformation. In Israel the patriarchate together with the Sanhedrin served as the central authority; in Babylonia the exilarch was the leader of the community along with the heads of rabbinical academies (*geonim*). In its daily life Jewry was bound by the *halakhah* (Jewish law), and synagogues, law courts, schools, philanthropic institutions and ritual baths constituted the framework for communal life. In North Africa and Spain, the *nagid* was the head of the community. Later in the medieval period, communal leadership in the Franco-German region was exercised by rabbinical authorities, and daily existence was regulated by traditional law. As in Babylonia, a wide range of institutions dealt with all aspects of community affairs, and taxes were raised to provide for a wide range of needs: ransoming captives, providing hospitality to Jewish visitors, visiting the sick, caring for the elderly, collecting dowries for poor brides, maintaining widows, and supervising Jewish baths. As elsewhere in the Jewish world, the focus of the community was the synagogue, which served as the centre for Jewish worship and study.

To regulate Jewish life, communal statutes (*takkanot ha-kahal*) were stipulated by the community's constitution – these were amplified by special ordinances and enactments. To ensure their enforcement, a court (*bet din*) was presided over by a panel of judges (*dayyanim*). In certain cases they excommunicated individuals or in the case of Jews who informed on fellow Jews, they passed sentences of death. The community's head (*parnas*) was recognized by secular or Church authorities as the representative of the Jewish populace; he and the local rabbi were frequently designated as *Magister Judaeorum* (Master of the Jews) or *Judenbischof* (Bishop of the Jews). From the fourteenth century, Polish Jewry gained dominance in Eastern Europe, and communal autonomy was often invested in the Jewish community of a central town which had responsibility for smaller communities in the region. In Poland-Lithuania the Council of the Four Lands functioned as a Jewish parliament. By contrast, in the Ottoman Empire, authority was vested in a chief rabbi (*hakham bashi*) who was recognized as the Jewish community's representative. Each province of the Empire had its own chief rabbi, and in Egypt this office replaced the *nagid*.

With the advent of the Enlightenment in the nineteenth century, the traditional pattern of Jewish life was transformed. Previously Jews were unable to opt out of the community; however, with full civil rights, Jews became full members of the wider community and membership in the Jewish community was voluntary. In modern times Jews have adjusted communal life to contemporary demands throughout the diaspora, and in Israel new forms of association have emerged. In contrast with previous centres where Jewish religious life was uniform in character, the community has fragmented into a number of differing religious groupings, each with its own character.

At the far right of the religious spectrum traditional Orthodoxy has attempted to preserve the religious beliefs and practices of the Jewish faith. From the late eighteenth century Orthodox Judaism opposed changes to Jewish existence brought about by the Enlightenment and the innovations advanced by Reform Jews. In essence Orthodoxy is synonymous with rabbinic Judaism as it developed through the centuries. Orthodox Jewry accepts the *Torah* as divinely revealed, and the process of rabbinic expansion of biblical law as guided by God's providence.

From the very beginning of the modern age Orthodox Jews rejected the values of the Enlightenment and proclaimed a ban of excommunication against Reformers. Such an approach was advocated by Mosheh Sofer of Pressburg (eighteenth to nineteenth century) and was characteristic of Hungarian Orthodoxy as well as Eastern European Jewry. In addition, it found expression in the anti-Zionist *Agudat Israel* movement. Other Orthodox leaders, however, attempted to integrate traditional Judaism and modern values. Such figures as Samson Raphael Hirsch (nineteenth century) Azriel Hildesheimer (nineteenth century) and members of the Breuer and Carlebach families formed the Neo-Orthodox movement from which centrist Orthodoxy later emerged in the West. A similar development occurred in Eastern Europe and can be traced from Elijah Gaon of Vilna (eighteenth century), Hayyim of Volozhin (eighteenth to nineteenth century) and the Berlin and Soloveichik families to Isaac Jacob Reines (nineteenth to twentieth century) and Abraham Isaac Kook (nineteenth to twentieth century).

In the United States the Orthodox movement underwent enormous growth with the arrival of Orthodox scholars, heads of *yeshivot* and Hasidic leaders during the first half of the twentieth century. From 1944 *Torah Umesorah* organized a network of Hebrew day schools and *yeshivot* throughout the country. Today there are about forty *yeshivot* for advanced talmudic studies. The most important Orthodox rabbinic institutions are Yeshivah University in New York and the Hebrew Theological College in Chicago. The largest Orthodox synagogue body is the Union of Orthodox Jewish Congregations of America. As elsewhere, Orthodoxy in the USA is divided into two distinct groups: traditionalists and modernists. The institutions of Orthodox traditionalists include: the Union of Orthodox Rabbis, the Rabbinical Alliance, and *Agudat Israel*. Modern Orthodoxy's religious leadership on the other hand is found in the Rabbinical Council of America. Elsewhere in the diaspora Orthodox Judaism constitutes the largest religious body. In France, for example, several traditional *yeshivot* have emerged alongside the old-fashioned *École Rabbinique*. In Great Britain a large network of congregations is maintained by the United

Synagogue; parallel with this body is the Federation of Synagogues and the Spanish and Portuguese Jews Congregation. On the traditional right is the Union of Orthodox Hebrew Congregations and the *yeshivah* community of Gateshead.

In Israel Orthodoxy is the formally recognized religious body of the State. Rabbinical courts exercise exclusive jurisdiction in matters of personal status and Orthodox religious judges are presided over by the two Chief Rabbis (Sephardi and Ashkenazi). At the local level Orthodox religious councils cater to religious needs: the provision of ritual baths, burial facilities, registration of marriages, care of synagogues, and the promotion of religious education. In addition, a state religious school system run on Orthodox lines exists alongside the state school system. Within the government Orthodox religious parties represent both religious Zionists and the non-Zionist *Agudat* camp.

Within the Orthodox camp Hasidism plays an important role. Founded by Israel ben Eleazer (Baal Shem Tov) in the eighteenth century as a reaction against arid rabbinism, the Hasidic movement spread to Southern Poland, the Ukraine and Lithuania. This popular mystical movement was initially condemned by Orthodox leaders such as the Gaon of Vilna (eighteenth century); eventually, however, it became a major force in Jewish life. Prior to World War Two hundreds of Hasidic dynasties flourished in Eastern Europe, but after the Holocaust most of the remaining leaders (*rebbes*) escaped to Israel and the United States. Today the best known groups (named after their town of origin) are: Belz, Bobova, Gur, Klausenburg-Zanz, Lubavich, Satmar and Vizhnits. Each of these groups preserves its traditions, including a distinctive type of dress worn by noblemen in the eighteenth century. Like the Orthodox generally, the Hasidim rigidly adheres to traditional Jewish practices as codified in the *Code of Jewish Law*.

Moving to the centre of the religious spectrum, Conservative Judaism constitutes one of the major developments in modern Jewish life. Founded by Zacharias Frankel in the middle of the nineteenth century, it advocates a middle of the road stance in which traditional Jewish law is observed, but modified according to contemporary needs. According to Frankel, Judaism should be understood as an evolving religious way of life. In the United States this ideology was propounded by the Jewish Theological Seminary founded in 1956. Later its president,

Solomon Schechter, founded the United Synagogue as the movement's lay organisation. From 1940–72 the Seminary was headed by Louis Finkelstein; during this time a West Coast affiliate of the Seminary (the University of Judaism) was established in Los Angeles. Through its rabbinical body (the Rabbinical Association) and its synagogual association (the United Synagogue of America), the movement grew in strength and founded a variety of innovative institutions including a camping programme (*Ramah* as well as United Synagogue Youth), radio and TV programmes, Solomon Schechter Day Schools, and New York's Jewish Museum. In 1972 Finkelstein was succeeded by Gerson D. Cohen who introduced far reaching changes, including the ordination of women. By 1985 830 congregations were affiliated to the United Synagogue of America with a membership of 1,250,000. Elsewhere, the movement is represented by the World Council of Synagogues. An offshoot of the Conservative movement, Reconstructionist Judaism, has also made an important impact on Jewish life. This new religious body was founded by Mordecai Kaplan who rejected supernaturalism and instead propounded a new view of Judaism. Currently, Reconstructionist Judaism has its headquarters at the Rabbinical College in Pennsylvania; affiliated congregations are organized in the Federation of Reconstructionist Congregations.

On the far left of the religious spectrum is Reform Judaism. At the beginning of the nineteenth century the communal leader, Israel Jacobson, initiated a programme of educational and liturgical reform. Following this initiative, Reform temples were established in Germany and elsewhere. The central aim of the early Reformers was to adapt Jewish worship to contemporary aesthetic standards. For these innovators, the informality of the traditional service seemed foreign and undignified, and they therefore insisted on greater decorum, more participation in prayer, a choir and hymns as well as alterations in prayers and the length of the service. Despite the criticisms of the Orthodox, the Reform movement underwent considerable growth, and during the nineteenth century a series of Reform synods took place in Europe.

In the United States Reform first appeared in Charleston, South Carolina in 1824; in subsequent years German immigrants founded a number of congregations throughout the country. Under the leadership of Isaac Mayer Wise the first

Conference of American Reform Rabbis took place in Philadelphia in 1869; this was followed in 1873 by the founding of the Union of American Hebrew Congregations. Two years later Wise established the Hebrew Union College, the first American rabbinical seminary. In 1885 the principles of the Reform movement were formulated by a group of rabbis in the Pittsburgh Platform. In 1889 the Central Conference of American Rabbis was established with Isaac Mayer Wise as president. Dissatisfaction with the Pittsburgh Platform led to the adoption of a more traditionalist position (the Columbus Platform), in 1937. In recent years Reform Judaism has undergone further development: by 1980, 739 congregations were affiliated with the Union of American Hebrew Congregations; during the latter half of this century the Jewish Institute of Religion in New York combined with the Hebrew Union College and branches were established in Los Angeles and Jerusalem. Elsewhere Reform Judaism is represented in South Africa, Asia, Australia, and Europe; these congregations are affiliated with the World Union for Progressive Judaism.

21

Jewish Literature

The Jewish faith is a revealed religion. Its basis is the Bible. The Hebrew name for the canon of Scripture is *Tanakh*: the Hebrew term is an abbreviation of the principle initial letters of the words standing for its three divisions: *Torah* (teaching); *Neviim* (prophets); *Ketuvim* (writings). The Torah consists of Genesis, Exodus, Leviticus, Numbers and Deuteronomy; according to tradition these five books were revealed by God to Moses on Mount Sinai. The second division of the Jewish Bible – Prophets – is divided into two parts. The first – Former Prophets – contains the books of Joshua, Judges, 1 and 2 Samuel, and 1 and 2 Kings. The second part – Latter Prophets – is composed of the major prophets (Isaiah, Jeremiah, and Ezekiel) and the minor prophets (Hosea, Joel, Amos, Obadiah, Jonah, Micah, Nahum, Habbakuk, Zephaniah, Haggai, Zechariah and Malachi). The third division consists of a variety of divinely inspired books: Psalms, Proverbs, Job, Song of Songs, Ruth, Lamentations, Ecclesiastes, Esther, Daniel, Ezra, Nehemiah and 1 and 2 Chronicles.

During the Second Temple period and afterwards, a large number of other books were written by Jews in Hebrew, Aramaic and Greek which were not included in the biblical canon. None the less, these texts did gain canonical status in the Roman Catholic and Eastern Orthodox Churches. Known as the Apocrypha, they had an important impact on Christian thought. The most substantial is the Wisdom of Jesus Son of Sirah (also known as Ben Sira or Ecclesiasticus). Other works include: the Wisdom of Solomon, 1 and 2 Macabees, Tobit and Judith. Additional literary sources of the Second Temple period are known as the Pseudepigrapha – these non-canonical books consist of such works as the Testament of the Twelve Patriarchs, 1 and 2 Enoch and Jubilees. Recent archaeological discoveries have also unearthed other works of this time: the Dead Sea Scrolls contain such texts as the Thanksgiving Psalms,

Manual of Discipline, and Scroll of War of the Children of Light against the Children of Darkness. In addition to these texts the writings of Philo and Josephus, as well as the New Testament, contribute further to Jewish literary activity during the Second Temple period.

After the Babylonian exile, a new phase of Jewish writing began. As tradition relates, this shift in Jewish life was initiated and carried on by the Men of the Great Assembly and the Scribes, and subsequently by the rabbis. Once the Temple was destroyed in AD 70 Pharisaic Judaism became the norm for Jews in Palestine and the diaspora. Its teachers, known as rabbis, engaged in the interpretation of Scripture; this practice (referred to as *midrash*) focused on both the legal and the narrative sections of the Bible. During the age of the *tannaim* (AD 70–200), Jewish sages produced teachings dealing with Jewish law which were codified in the *Mishnah* by Judah Ha-Nasi in about AD 200. This work is a compilation of oral traditions (Oral Law); it is divided into six orders (which are subdivided into sixty-three tractates). The first order, *Zeraim* (seeds) deals largely with agricultural law although it begins with a tractate about prayer. The second order, *Moed* (season) treats the sacred calendar. In the third order, *Nashim* (women), matrimonial law is discussed in extensive detail. The fourth order, *Nezikim* (damages) contains both civil and criminal law and also contains a tractate of moral maxims (known as *avot*). The fifth order, *Kodashim* (holy things) gives a detailed account of the rules for sacrifice. Finally, the sixth order, *Tohorot* (purity) deals with ritual purity. Although the *Mishnah* is comprehensive in scope, it does not contain all the traditions of the *tannaim*. The traditions not found worthy to be included were recorded in the *Tosefta*. Any teaching of this period which was not included in the *Mishnah* is known as a *baraita* (they are found not only in the *Tosefta*, but also in rabbinic *midrashim* as well as the *Talmud*).

Parallel with the legal tradition, the rabbis also expounded the narrative parts of Scripture. In the tannaitic period such *midrashim* dealt with the Pentateuch (Five Books of Moses). Some of these traditions allegedly derive from the School of Akiva; others are attributed to the School of Ishmael. These midrashic sources are: the *Mekilta* on the book of Exodus, the *Sifra* on Leviticus, and the *Sifrei* on Numbers and Deuteronomy. Other midrashic sources deal with material from the amoraic period (AD 200–500). Like the tannaitic *midrashim*, some are in the form of running commentaries known as exegetical *midrashim*; others consist of collections of sermons arranged according to the Sabbaths or festivals for which they were written – they are known as homiletical *midrashim*. The largest collection of *midrashim* is *Midrash Rabbah* consisting of works that were separate commentaries on the Pentateuch plus the Five Scrolls (the Song of Songs, Ruth, Lamentations, Ecclesiastes, Esther). Homiletical *midrashim* are exemplified by *Pesikta de-Rav Kahana*, *Pesikta Rabbati* and *Midrash Tanhuma* (also referred to as *Yelammedenu*).

In the centuries following the composition of the *Mishnah* and the early rabbinic *midrashim*, Jewish sages in Palestine and Babylonia continued to expand Jewish law. By the fourth century scholars in Israel had collected together the teachings of generations of rabbis in the academies of Tiberius, Caesarea and Sepphoris. The extended discussions of the *Mishnah* became the Palestinian *Talmud*. The text of this multi-volume work covers four sections of the *Mishnah* (seeds, set feasts, women and damages), but here and there various tractates were missing. No doubt the discussions in these academies included matters on these missing tractates, but it is not known how far the recording, editing and transmission of these sections had progressed before they were lost.

The views of these Palestinian sages (known as *amoraim*) had an important influence on scholars in Babylonia, though their work never attained the same prominence as that of the Babylonian *Talmud*. In Babylonia scholars completed the redaction of the Babylonian *Talmud* by the sixth century – an editorial task begun by Rav Ashi in the fifth century. This massive work is largely a summary of the amoraic discussions that took place in the Babylonian academies. Although the Babylonian *Talmud* deals with slightly fewer Mishnaic tractates, it is nearly four times larger than the Palestinian *Talmud* and came to be regarded as more authoritative.

The text of these *Talmuds* consists largely of summaries of rabbinic discussion: a phrase of *Mishnah* is interpreted, discrepancies are resolved and redundancies are explained. In this compilation conflicting opinions of the earlier *tannaim* are contrasted, unusual words are explained and anonymous opinions are identified. Frequently, individual teachers cite specific cases to support their views and hypothetical eventualities are examined to reach a solution on the discussion. Debates between outstanding scholars in one generation are often cited, as are differences of opinion between contemporary members of an academy or a teacher and his students. The range of talmudic exploration is much broader than that of the *Mishnah* itself and includes a wide range of rabbinic teachings about such subjects as theology, philosophy and ethics.

Although many midrashic sources were edited in posttalmudic times, there was a growing need for more explanatory exegesis of the biblical text which led to the publication of a variety of biblical commentaries in the medieval and early modern period. Prominent commentators included Solomon ben Isaac (Rashi) (eleventh century), Abraham ibn Ezra (twelfth century), Samuel ben Meir (Rashbam) (twelfth century), David Kimchi (Radak) (thirteenth century), Moses ben Nachman (Ramban) (thirteenth century), Levi ben Gershon (Gersonides) (fourteenth century), Don Isaac Abravanel (sixteenth century), and Obadiah Sforno (sixteenth century). Many commentaries were also written on rabbinic sources during this era. The most important were composed by Moses Maimonides (Rambam) (twelfth century), Solomon ben Isaac (Rashi) (twelfth century), and Obadiah Bertinoro (sixteenth century).

One of the most important developments of post-talmudic Judaism was the development of 'responsa' literature, consisting of replies to queries posed to leading legal authorities. The most important respondents include Sheira Gaon (eleventh century), Hai Gaon (eleventh to twelfth century), Rabbenu Gershom (tenth to eleventh century), Rabbenu Tam (twelfth century), Maimonides (twelfth century), Meir of Rothenburg (thirteenth century), Solomon ben Adret (Rashba) (thirteenth to fourteenth century), Asher ben Yechiel (thirteenth to fourteenth century), Isaac ben Sheshet Barfat (Ribash) (fourteenth to fifteenth century), Joseph Colon (Maharik) (fifteenth century), David ben Zimra (Radbaz) (fifteenth to sixteenth century), Jacob Emden (Yaavetz) (sixteenth to seventeenth century), Ezekiel Landau (eighteenth century), Moses Schreiber (eighteenth to nineteenth century), Solomon Kluger (eighteenth to nineteenth century), Joseph Saul Nathanson (nineteenth century), Isaac Elchanan Spektor (nineteenth century), David Hoffman (nineteenth to twentieth century), and Benzion Uziel (nineteenth to twentieth century).

After the completion of the *Talmud* and *responsa*, there was a need for a systematic presentation of Jewish law which would distil all previous legislation. The first attempt to produce such a code took place in the eleventh century in North Africa and Spain by Isaac Alfasi (Rif). Subsequently Moses Maimonides (Rambam) published the *Mishneh Torah* (also known as the *Yad ha-Hazakah*). Other codes included those of Mordecai ben Hillel (thirteenth century), Asher ben Yechiel (thirteenth century), and his son Jacob ben Asher (thirteenth to fourteenth century). The code by Jacob ben Asher (*Arbaah Turim*) was divided into four sections: (1) *Orah Hayyim* dealing with prayer, worship, Sabbath and festivals; (2) *Yoreh Deah* detailing a wide variety of ritual law; (3) *Even ha-Ezer* concerning matrimonial law; and (4) *Hoshen ha-Mishpat* focusing on civil and criminal law. This code served as the model for the most authoritative code, the *Shulhan Arukh* by Joseph Caro (fifteenth to sixteenth century). To this code were subsequently added glosses (*mappah*) by Moses Isserles (sixteenth century). The publication of the *Shulhan Arukh* subsequently led to the composition of numerous commentaries by such scholars as Joshua Falk (sixteenth to seventeenth century), David ben Saul Ha-Levi (sixteenth to seventeenth century), Moses Lima (seventeenth century), Shabbetai Cohen (seventeenth century), Abraham Gabiner (seventeenth century) and Saul ben Levi Phorbus (seventeenth century).

Parallel with these legal developments, Jewish mysticism underwent an efflorescence during the medieval period. Known as *kabbalah*, it drew on earlier midrashic and talmudic sources. Toward the end of the thirteenth century, the *Sefer ha-Zohar* (*Zohar*) was compiled by Moses ben Leon in Spain. This work exercised a profound influence on later Jewish mystics especially in Safed in Palestine such as Moses Cordovero (sixteenth century) and Isaac Luria (sixteenth century). The *kabbalah* also affected Hasidism in the eighteenth century. Prominent among Hasidic kabbalists was Shneur Zalman of Lyady (eighteenth to nineteenth century) who founded the *Habad* movement. Other thinkers included Nachum of Bratzlav (eighteenth to nineteenth century).

Another major development of post-talmudic Judaism was the revival of Jewish philosophy and theology in the medieval period. The earliest philosopher of the Middle Ages was Saadiah Gaon who produced the first major Jewish theological treatise, *The Book of Beliefs and Opinions*. This was followed in the eleventh century by the work in the neo-Platonic tradition, *Fountain of Life*, by Solomon ibn Gabirol. Another writer of this period, Bahya ibn Pakuda, drew on neo-Platonic ideas in the composition of his ethical work, *Duties of the Heart*. Another important philosopher of this period was Abraham ibn Daud (twelfth century) who wrote *The Exalted Faith*, in which he attempted to harmonize the Bible with rational thought. In opposition to this approach, Judah Halevi (eleventh to twelfth century) composed *The Book of the Khazars* to demonstrate that Judaism cannot be understood by the intellect alone. The greatest Jewish philosopher of the twelfth century was Moses Maimonides whose *Guide for the Perplexed* had a powerful impact on later Jewish thought. Prominent philosophers of later centuries included Levi ben Gerson (Gersonides) (thirteenth to fourteenth century); Hasdai Crescas, Simon ben Zemah Duran and Joseph Albo (all fourteenth to fifteenth century); Isaac Arama and Isaac Abrabanel (both fifteenth to sixteenth century). In the modern period important Jewish philosophers and theologians included Moses Mendelssohn in the eighteenth century and in the nineteenth century, Samson Raphael Hirsch, Solomon Formstecher, Solomon Hirsch and Solomon Ludwig Steinheim; Leo Baeck, Herman Cohen, and Franz Rosenzweig (nineteenth to twentieth century); and Mordecai Kaplan, Abraham Joshua Heschel and Martin Buber (all twentieth century).

22

Education

According to tradition, it is the duty of parents to educate their children. Thus, Deuteronomy 6.7 declares of biblical laws: 'And you shall teach them diligently to your children, and shall talk of them when you sit in your house, and when you walk by the way, and when you lie down and when you rise.' In addition, Scripture repeatedly refers to a father's obligation to tell his children about the Exodus from Egypt: 'You may tell in the hearing of your son and of your son's son how I have made sport of the Egyptians and what signs I have done among them' (Exod. 10.2); 'And you shall tell your son on that day, "It is because of what the Lord did for me when I came out of Egypt" ' (Exod. 13.8); 'When your son asks you in time to come, "What is the meaning of the statutes and the ordinances which the Lord our God has commanded you?" then you shall say to your son, "We were Pharaoh's slaves in Egypt; and the Lord brought us out of Egypt with a mighty hand" ' (Deut. 6.20–1). In addition to such parental obligations, it was the duty of the Levites to teach the people: 'They shall teach Jacob thy ordinances, and Israel the law' (Deut. 33.10).

Hence from the earliest period the study of the traditions was of fundamental importance. For this reason Scripture contains numerous references to the process of learning. The Book of Joshua for example states: 'This book of the law shall not depart out of your mouth, but you shall meditate on it day and night, that you may be careful to do according to all that is written in it' (Josh. 1.8). Again, the Book of Proverbs contains various references to the process of education: 'He who spares the rod hates his son' (Prov. 13.24); 'Train up a child in the way he should go, and when he is old he will not depart from it' (Prov. 22.6).

When the ancient Israelites returned from the Babylonian exile, the Bible records that Ezra gathered the people and taught them the Law (Nehemiah chapter 8). When the nation heard his words, they were profoundly moved and vowed to observe the religious practices and festivals of their ancestors, such as the pilgrim festivals, the New Year celebration, and the Day of Atonement. According to the rabbis, it was Ezra who instituted the *Torah* reading on Monday and Thursday when the people attended local markets.

In the rabbinic era sages continued this process of education. Thus Judah ben Tema declared in *Sayings of the Fathers* (as recorded in the *Mishnah*): 'Five years old (is the age) for (the study of) the Bible, ten years old for the *Mishnah*, thirteen for (the obligation to keep) the commandments, fifteen years old for *Gemara* (rabbinic commentary on the *Mishnah*).' According to Jewish law, parents are obliged to begin a child's education at the earliest possible time; as soon as a child begins to speak he must be taught the verse: 'Moses commanded us a law, as a possession for the assembly of Jacob' (Deut. 33.4). During this period Simeon ben Shetah (first century AD) established schools and urged parents to send their sons to them. However it was Joshua ben Gamla (first century AD) who is credited with creating a formal system of education. About him the *Talmud* declares: 'May Joshua ben Gamla be remembered for good, for had it not been for him, the *Torah* would have been forgotten from Israel.' Prior to Joshua ben Gamla, only those with fathers were taught the tradition, whereas those without fathers were deprived of instruction. To remedy this situation Joshua ben Gamla decreed that teachers had to be engaged in each locality at the community's expense and all children were to be given an education. Later the *Talmud* stipulated the size of classes: one teacher was permitted to handle up to twenty-five students; if students exceeded this number an assistant was to be hired. More than forty students required two teachers.

Although the *Talmud* does not provide a systematic programme of study, it emphasizes the importance of parental instruction: 'One who does not teach his son an occupation, teaches him to be a brigand'. Among the duties imposed on the father is the obligation to teach his son the *Torah*. As in Babylonia such instruction in the Law was carried out in the Palestinian academy. Initially it was founded in Jabneh after the destruction of the temple in AD 70. According to tradition, Johanan ben Zakkai arranged to have himself smuggled out of the city in a coffin; he was then brought before the Roman commander, Vespasian, and requested permission to found a centre of learning. This institution took over from the Great Sanhedrin. Subsequently other academies flourished under Johanan ben Zakkai's disciples. In the second century following the devastation of central and southern Palestine during the Bar Kokhba revolt, many scholars emigrated and the Jabneh academy was transferred to Galilee.

In Babylonia schools of higher learning were established in the first century AD. In the next century under the leadership of Rav Shila and Abba bar Abba, the academy of Nehardea became the Babylonian spiritual centre, maintaining contact with the Palestinian Jewish community. When Rav returned to Babylonia from Palestine, he founded another academy at Sura in AD 220. In 259 the Nehardea academy was destroyed; under Judah ben Ezekiel it was transferred to Pumbedita where it remained for the next five hundred years. From then it functioned in Baghdad until the thirteenth century. These academies attracted students from throughout the Jewish world; twice a year during the months of *Adar* and *Elul* individual study sessions (*kallah*) were held for large audiences.

During the period between the completion of the *Talmud* (sixth century AD) and the Enlightenment, the majority of male Jews received some sort of education. This was generally limited to the study of sacred texts; however in some periods secular subjects were also included. In twelfth and thirteenth century Spain, for example, Jewish scholars engaged in secular studies. In this context the medieval talmudist Joseph Ibn Aknin argued that there is no contradiction between studying sacred works and such subjects as logic, rhetoric, arithmetic, geometry, astronomy, music, science and philosophy.

Prior to Jewish emancipation, the typical pattern of Jewish education involved a teacher with several students who studied religious texts – this was known as a *heder* (room). Although these study circles were not schools in the modern sense, they did have some parallels. Students were able to graduate from one teacher to another as they progressed in their education. In some communities there was a formally structured *Talmud Torah* which had several classes; here too the subjects of study were exclusively religious. Most students were exposed to several years of such formal education before they went to work; only a few were able to have an extensive educational training.

In the nineteenth century organized *yeshivot* (rabbinic academies) emerged in Eastern Europe in such centres as Tels, Ponevezh and Slobodka as well as at Hasidic centres. In these colleges students progressed from one level to another – the best students often went on to a lifetime of *Torah* study. Throughout the subject matter was the *Talmud* and *halakhah* – secular studies were not permitted. With the emancipation of Jewry, however, many Jews became proficient in other fields of study including languages, mathematics, and the sciences. This marked the beginning of the *Haskalah* (enlightenment) movement. In most cases such secular investigation was done secretly, particularly in Eastern Europe.

However, in Western Europe new types of schools were founded with combined religious and secular education. In this century the neo-Orthodox thinker Samson Raphael Hirsch formulated the principles of such an educational system in his *Torah im Derkeh Erets*. Eventually even Eastern European *yeshivot* broadened their curriculum to include ethics as a result of the influence of the *Musar* movement. The Alliance Israélite Francaise also advanced the combination of religious and secular studies in new schools in North Africa and the Middle East.

Once Jews were permitted to study at secular schools, there was a growing need for supplementary Jewish education. In most cases *heders* or *Talmud Torah* schools were held in the afternoon or on Sundays. In some cases Jewish day schools were established to provide a more extensive Jewish education. By the middle of the twentieth century, there was an increasing awareness that such supplementary Jewish education was inadequate, and the number of day schools proliferated. In the United States the Orthodox *Torah U-Meshorah* day school network expanded from 100 schools prior to World War Two to the current number of 600. In addition, both the Conservative and Reform movements have recently established religious day schools. In other countries day schools have been encouraged by the Zionist movement. In Yiddish circles day schools were also founded, but most have either closed or amalgamated with other schools.

During the period of emancipation non-Orthodox rabbinical seminaries were established in the United States. Thus, in the last quarter of the nineteenth century the Reform seminary,

the Hebrew Union College, and the Conservative Jewish Theological Seminary were created on the pattern of their predeces-
sors in Berlin and Breslau. At this time New York's Yeshiva
University was founded on neo-Orthodox lines; its curriculum
combines religious with secular studies. Eventually all these
seminaries developed graduate schools in a wide range of fields
including Jewish education, communal services, sacred music,
biblical studies, and rabbinics.

Until the period of the Enlightenment, Jewish education was
limited to the education of male Jews. However, as Jews
assimilated into Western society, the education of women
became a priority. Thus in 1917 Sara Schnirer, with the
encouragement of a number of Orthodox rabbis, established the
Beth Jacob Orthodox system in which women were provided
with an official educational programme, although these institutions refused to teach *Mishnah* and *Talmud*. By contrast, the
Stern College for Women in Yeshiva University provides a wide
range of courses including talmudic study. In the Conservative,
Reconstructionist and Reform movements, the education of
women has been a fundamental principle, and in the last few
decades all three religious bodies have ordained women as
rabbis.

In recent years there has also been a large growth in
traditional *yeshivot* for post-high school students, particularly in
Israel and the United States. In addition, a considerable number
of *yeshivah* graduates have gone on to spend several years
studying in *kolels* (advanced institutes for *Talmud* study). In
addition, Jewish studies have become an integral part of
university and college studies since World War Two. Throughout the world, Jewish studies' departments have been created
where thousands of Jewish as well as non-Jewish students are
able to take courses in a wide range of Jewish subjects.

23

The Jewish Calendar

In the Jewish religion the act of creation is the starting point of year One in the calendar. According to tradition the first work of chronology is the *Seder Olam* attributed to Yose ben Halafta (second century). In this work the calculation is based on biblical geneological tables, the length of lives recorded in Scripture, and the creation of the world in six days: on this reckoning the year of creation was 3761 BC. The Jewish calendar itself is based on a lunar year of twelve months (of twenty-nine or thirty days). The year is thus approximately 354 days. The shortage of eleven days between lunar and solar years is made up by adding a thirteenth month in certain years. In AD 356 the patriarch Hillel II introduced a permanent calendar based on mathematical and astrological calculations – this calendar has remained in force with only minor modifications.

The names of the months in the Jewish year are of Babylonian origin. In the pre-exilic books they are generally identified by their numerical order. Regarding the days themselves, they begin at sunset and end at nightfall on the following day: as a result the Sabbath begins at sundown on Friday and ends the next night with the appearance of three stars. This same pattern also applies to all holy days. The Hebrew date is normally given by indicating the name of the month first, then the date, followed by the year. When the year is written in Hebrew, it is usual to omit the thousands.

In recent times there have been a number of attempts at calendar reform so as to arrange a calendar with the same number of days in each month. This would result in a uniform pattern so that the same date would fall on the same day of the week each year. In addition, the year would be divisible into two equal halves and four quarters. The central objection to such an alteration is that it would disturb the regularity of a fixed Sabbath after every six working days – if the reform were carried out, it would fall on a different day each year.

THE JEWISH YEAR

(1) *NISAN*

	Shabbat ha-Gadol	This Sabbath takes place before Passover.
14th	The Fast of the First-Born	A fast is observed on this day by every male first-born in gratitude for God's deliverance at the time of the Exodus.
15th–22nd	Passover	This eight day festival commemorates God's redemption of the Israelites from Egyptian bondage. It is also referred to as the Festival of Unleavened Bread – this term refers to the unleavened bread which the Israelites baked in their hurried departure.
16th	The Counting of the *Omer*	The Israelites were commanded to count forty-nine days from the second day of Passover (when the *Omer* was brought to the Temple). The fiftieth day was celebrated as the wheat harvest.
17th–20th	*Hol Hamoed*	The intermediate days of Passover and *Sukkot*. They are observed as semi-holy days.

| 23rd | *Isru Hag* | The day after the festival of Passover. |

(2) IYYAR

5th	*Yom ha-Atsmaut*	Israel Independence Day commemorates the proclamation of Israel's independence on 5th *Iyyar*, 1948.
	Second, Fifth and Second (Days of the Week)	During the months of *Iyyar* and *Marheshvan* these days are kept as fast days to atone for any sins committed on the preceding Passover or *Sukkot*.
14th	Second Passover	The Paschal lamb was to be sacrificed only on 14th *Nisan*. Those who were not able to make this sacrifice because they were in a state of impurity or a long way from home, could make this offering on 14th *Iyyar*.
18th	*Lag Ba-Omer*	The period between Passover and *Shavuot* was frequently a time of tragedy. During the time of Akiva a plague occurred among his disciples and only ceased on 18th *Iyyar* (33rd day of the *Omer*). This day subsequently became known as the Scholars' Feast. The Day itself is a day of joy. In Israel pilgrims go to Meron where Simeon ben Yochai is buried.

(3) SIVAN

3rd–5th	Three Days of Bordering	This day commemorates the days when the Israelites prepared themselves for the revelation on Mount Sinai.
6th–7th	*Shavuot*	This festival is celebrated after seven weeks have been counted from the bringing of the *Omer* on the second day of Passover. It commemorates the giving of the *Torah* on Mount Sinai.
8th	*Isru Hag*	The day after *Shavuot*.

(4) TAMMUZ

17th	The Fast of the 17th of *Tammuz*	This fast commemorates the day when the walls of Jerusalem were breached by the Romans, as well as other disasters.

(5) AV

	The Sabbath of the 'Vision'	The Sabbath before *Tishah B'Av*.
9th	*Tishah B'Av*	This fast commemorates the day on which the First Temple was destroyed by Nebuchadnezzar, and the Second Temple by Titus.
	The Sabbath of 'Comfort Ye'	The Sabbath after *Tishah B'Av*.

15th	The 15th of *Av*	This was a joyous day in ancient times when the people participated in a wood offering.

(6) *ELUL* (The time of preparation for the Solemn Days)

(7) *TISHRI*

1st–10th	Ten Days of Penitence	This period begins with *Rosh Hashanah* and concludes with *Yom Kippur*. It is time for religious reflection and penitence.
1st and 2nd	*Rosh Hashanah*	The New Year festival inaugurates the beginning of the spiritual year. It is observed for two days.
3rd	The Fast of Gedaliah	This fast commemorates the assassination of Gedaliah the Governor of the Jews appointed by Nebuchadnezzar.
10th	*Yom Kippur*	The Day of Atonement is the most solemn day of the Jewish year. Jews are commanded to fast and atone for their sins.
15th–21st	*Sukkot*	This festival commemorates God's protection of the Israelites in the wilderness. Booths are built during this festival to symbolize the temporary shelter used by the Israelites in their wanderings.

17th–21st	*Hol Hamoed*	These intermediate days of the festival are observed as semi-holy days.
21st	*Hoshanah Rabbah*	This name is given to the seventh day of *Sukkot* since seven circuits are made around the *Torah* while *Hoshanah* prayers are recited.
22nd and 23rd	*Shemini Atseret*	This festival is observed following *Sukkot*. The annual cycle of *Torah* readings is completed and begun again on this day. For this reason the festival is also known as *Simhat Torah*. Outside of Israel where two days of *Shemini Atseret* are observed, *Simhat Torah* is kept only on the second day.
23rd	*Simhat Torah*	On this festival the *Torah* is completed and recommenced.
24th	*Isru Hag*	The day after *Sukkot*.

(8) *MARHESHVAN*

	Second, Fifth and Second	During *Iyyar* and *Marheshvan* these days are kept by some as fast days to atone for sins committed during *Sukkot*.

(9) KISLEV

25th–2nd or 3rd of *Tevet*	*Hanukkah*	This festival is celebrated for eight days. It commemorates the re-dedication of the Temple by Judah Maccabee after the Seleucids were defeated in 165 BC.

(10) TEVET

10th	The Fast of the 10th of *Tevet*	This day commemorates the seige of Jerusalem by Nebuchadnezzar.

(11) SHEVAT

15th	New Year for Trees	This joyous festival is celebrated in Israel by the planting of trees.
	Sabbath relating to the Shekels	This Sabbath takes place before or on the 1st of *Adar*.

(12) ADAR

	The Sabbath of 'Remember'	This Sabbath takes place before *Purim*.
13th	The Fast of Esther	This fast commemorates Queen Esther's fast before she asked Ahasuerus to revoke his decree against the Jews.
14th	*Purim*	This festival commemorates the defeat of Haman's plot to destroy the Jewish people. It is a

		joyous occasion during which the Scroll of Esther is read.
15th	*Shushan Purim*	This festival commemorates the victory of the Jews of Shushan.
	The Sabbath of the Red Heifer	This Sabbath occurs on the first or second Sabbath after *Purim*.
	The Sabbath of the Month	This Sabbath occurs before or on the 1st of *Nisan*.

24

Sanctuary, Temple and Synagogue

Scripture relates that Moses made a portable shrine (sanctuary) following God's instructions (Exodus chapters 25—7). This structure travelled with the Israelites in the desert and it was placed in the centre of the camp in an open courtyard 1000 cubits by 50 cubits in size. The fence surrounding it consisted of wooden pillars from which a cloth curtain was suspended. Located in the eastern half of the courtyard, the sanctuary measured 30 cubits by 10 cubits; at its end stood the Holy of Holies, which was separated by a veil hanging on five wooden pillars on which were woven images of the cherubim. Inside the Holy of Holies was the Ark of the Covenant, the table on which the shewbread was placed, the incense altar, and the *menorah* (candelabrum). In the courtyard there was also an outer altar on which sacrifices were offered, as well as a brass laver for priests.

Eventually this structure was superseded by the Temple, which was built by Solomon in Jerusalem in the tenth century BC. Standing within a royal compound which also consisted of the palace, a Hall of Judgement, the Hall of Cedars, and a house for Solomon's wife, the Temple was 60 cubits long, 20 cubits wide, and 30 cubits high. The main part of the Temple was surrounded by a three-storey building divided into chambers with storeys connected by trapdoors – these were probably storerooms for the Temple treasures. The main building consisted of an inner room – the Holy of Holies – on the west, and an outer room measuring 20 by 40 cubits on the east. Around the Temple was a walled-in compound. At the entrance to the Temple stood two massive bronze pillars (Jachin and Boaz).

Within the Holy of Holies stood the Ark which contained the Two Tablets of the Covenant with the Ten Commandments. In the outer room stood an incense altar, the table for the shewbread, and ten lampstands made of gold. In front of the

Temple stood a bronze basin supported by twelve bronze cattle. A bronze altar also stood in the courtyard, which was used for various sacrifices.

From the time of Solomon's reign, the Temple served as the site for prayer and the offering of sacrifices to God. In addition to the communal sacrifices made daily, there were additional communal sacrifices offered on the Sabbath, festivals, and the New Moon. The Temple was also the site to which the *omer* (the first barley measure harvested on the second day of Passover) and the first fruits were brought on *Shavuot*. On Passover all families were required to come to Jerusalem to offer the paschal sacrifice. In the sixth century BC, however, the Temple was destroyed by the Assyrians when they invaded the country. After the exile in the sixth century BC, Jews in Babylonia established a new institution for public worship: the synagogue (meaning 'assembly' in Greek). There they came together to study and pray. On their return to Jerusalem in the latter part of the sixth century BC, the Jewish populace continued to gather in synagogues as well as offer sacrifice in the Temple. Thus the synagogue developed alongside the Second Temple.

In the synagogue itself, there are a number of elements which parallel the ancient Tabernacle and Temple. Firstly, there is the Holy Ark – this is symbolic of the Holy of Holies, the most important part of the Sanctuary and Temple. The Ark itself is located on the eastern wall so that Jews are able to pray in the direction of the Temple in Jerusalem. Secondly, the eternal light hangs before the Ark – this represents the lamp which burned continually in the Sanctuary. The third major element in the synagogue is the *Torah* (Five Books of Moses) which are placed in the Ark. The *Torah* is written in Hebrew by a scribe who uses a special ink on parchment. A breastplate covers the *Torah*, and over it hangs a pointer which is used for the chanting or recitation of the *Torah*. There are two rollers on which the *Torah* scroll is wrapped; in addition, various ornaments, usually in silver, adorn the Scroll: these are symbolic of the ornaments of the High Priest in Temple times. A fourth feature of the synagogue is the platform (or *bimah*) which was in previous times used only for the reading of the Law and the Prophets, as well as for rabbinical sermons. Finally, there is a separation between men and women, usually in the form of a balcony where women are seated during the service.

According to tradition, there were about 400 synagogues in Jerusalem when the Second Temple was destroyed. Although this figure may be exaggerated, there is considerable evidence of synagogue building in the Jewish world during the Second Temple period. The earliest concrete evidence comes from Egypt in the third century BC; two centuries later the Jewish philosopher Philo referred to the presence of synagogues in Rome. In addition, the Book of Acts mentions Paul's presence in synagogues in Damascus, Asia Minor and Cyprus. By the fifth century it was widely attested that wherever Jews lived, they built structures which became the focus of Jewish life and thought. Unlike the Temple where ritual was carried out exclusively by priests, the only requirement for synagogue worship was the presence of a quorum (*minyan*) of ten men – any service could be led by a lay person. This shift away from Temple hierarchy marked a fundamental democratization of Jewish life. Both halachic and aggadic sources testify to the importance of this institution: all synagogues were perceived as partaking of the holiness of the Temple. For this reason it became customary for men to cover their heads when worshipping in the synagogue.

From the third to the eighth century, over 100 synagogues existed in Israel, largely in Galilee. In general they followed several prototypes: the most common was the basilica form which consisted of a long hall divided by two rows of pillars into a central nave and two aisles. During this period it does not appear that there was a separate seating area for women. These buildings were impressive structures which dominated the surrounding Jewish settlement – frequently they were located at the highest point in a town or near a source of water. The interiors were usually unadorned so that worshippers would not be distracted from worship. At a certain stage, mosaic floors were introduced which contained geometrical designs and later depictions of biblical stories, as well as mythological figures drawn from the surrounding cultures.

In the Middle Ages the synagogue dominated Jewish life; in most communities it was located at the centre of the Jewish quarter. Three times a day men attended services, and frequently the local rabbinic court convened there. Classes took place in the sanctuary or in an annexe, and oaths as well as banns of excommunication were pronounced in its environs. In addition, communal offices, the ritual bath, a library, a hospice for travellers and a social hall were located in synagogue rooms or adjacent buildings. Throughout this period synagogue architecture was influenced by Romanesque and Gothic styles, and special sections for women became common. The readers' platform in the centre of the building together with the Ark served as the focal points of the structure. Because synagogues were not permitted to be higher than neighbouring churches, many European synagogues were built with the floors below street level to maximize their height.

In the early modern period synagogues were constructed in Western European ghettos (such as in Venice); in Poland wooden synagogues influenced synagogue architecture throughout Eastern Europe. In Muslim countries synagogues were modest in scale in accordance with Muslim law. From the nineteenth century, however, major innovations were introduced by reformers. Influenced by church architecture, Reform synagogues (temples) were large, imposing buildings containing organs. The section for women was abolished, and decorum during the service was emphasized. Head coverings for men were also abandoned, and the reader's platform was shifted from the centre to the area in front of the Ark. Yet despite such changes Reform temples, together with Orthodox synagogues, have reassumed the role of the social centre. Both generally contain social halls used for a wide variety of activities, classrooms for religious schooling, and offices for administrative staff. Thus no matter what their form, synagogues continue to dominate Jewish life and serve as the religious focus of the community in contemporary society.

25

Worship

For the Jewish people, prayer has served as the vehicle by which they have expressed their joys, sorrows and hopes: it has played a major role in the religious life of the Jewish nation, especially in view of the successive crises and calamities in which they have been involved throughout their history. In such situations Jews continually turned to God for assistance. Thus in the *Torah* the patriarchs frequently addressed God through personal prayer. Abraham, for example, begged God to spare Sodom since he knew that by destroying the entire population he would destroy the righteous as well as the guilty (Gen. 18.23–33). At Beth-el Jacob vowed, 'If God will be with me, and will keep me in this way that I go, and will give me bread to eat, and raiment to put on . . . then shall the Lord be my God' (Gen. 28.20–1).

Later Moses, too, prayed to God. After Israel had made a golden calf to worship, Moses begged God to forgive them for this sin (Exod. 32.31–2). Joshua also turned to God for help. When the Israelites went to conquer the city of Ai, their attack was repulsed; in desperation Joshua prayed to God for help in defeating Israel's enemies (Jos. 7.7). Later in the prophetic books, the Prophets also offered personal prayers to God, as did the Psalmist and others. This tradition of prayer continued after the canonization of Scripture, and as a consequence prayer has constantly animated the Jewish spirit – through personal encounter with the Divine, Jews have been consoled, sustained, and uplifted. In addition to personal prayer, Jews have throughout history turned to God through communal worship.

In ancient times Jewish communal worship centred on the Temple in Jerusalem. Twice daily – in the morning and afternoon – the priests offered prescribed sacrifices while the Levites chanted psalms. On Sabbaths and festivals additional services were added to this daily ritual. At some stage it became customary to include other prayers along with the recitation of the Ten Commandments and the *Shema* (Deut. 6.4–9, 11, 13–21; Num. 15.37–41) in the Temple service. With the destruction of the Second Temple in AD 70, sacrificial offerings were replaced by the prayer service in the synagogue, referred to by the rabbis as *avodah she-ba-lev* (service of the heart). To enhance uniformity, they introduced fixed periods for daily payer which correspon-ded with the times sacrifices had been offered in the Temple: the morning prayer (*shaharit*) and afternoon prayer (*minhah*) cor-respond with the daily and afternoon sacrifice; evening prayer (*maariv*) corresponds with the nightly burning of fats and limbs. By the completion of the *Talmud* in the sixth century, the essential features of the synagogue service were established, but it was only in the eighth century that the first prayer book was composed by Rav Amram, Gaon of Sura.

In the order of service the first central feature is the *shema*. In accordance with the commandment 'You shall talk of them when you lie down and when you rise' (Deut. 6.7), Jews are commanded to recite this prayer during the morning and evening service. The first section (Deut. 6.4–9) begins with the phrase '*Shema Yisrael*' ('Hear, O Israel: the Lord our God is one Lord'). This verse teaches the unity of God, and the paragraph emphasizes the duty to love God, meditate on his command-ments and impress them on one's children. In addition it contains laws regarding the *tefillin* and the *mezuzah*. *Tefillin* consist of two black leather boxes containing scriptural passages which are bound by black leather straps on the arm and forehead in accordance with the commandment requiring that 'you shall bind them as a sign upon your hand, and they shall be as frontlets between your eyes' (Deut. 6.8). They are worn by men during morning prayer except on the Sabbath and festivals. The *mezuzah* consists of a piece of parchment contain-ing two paragraphs of the *shema* which is placed into a case and affixed to the right-hand side of an entrance. Male Jews wear an undergarment with fringes (the smaller *tallit*) and a larger *tallit* (prayer shawl) for morning services. The prayer shawl used is made of silk or wool with black or blue stripes with fringes (*tzitzit*) at each of the four corners.

The second major feature of the synagogue service is the *Shemoneh Esreh* (Eighteen Benedictions or *Amidah*). These prayers were composed over a long period of time and received their full form in the second century. They consist of eighteen separate prayers plus an additional benediction dealing with heretics which was composed by the sage Samuel the Younger at the request of Rabban Gamaliel in the second century. The first and last three benedictions are recited at every service; the thirteen other prayers are recited only on weekdays. On Sabbaths and festivals they are replaced by one prayer dealing with the Holy Day. They consist of the following:

1. Praise for God who remembers the deeds of the patriarchs on behalf of the community.
2. Acknowledgement of God's power in sustaining the living and his ability to revive the dead.
3. Praise of God's holiness.
4. Request for understanding and knowledge.
5. Plea for God's assistance to return to him in perfect repentance.
6. Supplication for forgiveness for sin.
7. Request for deliverance from affliction and persecution.
8. Petition for bodily health.
9. Request for God to bless agricultural produce so as to relieve want.
10. Supplication for the ingathering of the exiles.
11. Plea for the rule of justice under righteous leaders.
12. Request for the reward of the righteous and the pious.
13. Plea for the rebuilding of Jerusalem.
14. Supplication for the restoration of the dynasty of David.
15. Plea for God to accept prayer in mercy and favour.
16. Supplication for the restoration of the divine service in the Temple.
17. Thanksgiving for God's mercies.
18. Request for granting the blessing of peace to Israel.

On special occasions a number of special prayers are added to these benedictions.

From earliest times the *Torah* was read in public gatherings; subsequently regular readings of the *Torah* on Sabbaths and festivals were instituted. In Babylonia the entire *Torah* was read during a yearly cycle; in Palestine it was completed once every three years. The *Torah* itself is divided into fifty-four sections, each of which is known as the 'order' or 'section' (*sidrah*). Each section is subdivided into portions, (each of which is called a *parashah*). Before the reading of the *Torah* in the synagogue, the Ark is opened and the Scroll (or *Torah* scrolls) are taken out.

The number of men called up to the reading varies: on Sabbaths there are seven; on *Yom Kippur* six; on *Rosh Hashanah* and the Pilgrim festivals (Passover, *Sukkot*, and *Shavuot*), five; on *Rosh Hodesh* and *Hol Hamoed*, four; on *Purim*, *Hanukkah* and fast days, three; and on Sabbath afternoons and Monday and Thursdays mornings (when the first *parashah* of the forthcoming *sidrah* is read), three. In former times those who were called up to the *Torah* read a section of the weekly *sidrah*; subsequently an expert in *Torah* reading was appointed to recite the entire *sidrah* and those called up recited blessings instead. The first three people to be called up are: *Cohen* (priest), *Levi* (priest), and *Yisrael* (member of the congregation).

After the reading of the *Torah*, a section from the prophetic books (*Haftarah*) is recited. The person who is called up for the last *parashah* of the *sidrah* reads the *Haftarah* – he is known as the *maftir*. The section from the Prophets parallels the content of the *sidrah*. Once the *Torah* scroll is replaced in the Ark, a sermon is usually delivered based on the *sidrah* of the week.

Another central feature of the synagogue service is the *kaddish* prayer. Written in Aramaic, it takes several forms in the prayer book and expresses the hope for universal peace under the kingdom of God. There are five main forms:

1. Half *kaddish* recited by the reader between sections of the service.
2. Full *kaddish* recited by the reader at the end of a major section of the service.
3. Mourners' *kaddish* recited by mourners after the service.
4. Scholars' *kaddish* recited after the reading of talmudic midrashic passages in the presence of a *minyan* (quorum of ten men).
5. Expanded form of the mourners' *kaddish* which is recited at the cemetery after a burial.

A further feature of the service is the *Hallel* consisting of Psalms 113—18. In the talmudic period it was known as the 'Egyptian *Hallel*' because the second psalm (114) begins with the words: 'When Israel went forth from Egypt'. (This designation was used to distinguish this group of psalms from another psalm

(136) – the 'Great *Hallel*' – which is recited on the Sabbath and festivals during the morning service.) The complete *Hallel* is recited on the first two days of Passover, on both days of *Shavuot*, on the nine days of *Sukkot*, and the eight days of *Hanukkah*. Part of the *Hallel* is recited on the intermediate days (*Hol Hamoed*), and the last two days of Passover.

Since the thirteenth century the three daily services have concluded with the recitation of the *alenu* prayer which proclaims God as king over humanity. In all likelihood it was introduced by Rav in the third century as an introduction to the *malhuyot*, the section recited as part of the *musaf* service for *Rosh Hashanah*. In the Middle Ages this prayer was the death-song of Jewish martyrs. The first part of this prayer proclaims God as king of Israel; the second anticipates the time when idolatry will disappear and all human beings will acknowledge God as king of the universe.

The traditional liturgy remained essentially the same until the Enlightenment. At this time reformers in Central Europe altered the worship service and introduced new prayers into the liturgy in conformity with current cultural and spiritual developments. Influenced by Protestant Christianity, these innovators decreed that the service should be shortened and conducted in the vernacular as well as in Hebrew. In addition they introduced Western melodies to the accompaniment of a choir and organ and replaced the chanting of the *Torah* with a recitation of the *sidrah*. Prayers viewed as anachronistic were abandoned (such as the priestly blessing given by *Cohanim*, the *kol nidre* prayer on the Day of Atonement, and prayers for the restoration of the Temple and the reinstitution of sacrifice). Further, prayers of a particularistic character were amended so that they became more universalistic in scope.

The Conservative movement also produced prayer books in line with its ideology. In general the Conservative liturgy followed the traditional *siddur* except for several differences: (1) prayers for the restoration of sacrifice were changed; (2) the early morning benediction thanking God that the worshipper was not made a woman was altered; (3) prayers for peace were altered to include all of humanity; (4) in general the *yekum purkah* prayer for schools and sages in Babylonia was omitted; (5) *Cohanim* (priests) usually did not recite the priestly benediction; (6) the *amidah* was not usually repeated except on the high holy days.

In recent times all groups across the Jewish spectrum have produced new liturgies (such as those that commemorate Holocaust Remembrance Day, Israel Independence Day and Jerusalem Reunification Day). Moreover, a wide range of occasional liturgies exist for camps, youth groups and *havurot* (informal prayer groups). Among non-Orthodox denominations there is a growing emphasis on more egalitarian liturgies with gender-free language and an increasing democratic sense of responsibility. Thus prayer and worship continue to be of vital importance to the Jewish people, yet there have occurred a variety of alterations to its nature within all branches of the Jewish faith.

26

Sabbath

Genesis 2.1–3 declares 'The heaven and the earth were finished, and all the host of them. And on the seventh day God finished his work which he had done, and he rested on the seventh day from all his work which he had done. So God blessed the seventh day and hallowed it, because on it God rested from all his work which he had done in creation.' This passage serves as the basis for the decree that no work should be done on the Sabbath. During their sojourn in the wilderness of Zin, the Israelites were first commanded to observe the Sabbath. They were told to work on five days of the week when they should collect a single portion of manna; on the sixth day they were instructed to collect a double portion for the following day was to be 'a day of solemn rest, a holy sabbath of the Lord' (Exod. 16.23). On the seventh day when several individuals made a search for manna, the Lord stated: 'How long do you refuse to keep my commandments and my laws? See! The Lord has given you the sabbath, therefore on the sixth day he gives you bread for two days; remain every man of you in his place, let no man go out of his place on the seventh day' (Exod. 16.28–9).

Several weeks later God revealed the Ten Commandments, including prescriptions concerning the Sabbath day:

> Remember the sabbath day, to keep it holy. Six days you shall labour, and do all your work, but the seventh day is a sabbath to the Lord your God; in it you shall not do any work, you, or your son, or your daughter, your manservant, or your maid-servant, or your cattle, or the sojourner who is within your gates; for in six days the Lord made heaven and earth, the sea, and all that is in them, and rested the seventh day; therefore the Lord blessed the sabbath day and hallowed it (Exod. 20.8–11).

The Book of Deuteronomy contains a different version, emphasizing the exodus from Egypt:

> Observe the sabbath day, to keep it holy, as the Lord your God commanded you. Six days you shall labour, and do all your work; but the seventh day is a sabbath to the Lord your God; in it you shall not do any work . . . . You shall remember that you were a servant in the land of Egypt, and the Lord your God brought you out thence with a mighty hand and an outstretched arm; therefore the Lord your God commanded you to keep the sabbath day (Deut. 5.12–15).

According to the Book of Exodus, the Sabbath is a covenant between Israel and God:

> Say to the people of Israel, 'You shall keep my sabbaths, for this is a sign between me and you throughout your generations, that you may know that I, the Lord, sanctify you . . . Therefore the people of Israel shall keep the sabbath, observing the sabbath throughout their generations as a perpetual covenant (Exod. 31.12, 16).

By the time the Sanhedrin began to function, the observance of the Sabbath was regulated by Jewish law. Following the injunction in Exodus 20.10, the primary aim was to refrain from work. In the Five Books of Moses only a few provisions are delineated: kindling a fire (Exod. 35.3); ploughing and harvesting (Exod. 23.12); carrying from one place to another (Exod. 16.29). Such regulations were expanded by the rabbis who listed thirty-nine categories of work (which were involved in the building of the Tabernacle). According to the *Mishnah* they are:

1. sowing; 2. ploughing; 3. reaping; 4. binding sheaves; 5. threshing; 6. winnowing; 7. sorting; 8. grinding; 9. sifting; 10. kneading; 11. baking; 12. shearing sheep; 13. washing wool; 14. beating wool; 15. dyeing wool; 16. spinning; 17. sieving; 18. making two loops; 19. weaving two threads; 20. separating two threads; 21. tying; 22. loosening; 23. sewing two stitches; 24. tearing in order to sew two stitches; 25. hunting a deer; 26. slaughtering; 27. flaying; 28. salting; 29. curing a skin; 30. scraping the hide; 31. cutting; 32. writing two letters; 33. erasing in order to write two letters; 34. building;

35. pulling down a structure; 36. extinguishing a fire; 37. lighting a fire; 38. striking with a hammer; 39. moving something.

In the *Talmud* these categories were discussed and expanded to include within each category a range of activities. In order to ensure that individuals did not transgress these prescriptions, the rabbis enacted further legislation which serve as a fence around the Law. Yet despite such ordinances, there are certain situations which take precedence over Sabbath prohibitions. Witnesses of the New Moon, for example, who were to inform the Sanhedrin or *Bet Din* of this occurrence were permitted to do so on the Sabbath. Other instances include circumcision on the Sabbath; dangerous animals may be killed; persons are permitted to fight in self-defence; anything may be done to save a life or assist a woman in childbirth.

The Sabbath itself commences on Friday at sunset. About twenty minutes before sunset, candles are traditionally lit by the woman of the house who recites the blessing: 'Blessed are you, O Lord our God, King of the universe, who has hallowed us by your commandments and commanded us to kindle the Sabbath light.'

In the synagogue, the service preceding Friday *maariv* takes place at twilight. Known as *Kabbalat Shabbat*, it is a late addition dating back to the sixteenth century when kabbalists in Safed went out to the fields on Friday afternoon to greet the Sabbath queen. In kabbalistic lore the Sabbath represents the *Shekhinah* (divine presence). This ritual is rooted in the custom of Hanina (first century) who, after preparing himself for the Sabbath, stood at sunset and said: 'Come, let us go forth to welcome the Sabbath', and that of Yannai (third century) who said: 'Come Bride! Come bride!' On the basis of such sentiments Solomon Alkabets composed the Sabbath hymn *Lekhah Dodi* which has become a major feature of the liturgy. In the Sephardi rite Psalm 29 and *Lekhah Dodi* are recited, whereas the Ashkenazi rite is comprised of Psalms 95–9, *Lekhah Dodi* and Psalms 92–3. The Reform prayer book offers a variety of alternative services including abridged versions of these psalms and the entire *Lekhah Dodi*. The Reconstructionist service commences with biblical passages, continues with an invocation and meditation on the Sabbath, and then moves on to an invocation and meditation on the Sabbath, and proceeds to a reading of psalms and *Lekhah Dodi*.

Traditionally, when the father returns home from the synagogue, he blesses his children. With both hands placed on the head of a boy, he says: 'May God make you like Ephraim and Manasseh'; for a girl: 'May God make you like Sarah, Rebekah, Rachel and Leah.' In addition, he recites the priestly blessing. Those assembled then sing *Shalom Aleikhem* which welcomes the Sabbath angels. At the Sabbath table the father recites the *kiddush* prayer over a cup of wine:

> Blessed are you, O Lord our God, King of the universe, who has sanctified us by your commandments and has taken pleasure in us, and in love and favour has given us your holy Sabbath as an inheritance, a memorial of the creation, that day being the first of the holy convocations, in remembrance of the Exodus from Egypt. For you have chosen us and hallowed us above all nations, and in love and favour have given us your holy Sabbath as an inheritance. Blessed are you O Lord, who sanctifies the Sabbath.

This is followed by the washing of the hands and the blessing of the bread. The meal is followed by the singing of table hymns (*zemirot*), and concludes with the Grace after Meals (*Birkhatha-Mazon*). This, which Jews are obligated to recite after every meal, originally consisted of three paragraphs in which worshippers thank God for sustenance, the land and the *Torah*, and pray for the restoration of the Temple. Subsequently a fourth paragraph was added which contains the words: 'Who is good and does good'. Subsequently short prayers beginning with 'the All Merciful' were added. On the Sabbath an additional prayer is included dealing with the Sabbath day.

On Sabbath morning the liturgy consists of a morning service, a reading of the *Torah* and the *Haftarah*, and the additional service. In the service itself, introductory prayers prior to the *Shema* differ from those of weekdays, and the *Amidah* is also different. Seven individuals are called to the reading of the Law, and an eighth for a reading from the prophets. In the Reform movement the worship is abridged and has no additional service. On returning home, the morning *kiddush* and the blessing over bread are recited followed by the Sabbath meal and then the Grace after Meals. In the afternoon service the

Torah is read prior to the *amidah*; three persons are called to the *Torah*, and the first portion of the reading of the Law for the following week is recited. Customarily three meals are to be eaten on the Sabbath day; the third meal is known as the *Seudah Shelishit*. It should take place just in time for the evening service. At the end of the Sabbath, the evening service takes place and is followed by the *Havdalah* service.

The *Havdalah* ceremony marks the conclusion of the Sabbath period; it is divided and consists of four blessings. Three are recited over wine, spices and lights, and the service concludes with the *Havdalah* blessing. In the Sephardi, Ashkenazi and Yemenite rites, the blessings are similar, but the introductory sentences are different. The Ashkenazi rite contains biblical phrases with the term 'salvation'; the Sephardi requests the granting of bountifulness and success; the Yemenite prays for a successful week. The final blessing opens with the phrase, 'Blessed are you, O Lord our God, King of the universe, who distinguishes'; it is followed by a series of comparisons: between the holy and the profane, light and darkness, Israel and the nations, between the seventh day and the six days of the week. The hymn *Ha-Mavdil* follows the *Havdalah* ceremony and asks for forgiveness of sins and for the granting of a large number of children. A number of customs including filling a cup and extinguishing the *Havdalah* candle in wine poured from it are associated with the *Havdalah* ceremony. Within Reform Judaism an alternative *Havdalah* service incorporates additional readings with traditional blessings.

27

Special Sabbaths

In the Jewish tradition a number of Sabbaths are of importance in the Jewish calendar. Three are linked to the beginning of a month: *Shabbat Mevarekhim* (Sabbath before a New Moon); *Shabbat Mahar Hodesh* (Sabbath on the eve of a New Moon); and *Shabbat Rosh Hodesh* (Sabbath coinciding with the beginning of a month). Other special Sabbaths are *Shabbat Shuvah* (Sabbath during the Ten Days of Penitence between *Rosh Hashanah* and the Day of Atonement); *Shabbat Hol Hamoed* (Sabbath during the Intermediate Days of *Sukkot*); *Shabbat Bereshit* (when the new *Torah* reading commences); *Shabbat Hanukkah* (Sabbath during *Hanukkah*); *Shabbat Shirah* (Sabbath when the Song of Moses is recited); four Sabbaths during the spring (*Shekalim, Zakhor, Parah, ha-Hodesh*); *Shabbat ha-Gadol* (Sabbath before Passover); another *Shabbat Hol Hamoed* (Sabbath during the Intermediate Days of Passover); *Shabbat Hazon* (Sabbath before *Tishah B'Av*; *Shabbat Nahamin* (Sabbath after *Tishah B'Av*). In the Reform movement only a few of these Sabbaths are recognized.

These special Sabbaths are observed in various ways:

Shabbat Mevarekhim (The Sabbath of Blessing). On this Sabbath before a New Moon, worshippers using the Ashkenazi liturgy recite *yehi ratson*, a formula based on the sage Rav's prayer that, 'it will be God's will to renew the coming month for good service', with four *yehi ratson* expressions of hope that it will be God's intention to re-establish the Temple, rescue his people from all afflictions and disasters, maintain Israel's sages, and grant a month of good tidings. In both rites the service continues with the prayer, 'He who performs miracles', an announcement of the date of the New Moon, and a benediction. The *Torah* and *Haftarah* are the portions of the week.

Shabbat Mahar Hodesh. This Sabbath, which falls on the eve of the New Moon, has a biblical origin (1 Sam. 20.18). The *Torah* reading is that for the week. The *Haftarah* (1 Sam. 20.18–42) depicts the covenant between Jonathan and David on the eve of the New Moon.

Shabbat Rosh Hodesh. In the Sabbath service which falls on the New Moon the *Hallel* is recited after the morning service; in the additional service *Amidah*, the *Attah Yatsarta* sequence replaces *Tikkanta Shabbat*. The *Torah* reading is that for the week and the *maftir* (additional reading) is Numbers 28.9–15. The *Haftarah* is Isaiah 66.1–24.

Shabbat Shuvah. (The Sabbath of Return). The origin of the name of this Sabbath is derived from the opening words of the *Haftarah*: 'Return (*shuvah*), O Israel, to the Lord your God.' Since this Sabbath occurs during the Days of Penitence, it is also known as *Shabbat Teshuvah* (Sabbath of Repentance). The *Torah* reading is that prescribed for the week, and the *Haftarah* is either Hosea 14.2–10; Joel 2.15–27 in the Ashkenazi rite, or Hosea 14.2–10; Micah 7.18–20 in the Sephardi rite (in the diaspora, Ashkenazim read Micah 7.18–20 before the Joel passage).

Shabbat Hol Hamoed Sukkot. In the service for this Sabbath which occurs during the intermediate days of *Sukkot*, the *Hallel* and the Book of Ecclesiastes are read after the morning service. In some traditional congregations *piyyutim* (religious poems) are recited. The reading for the day is Exodus 33.12–34 and a selection from Numbers 29; the *Haftarah* is Ezekiel 38.18—39.16.

Shabbat Bereshit (The Sabbath of Genesis). The origin of the name of this Sabbath is derived from the opening words of the Book of Genesis which are included in the reading of the Law for this Sabbath (which follows the *Simhat Torah* festival): 'In the beginning (*bereshit*) God created'. On this Sabbath the annual reading cycle of the *Torah* commences with Genesis 1.1–6,8 and the *Haftarah* is that for the week. Included among those who are called to the *Torah* is the person chosen as 'bridegroom of Genesis' on *Simhat Torah*. He normally provides a festival meal to which all are invited after the Sabbath morning service.

Shabbat Hanukkah. This Sabbath takes place during the *Hanukkah* festival. After the morning service, the *Hallel* is recited. The *Torah* reading is that for the week; the *maftir* (additional reading) is Numbers 7.1–17. If the Sabbath also falls on the eighth day of *Hanukkah* the weekly portion is Genesis 41.1—44.17 and the *maftir* is Numbers 7.54—8.4. If this Sabbath coincides with the New Moon, Numbers 28.9–15 is recited from a second scroll before *maftir*. The *Haftarah* is Zechariah 2.14—4.7 (1 Kings 7.40–50 for second Sabbath; if it is New Moon, Isaiah 66.1–24 is substituted).

Shabbat Shirah (The Sabbath of the Song). The origin of the name of this Sabbath is the song which Moses and the Israelites sang at the Red Sea (Exod. 15.1–18) which is included in the *Torah* reading. In some congregations special religious poems are also recited. The *Torah* reading is the weekly portion (Exod. 13.17—17.16). The *Haftarah* is Judges 4.4—5.31 among Ashkenazim, and Judges 5.1–31 among Sephardim. In traditional communities a special form of cantillation is reserved for this song. Ashkenazim worshippers stand while this song is read, but not Sephardim. In Moroccan communities a liturgical poem referring to the eight biblical songs sung by Moses, Miriam, Joshua, Deborah and other Israelites is recited. Western Sephardi congregations have a double reading of the song to a traditional melody, and Exodus 14.30—15.18 is chanted before and as part of the *Torah* reading. Orthodox congregations of the United Synagogue in England have borrowed this Sephardi tune for their own cantillation of the song. Ashkenazim elsewhere use a traditional Eastern European mode.

Shabbat Shekalim (The Sabbath of the Shekel Tax). The origin of the name of this Sabbath which precedes or coincides with the New Moon *Rosh Hodesh Adar* is derived from the *Mishnah* which states that, 'on the first day of *Adar* they gave warning of the shekel dues.' The *maftir* (additional reading) concerns the half-shekel levy which was used to support the Sanctuary. In some congregations special religious poems are recited; the *Torah* reading is that for the week and the *maftir* is Exodus 30.11–16. The *Haftarah* is 2 Kings 12.1–17 among Ashkenazim, and 2 Kings 11.17—12.17 among Sephardim. In some congregations the rabbi urges that contributions be made to religious institutions in Israel.

Shabbat Zakhor (The Sabbath of Remembrance). On this Sabbath before *Purim*, the *maftir* (additional reading) emphasizes the obligation to 'remember what Amalek did to you' (since traditionally Haman was a descendant of Amalek). During the service special religious poems are read in some synagogues. The *Torah* reading is that of the week and the *maftir* is Deuteronomy 25.17–19. The *Haftarah* is 1 Samuel 15.2–34.

Shabbat Parah (Sabbath of the Red Heifer). This Sabbath precedes *Shabbat ha-Hodesh*. The *maftir* (additional reading) deals with the red heifer whose ashes were used for purification. Special poems are recited on this Sabbath, and the *Torah* portion is that of the week; the *maftir* is Numbers 19.1–22. The *Haftarah* is Ezekiel 36.16–18 among Ashkenazim, and Ezekiel 36.16–36 among Sephardim.

Shabbat ha-Hodesh (The Sabbath of the Month). The origin of the name for this Sabbath is derived from the opening words of the *maftir* (additional reading): 'This month (*ha-Hodesh*) shall mark for you the beginning of the months.' This Sabbath precedes or coincides with *Rosh Hodesh Nisan* (the month when Passover takes place). In some congregations special religious poems are recited. The *Torah* portion is that for the week, and the *maftir* is Exodus 12.1–20. The *Haftarah* is Ezekiel 45.16—46.18 among Ashkenazim, and Ezekiel 45.18—46.15 among Sephardim.

Shabbat ha-Godel (The Great Sabbath). The origin of the name of this Sabbath is uncertain but it may derive from the last verse of the *Haftarah*: 'Lo, I will send the prophet Elijah to you before the coming of the awesome (*gadol*), fearful day of the Lord' (Mal. 4.5). This Sabbath precedes Passover. Religious poems are read in some congregations, and the rabbi usually gives a lecture on Passover and preparations for the holiday. In the afternoon a portion of the *Haggadah* (Passover prayer book) is recited. The *Torah* reading is that of the week, and the *Haftarah* is Malachi 3.4—4.6.

Shabbat Hol Hamoed Pesah. This Sabbath takes place during the intermediate days (*Hol Ha-Moed*) of Passover. In the service the *Hallel* and Song of Songs are recited after the morning service. In some synagogues special religious poems are also recited. The *Torah* reading is Exodus 33.12—34.26, and the *maftir* (additional reading) is Numbers 28.19–25. The *Haftarah* is Ezekiel 37.1–14.

Shabbat Hazon (The Sabbath of Prophecy). The origin of the name of this Sabbath, which precedes the ninth day of Av, is derived from the *Haftarah* which refers to Isaiah's vision (*hazon*) about the punishments which will be inflicted on Israel. The *Torah* portion is Deuteronomy 1.1—3.22; the *Haftarah* is Isaiah 1.1–27. During the service the rabbi or a learned Jew chants the *Haftarah*. Congregants are to attend synagogue in plainer clothes than normal. The Ark is usually covered by a weekday or black curtain. Among Ashkenazim the *Lekhah Dodi* hymn is sung on Friday night to the tune of the *Eli Tziayyon* elegy.

Shabbat Nahamu (The Sabbath of Comfort). The origin of this name is derived from the opening words of the *Haftarah*: 'Comfort (*nahamu*), O comfort my people.' The *Torah* reading is Deuteronomy 3.23—7.11 which includes the Ten Commandments and the first paragraph of the *Shema*. The *Haftarah* is Isaiah 40.1–26.

28

Pilgrim Festivals

According to the Book of Deuteronomy, Jews are to celebrate three pilgrim festivals each year: 'Three times each year shall all your males appear before the Lord your God at the place which he will choose, at the feast of unleavened bread, at the feast of weeks, and at the feast of booths' (Deut. 16.16). On the basis of this commandment large numbers of pilgrims went to Jerusalem during the First and Second Temple periods from throughout the Holy Land and Babylonia. There they assembled in the Temple area to offer sacrifice and pray to God.

The first of these festivals is Passover, which is celebrated for eight days (seven in Israel) from the 15th–22nd of *Nisan*. The various names for this festival illustrate its different dimensions.

1. *Pesah* (Passover). This term is derived from the account of the tenth plague in Egypt when first-born Egyptians were killed, whereas God 'passed over' the houses of the Israelites (whose door-posts and lintels were sprinkled with the blood of the *paschal* lamb). This term is also applied to the Passover sacrifice which took place on the 14th of *Nisan*; its flesh was roasted and eaten together with unleavened bread and bitter herbs.

2. *Hag ha-Matzot* (The Festival of Unleavened Bread). This term refers to the unleavened bread baked by the Israelites on their departure from Egypt. In accordance with God's command to Moses and Aaron while the people were in Egypt, no leaven was to be eaten during future Passover celebrations, nor was it to be kept in the house. All vessels used for leavening must be put away, and their place taken by a complete set used only for Passover. Although no leaven may be eaten during this period, the obligation to eat *matzah* applies only to the first two nights during the *Sedar* service.

3. *Zeman Herutenu* (The Season of our Freedom). This term designates the deliverance from Egyptian slavery and the emergence of the Jewish people as a separate nation.

4. *Hag ha-Aviv* (The Festival of Spring). This name is used because the month of *Nisan* is described in Scripture as the month of *Aviv*, when ears of barley begin to ripen. In accordance with the biblical command, a measure of barley (*omer*) was brought to the Temple on the second day of Passover. Only when this was done could bread be made from the new barley harvest.

In preparation for Passover, Jewish law stipulates that all leaven must be removed from the house. On the 14th of *Nisan* a formal search is made for any remains of leaven. This is then put aside and burned on the following morning. The first night of Passover is celebrated in a home ceremony referred to as the *Seder*. This is done to fulfil the biblical commandment to relate the story of the Exodus to one's son: 'And you shall tell thy son on the day, saying: "It is because of what the Lord did for me when I came out of Egypt" ' (Exod. 13.8). The order of the service dates back to Temple times. During the ceremony celebrants traditionally lean on their left sides – this was the custom of freemen in ancient times.

The symbols placed on the *Seder* table serve to remind those present of Egyptian bondage, God's redemption, and the celebration in Temple times. They consist of:

(1) Three *matzot*: these three pieces of unleavened bread are placed on top of one another, usually in a special cover. The upper and lower matzot symbolize the double portion of manna provided for the Israelites in the wilderness. The middle *matzah* (which is broken in two at the beginning of the *Seder*) represents the 'bread of affliction'. The smaller part is eaten to comply with the commandment to eat *matzah*. The larger part is set aside for the *afikoman*, which recalls Temple times when the meal was completed with the eating of the *paschal* lamb. These three *matzot* also symbolize the three divisions of the Jewish people: *Cohen*, *Levi* and *Yisrael*.

(2) Four cups of wine: according to tradition, each Jew must

drink four cups of wine at the *Seder*. The first is linked to the recital of *kiddush*; the second with the account of the Exodus and the Blessing for Redemption; the third with the Grace after Meals; and the fourth with the *Hallel* and prayers for thanksgiving. These cups also symbolize four expressions of redemption in Exodus 6.6–7.

(3) The cup of Elijah: this cup symbolizes the hospitality awaiting the passer-by and wayfarer. According to tradition, the Messiah will reveal himself at the Passover, and Malachi declared that he will be preceded by Elijah. The cup of Elijah was also introduced because of the doubt as to whether five cups of wine should be drunk rather than four.

(4) Bitter herbs: these symbolize the bitterness of Egyptian slavery.

(5) Parsley: this is dipped in salt water and eaten after the *kiddush*. It is associated with spring.

(6) *Haroset*: this is a mixture of apples, nuts, cinnamon and wine. It is a reminder of the bricks and mortars that Jews were forced to use in Egypt.

(7) Roasted shankbone: this symbolizes the *paschal* offering.

(8) Roasted egg: this commemorates the festival sacrifice in the Temple.

(9) Salt water: this recalls the salt that was offered with all sacrifices. It also symbolizes the salt water of the tears of the ancient Israelites.

At the *Seder*, the *Haggadah* details the order of service. It is as follows:

1. The *kiddush* is recited.
2. The celebrant washes his hands.
3. The parsley is dipped in salt water.
4. The celebrant divides the middle *matzah* and sets aside the *afikoman*.

5. The celebrant recites the *Haggadah* narration.
6. The participants wash their hands.
7. The blessing over bread is recited.
8. The blessing over *matzah* is recited.
9. Bitter herbs are eaten.
10. The *matzah* and *maror* are combined.
11. The meal is eaten.
12. The *afikoman* is eaten.
13. Grace after Meals is recited.
14. The *Hallel* is recited.
15. The service is concluded.
16. Hymns and songs are sung.

The second pilgrim festival – *Shavuot* – is celebrated for two days (or one day in Israel), on the 6th and 7th of *Sivan*. The word '*shavuot*' means 'weeks' – seven weeks are counted from the bringing of the *omer* on the second day of *Pesach* (Lev.23.15). The festival is also referred to as Pentecost, a Greek word meaning 'fiftieth', since it was celebrated on the fiftieth day. Symbolically the day commemorates the culmination of the process of emancipation which began with the Exodus at Passover. It is concluded with the proclamation of the Law at Mount Sinai. Liturgically, the festival is also called *Zeman Mattan Toratenu* (the Season of the Giving of our *Torah*). This name relates to events depicted in Exodus chapters 19—20.

During the Temple period farmers set out for Jerusalem to offer a selection of first ripe fruits as a thank-offering. In post-Temple times, the emphasis shifted to the festival's identification as the anniversary of the giving of the Law on Mount Sinai. In some communities it is a practice to remain awake during *Shavuot* night. In the sixteenth century Solomon Alkabets and other kabbalists began the custom of *tikkun* in which an anthology of biblical and rabbinic material was recited. Today in those communities where this custom is observed, this lectionary has been replaced by a passage of the *Talmud* or other rabbinic literature. Some congregations in the diaspora read a book of psalms on the second night. Synagogues themselves are decorated with flowers or plants, and dairy food is consumed during the festival. The liturgical readings for the festival include the Ten Commandments preceded by the liturgical poem *Akdamut Millin* on the first day, and *Yetsiv Pitgam* before the *Haftarah* on the second day. The Book of Ruth is also recited. In many communities this festival marks the graduation of young people from formal synagogue education (or confirmation in Reform temples). In Israel, agricultural settlements hold a First Fruits celebration on *Shavuot*.

The third pilgrim festival – *Sukkot* – is also prescribed in the Bible: 'On the fifteenth day of this seventh month and for seven days is the feast of tabernacles to the Lord (Lev. 23.34). Beginning on the 15th of *Tishri*, it commemorates God's protection of the Israelites during their sojourn in the desert. Leviticus commands that Jews are to construct booths during this period as a reminder that the people of Israel dwelt in booths when they fled from Egypt (Lev. 23.42–3).

During this festival a *sukkah* (booth) is constructed and its roof is covered with branches of trees and plants. During the festival, meals are to be eaten inside the *sukkah*. Leviticus also declares that various agricultural species should play a part in the observance of this festival: 'And you shall take on the first day the fruit of goodly trees, branches of palm trees, and boughs of leafy trees, and willows of the brook; and you shall rejoice before the Lord your God seven days (Lev. 23.40). In compliance with this prescription the four species are used in the liturgy: palm, myrtle, willow and citron. On each day of the festival the *lulav* (palm branch) is waved in every direction before and during the *Hallel* – this symbolizes God's presence throughout the world. Holding the four species Jews make one circuit around the *Torah* which is carried on the *bimah* (platform) on each of the first six days. During this circuit, *hoshanah* prayers are recited. On the seventh day of *Sukkot* (*Hoshanah Rabba*) seven circuits are made around the *Torah* while reciting *hoshanah* prayers. During the service the reader wears a white *kittel* (robe).

In conformity with Leviticus 23.36, 'On the eighth day you shall hold a holy convocation . . . it is a solemn assembly', *Shemini Atseret* and *Simhat Torah* are celebrated on the same day (or on separate days in the diaspora). No work is permitted at this time. On *Shemini Atseret* a prayer for rain is recited, and the reader wears a white *kittel*. Ecclesiastes is recited at the end of the morning service on *Shabbat Hol Hamoed* (or on *Shemini Atseret* if it falls on the Sabbath). The ninth day of *Sukkot* is *Simhat Torah*. On this joyous day the reading of the *Torah* is completed and recommenced. The *Torah* scrolls are taken out of the Ark and members of the congregation carry them in a procession around the synagogue.

29

The New Year and Day of Atonement

In ancient times the Jewish New Year (*Rosh Hashanah*) took place on one day; it is presently observed for two days, both in Israel and the diaspora, on the 1st and 2nd of *Tishri*, marking the beginning of the Ten Days of Penitence which ends on the Day of Atonement (*Yom Kippur*). The term '*Rosh Hashanah*' occurs only once in Scripture (Ezek. 40.1). None the less, this festival has three other biblical designations: (1) *Shabbaton* – a day of solemn rest to be observed on the first day of the seventh month; (2) *Zikhron Teruah* – a memorial proclaimed with the blast of a horn (Lev. 23.24); and (3) *Yom Teruah* – 'a day of blowing the horn' (Num. 29.1). Later the rabbis referred to the New Year as *Yom ha-Din* (the Day of Judgement, and *Yom ha-Zikkaron* (the Day of Remembrance).

According to the *Mishnah* all human beings will pass before God on the New Year; the *Talmud* expands this idea by stressing the need for self-examination. In rabbinic literature each person stands before the throne of God, and judgement on every person is entered on the New Year and sealed on the Day of Atonement. The tractate *Rosh Hashanah* in the *Talmud* declares that, 'there are three ledgers opened in heaven: one for the completely righteous who are immediately inscribed and sealed in the Book of Life; another for the thoroughly wicked who are recorded in the Book of Death; and a third for the intermediate, ordinary type of person whose fate hangs in the balance and is suspended until the Day of Atonement.' In this light, *Rosh Hashanah* and *Yom Kippur* are also called *Yamim Noraim* (Days of Awe).

On *Rosh Hashanah* the Ark curtain, reading desk and *Torah* scroll mantles are decked in white, and the rabbi, cantor and person who blows the *shofar* (ram's horn) all wear a white *kittel* (robe). In the synagogue service the *Amidah* of the *musaf* service contains three sections relating to God's sovereignty, providence and revelation: *Malkhuyyot* (introduced by the *alenu* prayer) deals with God's rule; *Zikhronot* portrays God's remembrance of the ancestors of the Jewish people when he judges each generation; *Shofarot* contains verses relating to the *shofar* (ram's horn) and deals with the revelation on Mount Sinai and the messianic age. Each introductory section is followed by three verses from the *Torah*, three from the Writings, three from the Prophets, and a final verse from the *Torah*. On the first and second day of *Rosh Hashanah* the *Torah* readings concern the birth of Isaac (Genesis 12.1–34) and the binding of Isaac or *Akedah* (Genesis 22.1–24). The *Haftarah* for the first day is 1 Samuel 1.29—2.10 which depicts the birth of Samuel, who subsequently dedicated his life to God's service; on the second day the *Haftarah* deals with Jeremiah's prophecy (Jer. 31.2–20) concerning the restoration of Israel.

On both days of *Rosh Hashanah* (except when the first is on the Sabbath) the *shofar* is blown at three points during the service: thirty times after the reading of the Law; thirty times during *musaf* (ten at the end of the three main sections); thirty times after *musaf*, and ten before *alenu*. In the liturgy there are three variants of the blowing of the *shofar*: *tekiah* (a long note); *shevarim* (three tremulous notes), and *teruot* (nine short notes). According to Maimonides the *shofar* is blown to call sinners to repent. As he explains in the *Mishneh Torah*: 'Awake you sinners, and ponder your deeds; remember your creator, forsake your evil ways, and return to God.' In the Ashkenazi rite the *U-Netanneh Tokef* prayer concludes the service on a hopeful note as congregants declare that, 'Repentance, prayer and charity can avert the evil decree.'

Traditionally it was a custom to go to the sea-side or the banks of a river on the afternoon of the first day (or on the second day if the first falls on a Sabbath). The ceremony of *Tashlikh* symbolizes the casting of one's sins into a body of water. The prayers for *Tashlikh* and three verses from the book of Micah (Mic. 7.18–20) express confidence in divine forgiveness. In the home after *kiddush* a piece of bread is dipped in honey followed by a piece of apple, and a prayer is recited that the year ahead may be good and sweet. It is also a custom to eat the new season's fruit on the second night of *Rosh Hashanah* to justify reciting the *Sheheheyanu* benediction on enjoying new things. The *hallah* loaves baked for this festival are usually round or have a plaited crust shaped like a ladder to represent hopes for a good round year, or the effort to direct one's life upward to God.

The Ten Days of Penitence begin with the New Year and last until the Day of Atonement. This is considered the most solemn time of the year when all are judged and their fate determined for the coming year. During the Ten Days a number of additions are made to the liturgy, especially in the morning service. *Selihot* (penitential prayers) are recited during the morning service, and various additions are made to the *Amidah* and the reader's repetition of the *Amidah*. The reader's repetition is followed by the *Avinu Malkenu* prayer. In some synagogues it is customary to recite Psalm 130.1 in the morning service. It is also traditional to visit the graves of close relatives at this time. The Sabbath between the New Year and the Day of Atonement is *Shabbat Shuvah*.

The holiest day of the Jewish calendar is the Day of Atonement which takes place on the 10th of *Tishri*. Like other major festivals its observance is prescribed in Scripture: 'On the tenth day of this seventh month is the Day of Atonement; and you shall afflict yourselves. It shall be to you a sabbath of solemn rest, and you shall afflict yourselves; on the ninth day of the month beginning at evening, from evening to evening' (Lev. 23.27,32). According to the sages, afflicting one's soul involved abstaining from food and drink. Thus every male over the age of thirteen and every female over twelve is obliged to fast from sunset until nightfall the next evening. Sick people, however, may take medicine and small amounts of food and drink; similarly, those who are ill may be forbidden to fast.

During the day normal Sabbath prohibitions apply, but worshippers are to abstain from food and drink, marital relations, wearing leather shoes, using cosmetics and lotions, and washing the body except for fingers and eyes. The rabbis stress that the Day of Atonement enables human beings to atone for sins against God; however, regarding transgressions committed against others, pardon cannot be obtained unless forgiveness has been sought from the persons injured: as a consequence, it is customary for Jews to seek reconciliation with anyone they might have offended during the year. Previously lashes (*malkot*) were administered in the synagogue to impart a feeling of repentance, but this custom has largely disappeared. The *kapparot* ritual still takes place before the Day of Atonement among Sephardi and Eastern communities as well as among some Ashkenazim. During this ceremony a fowl is slaughtered and either eaten before the fast or sold for money which is given to charity – its death symbolizes the transfer of guilt from the person to the bird that has been killed. In many congregations Jews substitute coins for the fowl, and charity boxes are available at the morning and afternoon services before *Yom Kippur*.

Customarily Jews were able to absolve vows on the eve of *Yom Kippur*. In addition, afternoon prayers are recited earlier than normal, and the *Amidah* is extended by two formulas of confession (*Ashamnu* and *Al Het*). Some pious Jews immerse themselves in a *mikveh* (ritual bath) in order to undergo purification before the fast. In the home a final meal (*seudah mafseket*) is eaten, and prior to lighting the festival candles, a memorial candle is kindled to burn throughout the day. Further, leather shoes are replaced by non-leather shoes or slippers. The prayer shawl (*tallit*) is worn throughout all the services, and a white curtain (*parokhet*) adorns the synagogue Ark and the scrolls of the Law. The reader's desk and other furnishings are also covered in white. Among Ashkenazim, rabbis, cantors and other officiants also wear a white *kittel*.

On *Yom Kippur* five services take place. The first, *Kol Nidre* (named after its introductory declarations), ends with the concluding service (*neilah*). Except for the extended *Amidah*, each service has its own characteristic liturgy. In all of them, however, the confession of sins (*viddui*) is pronounced – shorter confessions as well as longer ones are in the first person plural to emphasize collective responsibility. In some liturgies there are also confessions of personal transgressions. Of special importance in the liturgy is the *Avinu Malkenu* prayer in which individuals confess their sins and pray for forgiveness.

In most congregations the *Kol Nidre* (declaration of annulment of vows) is recited on the eve of Yom Kippur. Among the Orthodox it was a custom to spend the night in the synagogue reciting the entire book of Psalms as well as other readings. Among Sephardim and Reform Jews the memorial prayer is recited on *Kol Nidre*. In addition to *selihot* and other hymns, the morning service includes a *Torah* reading (Leviticus chapter 16) describing the Day of Atonement ritual in the Sanctuary, and a *maftir* (additional) reading (Num. 29.7–11) concerning the festival sacrifices. The *Haftarah* (Isa. 57.14—58. 14) describes the fast that is required. Ashkenazim (excluding Reform Jews) then recite memorial prayers (*yizkor*). Among Sephardi Jewry and Eastern communities, the *Hashkavah* service is repeated.

Before the *musaf* service a special prayer (*Hineni He-Ani Mi-Maas*) is recited. A number of liturgical hymns are also included in the reader's repetition of the *Amidah*, including the *U-Netanneh Tokef* passage. Interpolated in among the *selihot* and confessions toward the end of *musaf* is the *Elleh Ezkerah* martyrology. Based on a medieval *midrash*, this martyrology describes the plight of the Ten Martyrs who were persecuted for defying Hadrian's ban on the study of *Torah*. In some rites this part of the service has been expanded to include readings from Holocaust sources. In the afternoon service Leviticus chapter 18 is read, dealing with prohibited marriages and sexual offences; the *Haftarah* is the book of Jonah.

Before the concluding service (*neilah*), the hymn *El Nora Alilah* is chanted among Sephardim. This part of the liturgy is recited as twilight approaches. During this time hymns such as *Petah Lanu Shaar* serve to remind congregants that the period for repentance is nearly over. In many congregations the Ark remains open and worshippers stand throughout the service. Worshippers ask God to inscribe each person for a good life and to seal them for a favourable fate. *Neilah* concludes with the chanting of *Avinu Malkenu*. This is followed by the *Shema*, the threefold recital of *Barukh Shem Kevod Malkhuto*, and a sevenfold acknowledgement that the Lord is God. The *shofar* is then blown, and the congregants recite *La-Shanah ha-Baah Bi-Yerushalayim* (Next year in Jerusalem). After the service concludes it is customary to begin the construction of the booth (*sukkah*).

30

Days of Joy

In the Jewish calendar there are a number of joyous festivals on which Jews are permitted to follow their daily tasks:

(1) *Hanukkah*. This festival (meaning 'dedication') is celebrated for eight days beginning on 25th of *Kislev* – it commemorates the victory of the Maccabees over the Seleucids in the second century BC. At this time the Maccabees engaged in a military struggle with the Seleucids who had desecrated the Temple of Jerusalem. After a three year struggle (165–163 BC), the Maccabees under Judah Maccabee conquered Jerusalem and rebuilt the altar. According to Talmudic legend, one day's worth of oil miraculously kept the *menorah* burning in the Temple for eight days. *Hanukkah* commemorates this miracle.

The central observance of this festival is the kindling of the festive lamp on each of the eight nights. This practice gave this holiday the additional name of *Hag ha-Urim* (Festival of Lights). In ancient times this lamp was placed in the doorway or in the street outside; subsequently the lamp was placed inside the house. The lighting occurs after dark (except on Friday evenings when it must be done before the kindling of the Sabbath lights). The procedure for lighting the *Hanukkah* candles is to light one candle (or oil lamp) on the first night, and an additional candle each night until the last night when all eight candles are lit. The kindling should go from left to right. An alternative tradition prescribes that the eight candles are lit on the first night, seven on the second night, and so forth. These candles are lit by an additional candle called the *shammash* (serving light). In addition to this home ceremony, candles are lit in the synagogue.

In the synagogue liturgy this festival is commemorated by the recitation of the *Al ha-Nissim* prayer in the *Amidah*, and Grace after Meals. In the morning service the *Hallel* is recited, and a special reading of the Law takes place on each day of the holiday. In both the home and the synagogue the hymn *Maoz Tsur* is sung in Ashkenazi communities; the Sephardim read Psalm 30 instead. During *Hanukkah* it is customary to hold parties which include games and singing. The most well-known game involves a *dreydel* (spinning top). The *dreydel* is inscribed with four Hebrew letters (*nun, gimmel, he, shin*) on its side – this is an acrostic for the phrase '*nes gadol hayah sham*' (a great miracle happened here). During *Hanukkah* it is customary to eat *latkes* (potato pancakes) and *sufganiyyot* (doughnuts). In modern Israel the festival is associated with national heroism, and a torch is carried from the traditional burial site of the Maccabees at Modiin to various parts of the country.

(2) Another festival of joy is *Purim* celebrated on 14th of *Adar* to commemorate the deliverance of Persian Jewry from the plans of Haman, the chief minister of King Ahasureus. The name of this holiday is derived from the Akkadian word '*pur*' (lots) which refers to Haman's casting of lots to determine a date (13th *Adar*) to destroy the Jewish people (Esth. 3.7–14). In remembrance of this date the Fast of Esther is observed on 13th of *Adar* – on this day Queen Esther proclaimed a fast before she interceded with the king. On the next day *Purim* is celebrated as the Feast of Lots which Mordecai, Esther's cousin, inaugurated to remember the deliverance of the Jewish people (Esth. 9.20ff). The 15th of *Adar* is *Purim Shoshan* since the conflict between the Jews and Haman's supporters in ancient Susa did not cease until the 14th, and Ahasureus allowed the Jews an extra day to overcome their foes. This means that the deliverance could only be celebrated a day later (Esth. 9.13–18).

The laws regarding the observance of *Purim* are specified in the tractate *Megillah* in the *Talmud*. In the evening and morning services the Esther scroll is chanted to a traditional melody. In most congregations *Purim* resembles a carnival – children frequently attend the reading from the scroll in fancy dress, and whenever Haman's name is mentioned, worshippers stamp their feet and whirl noisemakers (*greggers*). In the *Amidah* and Grace after Meals a prayer of thanksgiving is included; however, the *Hallel* psalms are excluded. During the afternoon a special festive meal takes place including such traditional dishes as *Hamentashen* (Haman's hats) – triangular buns or pastries filled with poppyseed, prunes, dates, etc. It is usual for parents and relatives to give children money (*Purim gelt*). On *Purim* it is customary to stage plays, and in *yeshivot* students mimic their teachers. In modern Israel parades take place with revellers dressed in *Purim* costumes.

(3) *Rosh Hodesh* is another festival of joy which occurs with the New Moon each month. Since the Jewish calendar is lunar, each month lasts a little more than twenty-nine days. Because it was not possible to arrange the calendar with months of alternative length the Sanhedrin declared whether a month had twenty-nine or thirty days. If the outgoing month had twenty-nine days, the next day was *Rosh Hodesh*. When a month had thirty days, the last day of the outgoing month and the first day of the new month constituted *Rosh Hodesh*. In early rabbinic times, the Sanhedrin was responsible for determining the day of the New Moon on the basis of eye witnesses who had claimed to see the new moon. Only in the fourth century was a permanent calendar fixed by Hillel II.

During the period of the First Temple, *Rosh Hodesh* was observed with the offering of special sacrifices, the blowing of *shofars*, feasting and a rest from work. By the end of the sixth century BC *Rosh Hodesh* became a semi-holiday. Eventually even this status disappeared, and *Rosh Hodesh* became a normal working day except for various liturgical changes. The liturgy for *Rosh Hodesh* includes the *Yaaleh Ve-Yavo* prayer, read in the *Amidah* and in Grace after Meals, which ask God to remember his people for good, for blessing and for life. In the morning service the *Hallel* psalms of praise are recited. The Bible reading is from Numbers chapter 28 which describes the Temple service for the New Moon. An additional service is also included, corresponding to the additional sacrifice which was offered on the New Moon.

(4) A further joyous festival is the *New Year for Trees* (*Tu Bi-Shevat*) which takes place on 15th of *Shevat*. Although this festival is not referred to in the Bible, it appeared in the Second Temple period as a fixed cut-off date for determining the tithe levied on the produce of fruit trees. Once the Temple was destroyed, the laws of tithing were no longer applicable; as a result, this festival took on a new character. Wherever Jews

resided, it reminded them of their connection with the Holy Land. During the fifteenth century, a number of new cere- monies and rituals were instituted by the mystics of Safed. Due to the influence of Isaac Luria, it became customary to celebrate the festival with gatherings where special fruits were eaten and hymns and readings from Scripture were recited. Among the fruits eaten on *Tu Bi-Shevat* were those of the Holy Land. In modern Israel new trees are planted during this festival.

(5) Another joyous occasion is the *Fifteenth of Av* which was a folk festival in the Second Temple period. At this time bachelors selected their wives from unmarried maidens. According to the *Mishnah*, on both this day and the Day of Atonement, young girls in Jerusalem dressed in white garments and danced in the vineyards where young men selected their brides. In modern times this festival is marked only by a ban on eulogies or fasting. In the liturgy the *Tananun* prayer is not recited after the *Amidah*.

(6) The final festival is Independence Day – this is Israel's national day, which commemorates the proclamation of its independence on 5th of *Iyyar*, 1948. The Chief Rabbinate of Israel declared it a religious holiday and established a special order of service for the evening and morning worship. This service includes the *Hallel*, and a reading from Isaiah (Isa. 10.32— 11.12). The rabbinate also suspended any fast which occurs on the day, the recital of the *Tahanun* prayer, and mourning restrictions of the *omer* period. In Israel the preceding day is set aside as a day of remembrance for soldiers who died in battle. *Yikzor* prayers (including the *kaddish*) are recited then, and next-of-kin visit the military cemeteries. At home memorial candles are lit, and Psalm 9 is recited in many synagogues.

31

Fast Days

In the ritual of the First Temple, fasting was a permanent feature; in addition, the death of a national leader (such as King Saul) could initiate a day-long fast (2 Sam. 12) or even a weekly fast (1 Sam. 31.13). The purpose of such fasting was manifold. Its most widely attested function was to avert or terminate calamities. Fasting also served as a means of obtaining divine forgiveness.

In the Bible there is no record of specific fast days in the annual calendar (except for the Day of Atonement). Fixed fast days were first mentioned in the post-exilic period by the prophet Zechariah who declared: 'Thus says the Lord of hosts: The fast of the fourth month, and the fast of the fifth, and the fast of the seventh, and the fast of the tenth, shall be to the houses of Judah seasons of joy and gladness, and cheerful feasts' (Zech. 8.19). According to tradition, these fasts commemorate the events which resulted in the destruction of the Temple: the 10th of *Tevet* – the beginning of the siege of Jerusalem; the 17th of *Tammuz* – the breaching of the walls; the 9th of *Av* – the destruction of the Temple; the 3rd of *Tishri* – the assassination of Gedaliah (the Babylonian-appointed governor of Judah). Thus the practice of fasting, which was a spontaneous phenomenon in the period of the First Temple, later entered the calendar as a recurring event in commemoration of historical calamities.

Jewish sources lay down a series of prescriptions to regularize the process of fasting. During the First Temple period the devout offered sacrifices, confessed sins and uttered prayers. From the Second Temple period onward, public fasts were also accompanied by a reading from Scripture. On solemn fasts four prayers (*shaharit, hazot, minhah,* and *neilat shearim*) were recited as well as *maariv*. The *Amidah* of the fast day consisted of twenty-four benedictions (the normal eighteen, plus six others) and the liturgy was elaborated with passages of supplication (*selihot*) and prayers for mercy. During the service the *shofar* was sounded, accompanied by horns. In the Temple the blowing of *shofarot* and trumpets was performed differently from other localities. Prayers were normally uttered in the open, and all the people tore their clothes, wore sackcloth, and put ashes or earth on their heads. Holy objects were also humiliated. It was not uncommon to cover the altar with sackcloth and the Ark, containing the *Torah* scrolls, was frequently taken into the street and covered with ashes. During the mass assembly, one of the elders rebuked the people for their failings, and the affairs of the community were scrutinized. It was normal for young children and animals to fast as well. (The sages, however, exempted young children and animals, the sick, those obliged to preserve their strength, and pregnant and nursing women).

Ordinary fast days lasted during the daylight hours; important fasts were twenty-four hours in length. Fasts were held either for one day or, on some occasions, for a series of three or seven days. In some cases they took place daily for a continued period. In unusual cases, fasts were held on Sabbaths and festivals – but it was normally forbidden to fast on these days. So as not to mar the celebration of joyful events in Jewish history, Hananiah ben Hezekiah ben Garon (first century AD) formulated a *Scroll of Fasting* which lists thirty-five dates on which a public fast should not be proclaimed. Eventually, however, this list was abrogated. It was customary to hold fast days on Mondays and Thursdays. After the destruction of the Second Temple, individuals took upon themselves to fast every Monday and Thursday; Jewish law specifies that in such cases these persons should fast during the afternoon of the preceding day. It was also possible to fast for a certain number of hours. On some occasions, the fast was only partial, and those who fasted refrained only from meat and wine.

According to tradition, fast days fall into three categories:

A. FASTS DECREED OR REFERRED TO IN THE BIBLE

1. The Day of Atonement (*Yom Kippur*) is to be a fast day in accordance with the declaration: 'You shall afflict your souls'. This is done so that individuals may be cleansed from sin (Lev. 16.29–31; 23.27–32; Num. 29.7ff).

2. The Ninth of *Av* (*Tishah B'Av*) was the day when Nebuchadnezzar destroyed the Temple in 586 BC and Titus later devastated the Second Temple in AD 70). The *Mishnah* (second century compilation of Law) also decrees that on this day God declared that the older Israelites should not enter the Promised Land (Num. 14.28ff). Betar was captured in AD 135, and Jerusalem was ploughed up on Hadrian's decree. Like *Yom Kippur* this fast is observed for a complete day, beginning at sunset on the eighth day of *Av* and ending at nightfall on the ninth. As a sign of mourning neither meat, drink, nor wine should be consumed from the first day of Av until noon on the tenth, except on the Sabbath and on a *Seudat Mitzvah* (a meal in honour of a religious act). In the synagogue service the Ark curtain and coverings are removed; congregants take off their shoes and sit on low chairs. During the morning service *tefillin* and *tallit* are not worn but are put on during the afternoon service. At the evening and morning services a number of elegies (*kinot*) are recited, which are connected with tragic events in the history of the Jewish people. The *Torah* reading at the morning service is taken from Deuteronomy 4.25–40 which deals with God's forgiveness of penitents. The *Haftarah* (Jer. 8.13—9.23) predicts the punishment which will befall the kingdom of Judah. At the afternoon service the *Torah* and *Haftarah* readings are the same as on other fast days. During the seven weeks between *Tishah B'Av* and *Rosh Hashanah* the *Haftarah* portions are taken from the Book of Isaiah, containing messages of consolation.

3. The Seventeenth of *Tammuz* commemorates the breaching of the walls of the Jerusalem. This occurred on 9th of *Tammuz* in the First Temple period (2 Kings 25.3–4) and in Second Temple times they were breached by the Romans on 17th of *Tammuz*. In addition, the *Mishnah* records that other disasters took place on 17th of *Tammuz*: Moses broke the tablets of stone on which the Ten Commandments were inscribed when he saw the ancient Israelites worship the golden calf; the communal burnt offerings ceased when Jerusalem was besieged; a Syrian officer, Apostomos, burnt the *Torah* scrolls and set up an idol in the Temple. The fast of 17th of *Tammuz* begins at sunrise on the day itself (rather than the previous night). In the morning service, Exodus 32.22–14 and 34.1–10 are read; in the afternoon, these passages are repeated and among

Ashkenazim, followed by a *Haftarah* taken from the Book of Isaiah (Isa. 55.6—56.8).

4. The Tenth of *Tevet* is a fast commemorating the commencement of the siege of Jerusalem by Nebuchadnezzar (2 Kings 25.1). This fast begins at dawn and lasts until nightfall. The liturgy for the day includes penitential prayers (*selihot*) and a reading from Exodus (parts of Exodus chapters 32 and 34) which deals with the worship of the golden calf and Moses' prayer for forgiveness for the nation. In the afternoon service the same passage is read with the addition of a *Haftarah* from Isaiah chapters 55 and 56. In Israel, 10th of *Tevet* is observed as a day of remembrance of the six million Jews who died at the hands of the Nazis in the Holocaust.

5. The Fast of Gedaliah takes place on 3rd of *Tishri* to commemorate the fate of Gedaliah, the governor of Judah who was assassinated on this day. Fasting takes place from dawn to dusk and penitential hymns (*selihot*) are recited during the morning service. (If the fast falls on a Sabbath, it is observed the next day).

6. The Fast of Esther takes place on 13th of *Adar* (the day before *Purim*).

B. FASTS DECREED BY THE RABBIS

1. Those who are especially pious are encouraged to fast during the Ten Days of Penitence and for as many days as possible during the month of *Elul*.

2. The first Monday and Thursday, and the following Monday after Passover and *Sukkot* are to be observed as fast days.

3. *ShOVaVIM Tat* (initial letters of the first eight weekly Bible portions of the Book of Exodus) is observed during the winter months of January and February.

4. A fast is observed during the Three Weeks of Mourning between 17th of *Tammuz* and 9th of *Av*.

5. 7th of *Adar* is a traditional date of the death of Moses; it is observed by members of the burial society who fast prior to their annual banquet held on the evening of that day.

6. *Yom Kippur Katan* is a fast day which takes place on the last day of each month.

7. The Fast of the First-Born takes place on 14th of *Nisan* to commemorate the sanctification of the first-born who were saved during the time of the last plague of Egypt.

8. Days commemorating calamitous events in the history of the Jewish nation.

C. PRIVATE FASTS

1. The anniversary of the death of a parent or teacher.

2. Grooms and brides fast on their wedding days.

3. Fasting occurs to prevent the consequences of nightmares taking place.

4. Fasting takes place if a *Torah* scroll is dropped.

32

From Birth to the Coming of Age

In Scripture the first commandment is to be fruitful and multiply (Gen. 1.28). In biblical times childbirth took place in a kneeling position (1 Sam. 4.19) or sitting on a special birthstool (Exodus chapter 16). Scriptural law imposes various laws on ritual purity and impurity on the mother: if she gives birth to a boy she is considered ritually impure for seven days; for the next thirty-three days she is not allowed to enter the Temple precincts or handle sacred objects. For the mother of a girl, the number of days are respectively fourteen and sixty-six. According to Jewish law, if a woman in childbirth is in mortal danger, her life takes precedence over that of the unborn child – only when over half of the child's body has emerged from the birth canal is it considered to be fully human.

In ancient times the birth of a child was accompanied by numerous superstitious practices, including the use of amulets to ward off the evil eye. After the birth, family and friends gathered nightly to recite prayers to ward off evil spirits such as Lilith, the female demon who allegedly attempts to kill off all new-born children. Among German Jewry, it was frequently the practice for parents of a son to cut off a strip of swaddling in which the child was wrapped during his circumcision; this is known as the *wimple*, and is kept until his *bar mitzvah*, when it is used for tying the scroll of the Law. From the medieval period Ashkenazi mothers visited the synagogue after the birth of a child to recite the *Gomel* blessing (which expresses gratitude to God), as well as other prayers. It is also the custom for the congregation to recite the *Mi She-Barakh* prayer for the welfare of the mother and the child.

The naming of a new-born child takes place on one of two occasions: a baby boy is named at the circumcision ceremony; a baby girl is named in the synagogue on the first time the *Torah* is read after her birth. The Hebrew form of the individual's name consists of the individual's name followed by *'ben'* (son) or *'bat'* (daughter) of the father. This form is used in all Hebrew documents as well as for the call to the reading of the *Torah*. In modern times it is still the practice to give a child a Jewish name in addition to a secular one. Ashkenazi Jews frequently name the child after a deceased relative; Sephardi Jews after someone who is still alive. Alternatively, a Hebrew name may be selected which is related to the secular name either in meaning or sound, or the secular name may be transliterated in Hebrew characters. Traditionally it was the custom to change the name of a person at the time of a serious illness; according to the rabbis, changing the name is a way of misleading the angel of death. On this basis, it became the custom to add a further name to the ill person's – from that point the individual was known by his original name, together with the new one.

The custom of redeeming first-born male children is based on the biblical prescription that first-born sons should be consecrated to the Temple. Just as first fruits and first-born animals had to be given to the priests, so first-born male children were dedicated to God. The obligation to redeem first-born sons from this service is referred to in Numbers 3.44–51: redemption is to take place by payment of five shekels to a priest. Detailed laws concerning the Redemption of the First-Born (*Pidyon ha-Ben*) are presented in the *Mishnah* tractate *Bekhorot*, and expanded in the talmudic commentary on the passage. According to this legislation, the sons of priests and Levites are exempt from redemption, as are first-born sons whose mother is the daughter of either a priest or Levite. In the geonic period, a ceremony was instituted in which the father of the child declares to the priest on the thirty-first day after its birth that the infant is the first-born son of his mother and father and that, as a father, he is obliged to redeem him. The priest then asks the father if he prefers to give his son to the priest or redeem him for five shekels. The father replies that he wants to redeem his son, and hands the priest the required amount. The father then recites a blessing concerning the fulfilment of the precept of redeeming the child, and another expressing gratitude to God. This procedure has served as the basis for the ceremony since the Middle Ages.

According to Jewish law, all male children are to undergo circumcision, in accordance with God's decree, and as a sign of the covenant between God and Abraham's offspring. As Genesis chapter 17 relates:

> God said to Abraham . . . 'This is my covenant which you shall keep between me and you and your descendants after you: every male among you shall be circumcised. You shall be circumcised in the flesh of your foreskins, and it shall be a sign of the covenant between me and you' (Gen. 17.9–11).

Jewish ritual circumcision involves the removal of the entire foreskin. It is to be performed on the eighth day after the birth of the child by a person who is properly qualified (*mohel*). Jewish law specifies that this ceremony can be performed even on the Sabbath, festivals, or the Day of Atonement; however, postponement is allowed if there is any danger to the child's health. The laws regulating this procedure are derived from biblical sources as well as rabbinic enactments. Traditionally the ceremony is to take place in the presence of a quorum of ten adult Jewish men (*minyan*). On the morning of the eighth day, the infant is taken from the mother by the godmother who hands him to the *sandak* (godfather). The *sandak* then carries the child into the room where the circumcision is to take place and hands him to the individual who places the child on a chair called the Chair of Elijah. Another person then takes him from the Chair of Elijah and passes him to the child's father who puts him on the lap of the godfather who holds the boy during the ceremony. The circumcision is performed by a *mohel*; formerly blood was drawn orally by the *mohel* but today an instrument is used. The infant is then handed to the person who will hold him during the ceremony of naming, and the ceremony concludes with a special blessing over a cup of wine, followed by the naming of the child.

At thirteen a boy attains the age of Jewish adulthood; from this point he is counted as part of a *minyan* (the quorum for prayer). According to the *Mishnah*, the thirteenth year is when a boy should observe the commandments. The term *bar mitzvah* ('son of the commandment') occurs five times in the Babylonian *Talmud*, but in all cases it is used merely to refer to someone obliged to fulfil Jewish law. The *Talmud* stipulates that male adolescence begins at the age of thirteen years and a day; none the less a boy was able to participate in religious ceremonies at an earlier age as long as he could appreciate their meaning. However, by the Middle Ages, a Jewish minor's participation in religious rituals had become limited.

Ashkenazim for example allowed a boy to wear *tefillin* only after he was thirteen; in addition, he was not allowed to be called to the reading of the Law until then. Sephardi congregations also imposed similar restrictions.

The essentials of the *bar mitzvah* ceremony involved prayer with *tefillin* for the first time, and reading from the *Torah*. Among East European Ashkenazim, a boy was normally called to the reading of the *Torah* on the first Monday or Thursday after his thirteenth birthday; then he would recite the *Torah* blessings and chant some verses from the weekly *sidrah*. In Western Europe on the other hand, a thirteen-year-old boy would be called to the reading at Sabbath morning services where he would recite the *Torah* blessings, chant a portion of the law (*maftir*), and read from the Prophets. This has now become a universally accepted practice. Once the *bar mitzvah* boy had completed the second *Torah* blessing, his father would recite a special prayer – *Barukh She-Petaroni*.

In both Ashkenazi and Sephardi communities the *bar mitzvah* ceremony included a discourse (*derashah*) by the *bar mitzvah* boy which demonstrated his knowledge of rabbinic sources. In time other practices became part of the *bar mitzvah* ceremony; some boys chanted the entire weekly reading; others were trained as prayer leaders; some conducted the Sabbath eve service on Friday night as well as the Sabbath morning service. In some Western communities the *bar mitzvah* boy reads a special prayer standing before the rabbi or the Ark. In modern times it is usual for the rabbi to address the *bar mitzvah* boy after the reading of the Law.

Initially a *bar mitzvah* meal for family and friends was held after the weekday morning service, or a *seudah shelishit* (third meal) was consumed after the Sabbath afternoon service. Subsequently this was expanded into a *kiddush* (blessing over wine and bread) at the Sabbath morning service, followed by a family meal. Today there is frequently a *bar mitzvah* reception on a more lavish scale. Among Oriental Jews other variations of such festivities take place. In many Eastern Sephardi communities, Hebrew poems (*piyyutim*) are composed for this occasion. In the nineteenth century Reform Judaism substituted a confirmation ceremony for both boys and girls in place of *bar mitzvah*; however, as time passed, most Reform congregations have instituted *bar mitzvah* as well. Since 1967 both Orthodox and non-Orthodox *bar mitzvahs* have taken place at the Western Wall in Jerusalem.

Unlike *bar mitzvah* there is no legal requirement for a girl to take part in a religious ceremony to mark her religious majority (at the age of twelve years and a day). None the less, a ceremonial equivalent of *bar mitzvah* has been designed for girls. In Orthodoxy this was the innovation of Jacob Ettlinger in the nineteenth century, and subsequently spread to other lands. In the late nineteenth century it was approved by Joseph Hayyim ben Elijah al-Hakam of Baghdad, who formulated various regulations, including the holding of a banquet and the wearing of a new dress so that the *bat mitzvah* girl could recite the *Sheheheyanu* benediction.

In the early twentieth century the Conservative scholar Mordecai Kaplan pioneered the *bat mitzvah* ceremony in the USA as part of the synagogue service, and since then this has become widely accepted by many American communities. In non-Orthodox communities, a twelve-year-old girl celebrates her coming of age on a Friday night or during the Sabbath morning service where she conducts the prayers, chants the *Haftarah*, and in some cases reads from the *Torah* and delivers an address. In Orthodox synagogues, however, the *bat mitzvah's* participation in the services is more limited. At a women's *minyan*, however, she is called to the reading of the *Torah* and may even chant one of the portions, together with the *Haftarah*.

Outside the USA the *bat mitzvah* ceremony takes various forms. In Reform congregations it is in line with the American pattern. Orthodox girls, however, do not participate in the synagogue service; rather a *bat mitzvah's* father is called to the *Torah* on the appropriate Sabbath morning and recites the *Barukh She-Petaroni* benediction. His daughter then recites the *Sheheheyanu* prayer, and the rabbi addresses her in the synagogue or at a *kiddush* reception afterwards. Alternatively, the ceremony takes place at home or in the synagogue hall on a weekday. In Britain and South Africa the procedure is different: *bat mitzvah* girls must pass a special examination enabling them to participate in a collective ceremony.

33

Marriage

According to tradition, marriage is God's plan for humanity, as illustrated by the story of Adam and Eve in the Book of Genesis. In the Jewish faith it is viewed as a sacred bond as well as a means to personal fulfilment. It is more than a legal contract, rather an institution with cosmic significance, legitimized through divine authority. The purpose of marriage is to build a home, create a family and thereby perpetuate society. Initially Jews were allowed to have more than one wife, but this was banned in Ashkenazi countries with the decree of Rabbenu Gershom in 1000. In modern society, all Jewish communities – Sephardic and Ashkenazic – followed this ruling.

In the Bible marriages were arranged by fathers: Abraham, for example, sent his servant to find a wife for Isaac (Gen. 24.10–53), and Judah arranged the marriage of his first-born son (Gen. 38.6). When the proposal of marriage was accepted by the girl's father (or elder brother in his absence), the nature and amount of the *mohar* (payment by the groom) was agreed. By Second Temple times, there was a degree of choice in the selection of a bride – on 15th of *Av* and the Day of Atonement, young men could select their brides from among the girls dancing in the vineyards.

According to tradition a period of engagement preceded marriage itself. The ceremony was a seven-day occasion for celebration during which love songs were sung in praise of the bride. In the talmudic period a major development occurred concerning the *mohar* – since it could be used by the father of the bride, a wife could become penniless if her husband divorced or predeceased her. As a result the *mohar* evolved into the formulation of a marriage document (*ketubbah*) which gave protection to the bride. In addition, the act of marriage changed from being a personal civil procedure to a public religious ceremony which required the presence of a *minyan* (quorum) and the recitation of prayers.

In biblical and talmudic times marriage occurred in two stages: betrothal and *Nissuin*:

1. *Betrothal*: The concept of betrothal has two stages: (a) the commitment of a couple to marry as well as the terms of financial obligations (*shiddukhin*), and (b) a ceremony establishing a nuptial relationship independent of the wedding ceremony (*kiddushin* or *erusin*). An early instance of *shiddukhin* is found in Genesis 34 where the term *mohar* is used for a sum of money the father of the groom is to pay the father of the bride. During the talmudic period, this term was not used; instead the *Talmud* stipulates that negotiations should take place between the respective parents concerning financial obligations. The term for such negotiations is *shiddukhin* (an Aramaic word meaning 'tranquillity'). The terms agreed upon were written in a document called a *shetar pesikta*; the amount given to the son was called *nedunyah*. From the medieval period to the present the prenuptial agreement was itself divided into two stages: a verbal understanding (*vort*) was made, followed by a ceremony (*kinyan*) symbolizing the acceptance of the obligation to marry. This normally occurred at a meal; the act of accepting was accomplished by taking an object (usually the corner of a handkerchief). The second stage involved the writing in a document (*tenaim*) of the terms undertaken. In addition the *tenaim* designated the date and place of the nuptial ceremony. The ceremony of the *tenaim* concludes with the mothers of the bride and groom breaking a pottery dish. This ceremony is frequently celebrated with a dinner, and during the following period the bride and groom exchange gifts.

In the Bible the betrothal or nuptial ceremony which takes place prior to the wedding is referred to as *erusin*: in the rabbinic period the sages who outlined this procedure called it *kiddushin* to indicate that the bride is forbidden to all men except her husband. According to the *Mishnah*, the bride could be acquired in marriage in three ways: by money, deed or intercourse. Traditionally the method involved placing a ring on the bride's finger. At this stage the groom declared: 'Behold, you are consecrated unto me with this ring according to the law of Moses and of Israel.' Then the blessing over wine was recited:

Blessed are you, O Lord our God, King of the Universe, who

has hallowed us by your commandments, and has commanded us concerning forbidden marriages; who has forbidden unto us those who are betrothed, but has sanctioned unto us such as are wedded unto us by the rite of the nuptial canopy and the sacred covenant of wedlock.

After this ceremony the bride continued to remain in her father's house until the stage of *nissuin*.

2. *Nissuin*: During the second stage of the procedure for marriage the seven blessings (*sheva berakhot*) are recited:

Blessed are you, O Lord our God, King of the Universe, who creates the fruit of the vine.

. . . Who has created all things to your glory.

. . . Creator of man.

Who has made man in your image, after your likeness . . .

. . . made she who was barren (Zion) be glad and exult when her children are gathered within her in joy. Blessed are you, O Lord, who makes Zion joyful through her children. O make these loved companions greatly to rejoice, even as of old you did gladden your creatures in the Garden of Eden. Blessed are you, O Lord, who makes bridegroom and bride to rejoice.

. . . Who has created joy and gladness, bridegroom and bride, mirth and exultation, pleasure and delight, love, brotherhood, peace and fellowship. Soon may there be heard in the cities of Judah and in the streets of Jerusalem, the voice of joy and gladness, the voice of the bridegroom and the voice of the bride, the happy sound of bridegrooms from their canopies, and of youths from their feasts of song.

Blessed are you, O Lord, who makes the bridegroom to rejoice with the bride.

From the Middle Ages, it became customary for Ashkenazic Jewish communities to postpone the betrothal ceremony until immediately prior to the *nissuin* wedding ceremony – this also became customary among Sephardi Jews. In Hasidic communities, however, the traditional *tenaim* ceremony is still usually observed.

According to Jewish law, a marriage cannot be contracted in certain instances. Prohibited marriages are divided into two classes: permanent and temporary.

1. *Permanent prohibitions*: Leviticus chapters 18 and 29 outlines types of relationships between relatives which are not permitted for marriage, including a man's parents, stepmother, sister, granddaughter, aunt, daughter-in-law, sister-in-law, stepdaughter, step-granddaughter, and wife's sister (during his wife's lifetime). Other prohibited liaisons include the following cases: (a) if a husband has divorced his wife and she remarried and was subsequently divorced or became a widow, he may not remarry her; (b) a wife who had willingly committed adultery is prohibited to her husband as well as the adulterer. If she was raped she is prohibited to her husband if he is a priest (*Cohen*); (c) a woman is not allowed to marry anyone who represented her in her divorce case or witnessed her husband's death; (d) a priest is not allowed to marry a divorcee, a widow, or a harlot; (e) a *mamzer* (child of an illegitimate or incestuous relationship) may not marry a Jewish man or woman; (f) mixed marriage is forbidden.

2. *Temporary prohibitions*: Some marriages are prohibited only for limited periods such as: (a) a widow or divorcee may not remarry within ninety days of her husband's death or after receiving a bill of divorce (*get*); (b) a person may not marry within the thirty day period of mourning; a widower must wait until three festivals have occurred (unless he has no children or he has young children who need the care of a mother); one is not allowed to marry a pregnant woman, or a nursing woman until the child is twenty-four months; (c) a woman may not marry for a third time if her two successive husbands died due to accidents; (d) a married woman is not allowed to marry a second husband; she may only do so if she receives a bill of divorce.

Prior to the wedding itself, the bride is to immerse herself in a ritual bath (*mikveh*) usually on the evening before the ceremony. To facilitate this the wedding date is determined so that it does not occur during her time of menstruation, or the following week. In some Sephardi and Eastern communities this event is a public celebration. In most Sephardi communities a special celebration for the bride also takes place on the evening of the wedding. Referred to as the *hinnah*, women friends and family come to the house of the bride, whose hands are painted with red henna. Yeman women dress the brides in splendid clothes and jewellery to the accompaniment of singing, and then apply the henna. The aim of this ceremony is to ward off the evil eye.

On the Sabbath before the wedding in Ashkenazi communities, the groom is called to the reading of the Law and is showered with candies during the reading of the *Torah* blessings. In Sephardi and Eastern communities, the groom's Sabbath takes place on the Sabbath after the wedding. During the ceremony itself it is customary to shower the couple with rice and confetti. In some Ashkenazi circles, the bride when reaching the marriage canopy (*huppah*) is led around the groom seven times. The ceremony itself can be held anywhere, but from the Middle Ages the synagogue or synagogue courtyard was commonly used. It also became customary to hold it in the open air to symbolize God's promise to Abraham to make his descendants as numerous as the stars. Eventually, however, it has become customary to hold the ceremony in a hall.

In modern times the Orthodox wedding ceremony normally follows a uniform pattern based on traditional law. Normally the groom signs the *ketubbah*. If this takes place before evening, the afternoon service takes place and the groom who is fasting recites the *Yom Kippur* confession. He is then led to the bride and covers her face with her veil; the couple are led next to the marriage canopy (*huppah*) with their parents walking with the groom and the bride (or the fathers accompanying the groom and the mothers the bride). According to custom those leading the couple carry lighted candles. When the participants are under the canopy the rabbi recites the blessing over wine and the *erusin* blessing. Then the bride and groom drink from the cup. The groom then recites the traditional formula: 'Behold you are consecrated unto me with this ring according to the law of Moses and of Israel.' He then puts the ring on the bride's right index finger.

To demonstrate that the act of marriage consists of two ceremonies, the *ketubbah* is read prior to the *nissuim* ceremony. The seven blessings are then recited over a second cup of wine. The ceremony concludes with the groom stepping on a glass and breaking it. After the ceremony the bride and groom are led into a private room for *yihud* (seclusion). At the end of the wedding meal, the Grace after Meals is recited, and is followed by another reading of the Seven Blessings.

Within Conservative and Reform Judaism the wedding

service follows this traditional pattern with varying alterations. In most cases the custom of the groom covering the bride's face before the ceremony, the procession to the *huppah* with candles, and the *yihud* observance are omitted. In addition both movements have introduced a double ring ceremony in which the bride also puts a ring on the groom's finger (either with or without reciting the relevant blessing). The Reform ceremony is frequently accompanied by additional readings.

In the Orthodox community, the laws of ritual purity (*niddah*) are observed. Sexual intercourse even between married couples may only take place when the woman is ritually clean. During her menstrual period and for seven full days afterwards, a woman is forbidden to her husband. At the end of that time she must visit the ritual bath (*mikveh*) and immerse herself completely. Then they can resume marital relations. These laws are ignored by the non-Orthodox.

34

Divorce

Biblical law specifies the procedure for divorce. According to the Book of Deuteronomy, 'When a man takes a wife and marries her, if then she finds no favour in his eyes because he has found some indecency in her, and he writes her a bill of divorce and puts it in her hand and sends her out of his house' (Deut. 24.1). This verse stipulates that the power of divorce rests with the husband, and the act of divorce must be in the form of a legal document. Among early rabbinic scholars there was disagreement as to the meaning of the term 'indecency': the School of Shammai interpreted it as referring to unchastity, whereas the School of Hillel understood the term more widely. None the less, in two instances it was not permitted for divorce to take place: (1) if a man claimed that his wife was not a virgin at the time of marriage and his charge was disproved (Deut. 22.13–19); or (2) if he raped a virgin whom he later married (Deut. 22.28–9). Conversely, a man was not allowed to remarry his divorced wife if she had married another person and had been divorced or widowed (Deut. 24.2–4). Nor could a priest marry a divorced woman (Lev. 21.7).

In the talmudic period, the law of divorce underwent considerable development, including the elaboration of various situations under which the court could compel a husband to grant his wife a divorce. Thus a husband was compelled to divorce his wife if she remained barren over a period of ten years, if the husband contracted a loathsome disease, if he refused to support her or was not in a position to do so, if he denied his wife her conjugal rights, or if he beat her despite the court's warnings. In such cases the *Talmud* states that the husband is coerced by the court only to the extent that he would in fact want to divorce his wife.

The bill of divorce (*get*) is to be drawn up by a scribe following a formula based on mishnaic law. This document is written almost entirely in Aramaic on parchment. Once it has been given to the wife, it is retained by the rabbi who cuts it in criss-cross fashion so that it cannot be used a second time. The husband then gives the wife a document (*petor*) which affirms that he has been divorced, and may remarry. The wife is permitted to remarry only after ninety days, so as to ascertain whether she was pregnant at the stage of divorce. A typical bill of divorce is as follows:

> On the . . . day of the week, the . . . day of the month of . . . in the year . . . from the creation of the world according to the calendar reckoning we are accustomed to count here, in the city . . . which is located on the river . . . and situated near wells of water, I . . . the son of . . . who today am presently in the city . . . which is located on the river . . . and situated near wells of water, do willingly consent, being under no restraint, to release, to set free, and put aside you, my wife . . ., daughter of . . ., who is today in the city of . . ., which is located on the river . . . and situated near wells of water, who has been my wife from before. Thus I do set free, release you, and put you aside, in order that you may have permission and the authority over yourself to go and marry any man you may desire. No person may hinder you from this day onward, and you are permitted to every man. This shall be for you from me a bill of dismissal, a letter of release, and a document of freedom, in accordance with the laws of Moses and Israel.

This document must be witnessed by two males over the age of thirteen who are not related to each other or to the divorcing husband and wife.

The traditional procedure is based on the *Code of Jewish Law*. The officiating rabbi initially asks the husband if he gives the bill of divorce (*get*) of his own free will without duress and compulsion. After receiving the writing materials from a scribe, he instructs the scribe to write a *get*. He then instructs the witnesses to sign the *get*. The *get* is written and the witnesses must be present during the writing of the first line; the witnesses as well as the scribe then make a distinguishing mark on the *get*. When the *get* is completed and the ink is dry, the witnesses read the *get*. The rabbi then questions the scribe to ensure that the document was written by him on the instruction of the husband. Turning to the witnesses, the rabbi asks if they heard the husband instruct the scribe to write the *get*, as well as observed him writing it. In addition, the rabbi questions the witnesses about their signatures on the bill of divorce. Finally, the rabbi asks the husband if the *get* was given freely. The wife is then asked if she freely accepts the *get*:

> Rabbi: 'Are you accepting this *get* of your own free will?'
> Wife: 'Yes.'
> Rabbi: 'Did you bind yourself by any statement or vow that would compel you to accept this *get* against your will?'
> Wife: 'No.'
> Rabbi: 'Perhaps you have unwittingly made such a statement that would nullify the *get*. In order to prevent that, will you kindly retract all such declarations?'
> Wife: 'I revoke all such statements that may nullify the *get*, in the presence of the witnesses.'

The rabbi tells the wife to remove all jewellery from her hands and hold her hands together with open palms upward to receive the bill of divorce. The scribe holds the *get* and gives it to the rabbi. The rabbi then gives the *get* to her husband; he holds it in both hands and drops it into the palms of the wife and states: 'This be your *get* and with it be you divorced from this time forth so that you may become the wife of any man.' When the wife receives the bill of divorce, she walks with it a short distance and returns. She gives the *get* to the rabbi who reads it again in the presence of the witnesses; the rabbi then asks the scribe and the witnesses to identify the *get* as well as the signatures. Following this, the rabbi states: 'Hear all you present that Rabbenu Tam has issued a ban against all those who try to invalidate a *get* after it has been delivered.' The four corners of the *get* are cut, and it is placed in the rabbi's files. The husband and wife receive written statements certifying that their marriage has been dissolved in accordance with Jewish law.

It is customary for the husband and wife to be present during the divorce proceedings, but if this is not possible Jewish law stipulates that an agent can take the place of either party. The husband may appoint an agent to deliver the *get* to his wife; if this agent is unable to complete the task, he has the right to appoint another one, and the second agent yet another. The wife can also appoint an agent to receive the *get*. Thus it is possible for the entire procedure to take place without the husband or wife seeing one another; this is sometimes done to avoid the emotional strain of the husband and wife meeting each other if a bitter divorce has occurred.

In certain instances a *get* of benefit (*get zikkui*) may be arranged. Jewish law stipulates that the woman's consent to a divorce is not necessary, and the *get* can be given to her against her will. However the ordinance of Rabbenu Gershom (tenth to eleventh century) prohibits divorcing a woman without consent. According to talmudic scholars, a benefit can be conferred upon an individual even when that person is not present. That is, if the procedure can bring about a benefit for an individual, it is logical to assume that this person would give his or her consent if he or she knew about it. In the case of civil divorce, it can be assumed that if the husband and wife have already obtained a divorce from the secular authorities, she has given consent to divorce. In such a case, the rabbinical court (*bet din*) can appoint an agent to receive the *get* for her even without her consent. Here the wife would be receiving a benefit because she would be able to remarry according to the *Halakhah* without risking being considered an adulteress. In such instances the procedure of divorce is the same, except that instead of giving the bill of divorce to the wife, the husband gives the *get* to an agent who is appointed by the court.

Throughout history a number of modifications have been made to divorce legislation. In the Middle Ages Rabbenu Gershom brought about a fundamental change in the law of divorce among Ashkenazim as well as some Sephardi communities. In an enactment (*takkanah*), he decreed that a husband may not divorce his wife without her consent. This *takkanah* in essence made the rights of the wife nearly equivalent to those of the husband: from this time forth divorce could only be by mutual consent. Later halakhists strengthened this enactment by stating that any writ of divorce issued in violation of this ruling was null and void. Some time later Jacob Tam decreed that in certain emergencies the *takkanah* requiring mutual consent could be set aside, such as in the case of a woman who apostasized and left the Jewish community.

Yet despite such modifications, certain difficulties still remain about the granting of a *get*. Since it is the husband who must give the bill of divorce to his wife, if he cannot be located, this presents an insurmountable obstacle. Similarly in the diaspora rabbinic scholars have no authority to compel a husband to comply with their instructions. In both cases the wife has the status of being an *agunah* (a 'tied' woman) who is not able to remarry according to traditional Jewish law. In order to vitiate this difficulty the Rabbinical Assembly of the Conservative movement proposed a *takkanah* calling for the insertion of a clause in the marriage contract whereby both groom and bride in grave circumstances agree to abide by the decision of the religious court (*bet din*) of the Conservative movement:

> And both together agreed that if this marriage shall be dissolved under civil law, then either husband or wife may invoke the authority of the *bet din* of the Rabbinical Assembly and the Jewish Theological Seminary of America or its duly authorized representatives, to decide what action by either spouse is then appropriate under Jewish matrimonial law, and if either spouse should fail to honour the demand of the other or to carry out the decision of the *bet din* or its representatives, then the other spouse may invoke any and all remedies available in civil law and equity to enforce compliance with the *bet din's* decision and this solemn obligation.

Another solution proposed by the Conservative movement involves an antenuptial agreement signed by the bride and groom:

> On the . . . day of . . ., 19 . . ., corresponding to . . . 57 . . ., in . . ., the groom, Mr . . ., and the bride, Mrs . . ., of their own free will and accord entered into the following agreement with respect to their intended marriage.

The groom made the following declaration to the bride:

> I will betroth and marry you according to the laws of Moses and Israel, subject to the following conditions:
> (a) If our marriage be terminated by decree of the civil courts and if by expiration of six months after such a decree I give you a divorce according to the laws of Moses and Israel (a *get*), then our betrothal (*kiddushin*) and marriage (*nissuin*) will have been valid and binding.

(b) But if our marriage be terminated by decree of civil court and if by expiration of six months after such a decree I do not give you a divorce according to the laws of Moses and Israel (a *get*) then our betrothal (*kiddushin*) and marriage (*nissuin*) will have been null and void.

This document gives authority to the *bet din* to annul the marriage *ab initio* in the case where there is a refusal to authorize a *get*.

In a later enactment the Rabbinical Assembly of the Conservative movement invoked the power that the talmudic rabbis had to annul marriages. The formula ('You are betrothed unto me with this ring, according to the laws of Moses and Israel') is interpreted by the rabbis in the *Talmud* to imply that every bride and groom contract a marriage subject to the approval of rabbinical authorities. If the rabbinical authorities remove their approval then the marriage is null and void *ab initio*. Since this power was invoked in ancient times when the husband acted in an unjust manner, it was felt that in later times the power could be invoked again to resolve the problem of the *agunah*.

Within Reform Judaism the traditional practice of granting a bill of divorce has been abandoned. Instead civil divorce is regarded as valid. For this reason there has been no attempt within Reform Judaism to formulate a policy dealing with the status of the *agunah*.

35

The Home

In Judaism religious observance in the home is of fundamental importance. According to the sages, it is (to use Ezekiel's terminology) a *mikdash meat* (a minor sanctuary) – like the synagogue, it continues various traditions of the ancient Temple. The Sabbath candles, for example, recall the Temple *menorah* and the dining table symbolizes the altar. Most significantly, within the home, family life is sanctified. As head of the family, the father is to exercise authority over his wife and children. He is obligated to circumcise his son, redeem him if he is the first-born, teach him *Torah*, marry him off and teach him a craft. Further he is required to serve as a role model for the transmission of Jewish ideals to his offspring.

Regarding Jewish women, the prevailing sentiment is that the role of the wife is to bear children and exercise responsibility for family life. According to the *Halakhah*, womanhood is a separate status with its own specific sets of rules, obligations and responsibilities. In terms of religious observance, women were classed with slaves and children, disqualified as witnesses, excluded from the study of the *Torah* and segregated from men. Moreover, they were regarded as ritually impure for extended periods of time. In general, they were exempted from time-bound commands; as a result they were not obliged to fulfil those commandments which must be followed at a particular time (such as the recitation of prayer). The purpose of these restrictions was to ensure that their attention and energy be directed toward completing their domestic duties. In the contemporary period, however, a growing number of women have agitated for equal treatment – in consequence, the role of women has undergone a major transformation. None the less, there has been a universal recognition in all branches of Judaism that the Jewish wife should continue to play a central role in the home.

Children are expected to carry out the commandment to

honour (Exod. 20.12) and respect (Lev. 19.3) their parents. For the rabbis, the concept of honour refers to providing parents with food, drink, clothing and transportation. Reverence requires that a child does not sit in his parents' seat, nor interrupt them, and takes their side in a dispute. The *Talmud* extols such treatment: 'There are three partners in man, the Holy One, blessed be he, the father, and the mother. When a man honours his father and mother, the Holy One, blessed be he, says, "I ascribe (merit) to them as though I had dwelt among them and they had honoured me" '.

The Jewish tradition teaches that domestic harmony is the ideal of home life. The *Talmud* specifies the guidelines for attaining this goal: 'A man should spend less than his means on food, up to his means on clothes, and more than his means in honouring wife and children because they are dependent on him.' Such harmony is to be attained through give and take on the part of all, as well as through the observance of Jewish ritual which serves to unify the family. The Jewish home is permeated with sanctity when the family lives in accordance with God's commandments.

Symbols of the Jewish religion characterize the Jewish home, beginning with the *mezuzah* on each doorpost. In Scripture it is written that 'these words' shall be written on the doorposts (*mezuzot*) of the house (Deut. 6.4–9; 11.13–21). This prescription has been understood literally: these two passages must be copied by hand on a piece of parchment, put into a case, and affixed to the doorpost of every room in the house.

The first of these passages from Deuteronomy contains the *Shema* as well as the commandments to love God, study the *Torah*, express the unity of God, wear *tefillin*, and affix a *mezuzah*. The second passage connects prosperity with the observance of God's commandments. The *mezuzah* itself must be written by a scribe on parchment – the scroll is rolled and put into a case with a small opening through which the word *Shaddai* (Almighty) is visible. The *mezuzah* is placed on the upper part of the doorpost at the entrance in a slanting position. The following conditions should be met in placing the *mezuzah* on every right-hand entrance:

1. The room into which the doorway leads should be at least four by four cubits.

2. The doorway should have doorposts on both sides.
3. The doorway should serve as an entrance into a room with a ceiling.
4. The door should have a lintel.
5. The doorway should have doors that open as well as close.
6. The doorway should be at least forty inches high and sixteen inches wide.
7. The room must be for ordinary residence.
8. The room should be for human dwelling.
9. The room should be used as a dignified dwelling.
10. The room should be for continued habitation.

When the *mezuzah* is placed on the doorpost, a benediction is recited. Traditional Jews touch the *mezuzah* with their hand while entering or leaving the home.

Other home ritual objects of major importance are the Sabbath candles. At least two candles should be used in honour of the dual commandment to remember and observe the Sabbath day (Exod. 20.8; Deut. 5.12). This ceremony is performed before sunset on the eve of Sabbaths (as well as festivals), symbolizing light and joy. Lighting the candles is normally the task of the wife, but it may be done by any member of the family.

At the beginning of the Sabbath the *kiddush* prayer is recited over wine prior to the evening meal. It consists of two sections: the blessing over the wine and the benediction of the day. The introductory biblical passages which precede this prayer are Genesis 1.31 and 2.1–3. The blessing for wine is then recited, following by the benedictions for the sanctification of the day. The blessing which follows includes the assertion that Israel was made holy through God's commandments, that it was favoured by having been given the Sabbath as an inheritance in remembrance of creation, and that the Sabbath is the first of the holy convocations and commemorates the Exodus from Egypt. This is followed by a sentence whose form is reminiscent of the festival *kiddush*. The festival *kiddush*, which is also recited at home, consists of the blessing over wine as well as the blessing over the day; this is followed by the recitation of the *sheheheyanu* prayer ('Blessed are you, Lord our God, King of the universe, who has kept us alive, sustained us, and brought us to this season'). Wine goblets reserved for this occasion are frequently made of silver and bear an inscription such as, 'Observe the

Sabbath day and keep it holy'. It is usual for participants to wash their hands after the *kiddush* is recited.

Before meals on the Sabbath as well as on ordinary days, a blessing over food is recited. Over food the blessing is, 'who brings forth bread from the earth'; over wine, 'who creates the fruit of the vine'; over fruit, 'who creates the fruit of the tree'; over vegetables, 'who creates the fruit of the ground'. Alternatively, there is a more general blessing for things for which there are no specific blessings: 'By whose word all things were brought into being'.

After the meal is completed a Grace after Meals is recited. This prayer, *Birkat ha-Mazon*, is comprised of a series of blessings and prayers. Structurally the Grace consists of four benedictions interspersed with various prayers and petitions. The first blessing praises God for sustaining his creatures with food; the second is a national expression of thanks for deliverance from Egypt, God's covenant with his chosen people, and the land which he gave to them; the third asks God to provide Israel with relief from want and humiliation, and to vindicate his people by restoring Jerusalem; the fourth blessing acknowledges the benefits for which God is to be thanked. This is followed by a series of petitions which invoke 'the Compassionate One' (*Ha-Rahaman*).

The cycle of the year provides various opportunities for home observances. On Passover normal dishes are replaced. Traditional law excludes the use of all domestic utensils, crockery and cutlery. As a result sets are kept especially for this holiday. The *Seder* itself is observed on the first two nights of Passover (except in Israel and among most Reform Jews). The purpose of this festival is to commemorate the redemption of the Jewish people from slavery. During the service the *Haggadah* (Prayer Book) is read, and a special *Seder* dish is prepared which includes: a roasted hard-boiled egg symbolizing the Temple sacrifice; a roasted bone symbolizing the *paschal* lamb; bitter herbs symbolizing bitter oppression; *charoset* reminiscent of the mortar prepared by the Israelites in making brick; parsley in imitation of the *hors-d'oeuvres* of Roman nobility; and salt water representing the tears shed by the Israelites in bondage. During the *Seder* participants eat *matzot* (unleavened bread) and drink four glasses of wine. Prayers and narratives are recited both before and after the meal. In recent times revised versions of the *Haggadah* have been composed for various non-Orthodox communities.

On *Sukkot* it is customary to dwell in a temporary structure (*sukkah*) built for the festival in a yard, garden or balcony. It is covered by foliage through which the stars can be seen at night. All the meals which take place during this festival should be eaten in the *sukkah* if possible. During *Hannukah* a festival lamp is kindled at home on each day of the festival in memory of the victory of the Maccabbees over the Seleucids. In ancient times a lamp was put in the doorway or even in the street outside; in modern times it is placed within the home. The custom is to light a candle on the first night and an additional candle for each night until the last night when eight candles are kindled. On *Purim* families frequently exchange gifts and enjoy a festive meal.

Life cycle events also provide an occasion for special observances in the home. At the birth of a male child, a *Shalom Zakhor* gathering takes place on the Friday night after the birth; the circumcision ceremony takes place on the eighth day; and the redemption of the first-born on the thirtieth day. All these occasions are times for festivity. Similarly *bar* and *bat mitzvah* are times of festivity in the home. Again, during the week after a marriage, a nightly feast is held where the Seven Benedictions are recited. Finally, at the time of mourning, friends and visitors come to the home during the seven days of mourning (*shivah*) where a *minyan* recites the morning and evening prayers.

In contemporary society Orthodox Judaism continues to carry out these home activities; however, within the various branches of non-Orthodox Judaism various modifications have been made to those traditions, and a number of home festivities have been eliminated because they are no longer viewed as spiritually meaningful. None the less there is a universal recognition among Jewry that the home is central to Jewish existence and survival.

36

Dietary Laws

According to the Jewish tradition, food must be ritually fit (*kosher*) if it is to be eaten. The Bible declares that laws of *kashrut* (dietary laws) were given by God to Moses on Mount Sinai: thus Jews are obligated to follow this legislation because of its divine origin. None the less, various reasons have been adduced for observing these prescriptions. Allegedly forbidden foods are unhealthy; that is why they are forbidden. Another justification is that those who refrain from eating particular kinds of food serve God even while eating, and thereby attain an elevated spiritual state. Indeed some of these laws – such as refraining from eating pork – have gained such symbolic significance that Jews were prepared to sacrifice their lives rather than violate God's decree. In this way these martyrs demonstrated their devotion to the Jewish faith.

The laws concerning which animals, birds and fish may be eaten are contained in Leviticus chapter 11 and Deuteronomy 14.3–21. According to Scripture, only those animals which both chew the cud and have split hooves may be eaten. Such animals include domestic animals like cows and sheep. No similar formula is stated concerning which birds may be consumed; rather a list is given of forbidden birds such as the eagle, the owl and the raven. Although no reasons are given to explain these choices, it has been suggested that forbidden birds are in fact birds of prey; by not eating them human beings are able to express their abhorrence of cruelty as well as the exploitation of the weak over the strong. Regarding fish, the law states that only fish which have both fins and scales are allowed. Again, no reason is given to support this distinction; however, various explanations have been proposed, such as the argument that fish that do not have fins and scales frequently live in the depths of the sea, which was regarded as the abode of the gods of chaos – on this basis, this law constitutes a protest against idolatry.

A further category of *kashrut* deals with the method of killing animals for food (*shehitah*). Although the *Torah* does not offer details of this procedure, the *Talmud* states that this method has divine authority because it was explained by God to Moses on Mount Sinai. According to tradition, the act of slaughter must be done with a sharpened knife without a single notch, since that might tear the animal's food pipe or windpipe.

Numerous other laws govern this procedure, and a person must be trained in the law if he is to be a *shohet* (slaughterer). According to scholars such as Maimonides (twelfth century), the central idea underlying the laws of ritual slaughter is to give the animal as painless a death as possible. Judaism does not require that the devout become vegetarians, but when animals are killed for food this must be done so as to cause the least amount of suffering possible.

Another feature of ritual slaughter is the concern that no animal is eaten if it has a defect; in such cases it is referred to as '*terefah*' (meaning 'torn'). The prohibition against *terefah* is based on Exodus 22.31: 'You shall be men consecrated to me; therefore you shall not eat any flesh that is torn by beasts in the field; you shall cast it to the dogs.' This prescription is elaborated in the *Mishnah* where the rabbis decree that *terefah* refers not only to the meat of an animal torn by wild beasts, but to any serious defect in an animal or bird's organs. In this section of the *Mishnah* such defects are listed in detail. On the basis of this law, the *shohet* is obliged to examine the lungs of an animal after it has been slaughtered to ensure that no defect is found. Similarly, if any irregularity is found in an animal which has been slaughtered, it should be taken to a rabbi to determine if it is *kosher*. In the preparation of meat, it is important that adequate salting takes place. This prescription is based on the biblical prohibition against blood. Although it is theoretically possible to extract a large quantity of blood from meat, the process can be aided by salting it. While being salted, meat is soaked in cold water for half an hour – this softens the texture of the meat and makes it easier for salt to extract the blood. The meat is then put on a sloping draining board so that the water drains away. Subsequently salt is placed on the meat and left for an hour. The meat is then rinsed in water three or four times.

Another restriction concerning ritual food is the prohibition against eating milk and meat together. This stipulation is based on Exodus 23.19: 'Thou shalt not boil a kid in its mother's milk.'

213

According to the rabbis, this rule refers not only to the act of boiling a kid in its mother's milk, but to any combination of meat and milk. Tradition stipulates that it is forbidden to cook meat and milk together. Later, this prohibition was expanded to eating milk and meat products at the same time. Eventually the law was introduced that dairy dishes should not be eaten after meat until a stipulated period of time had passed. The required amount of time has varied according to local custom: some Jews wait three hours; others six. Meat, on the other hand, may be eaten after dairy products; none the less, it is usual to wash the mouth out beforehand.

A number of explanations have been given to account for this prohibition. According to Maimonides (twelfth century), it is because a mixture of milk and meat cannot be digested easily; in addition, the practice of cooking meat in milk was a pagan practice which was forbidden to the Israelites. Another explanation is that meat represents death whereas milk symbolizes life: life and death must be kept apart. Others maintain that this prohibition serves as a reminder to make distinctions in life – in this way the thinking of a Jew is sharpened.

Not only should milk and meat products not be consumed at the same time, dairy food should not be cooked in meat utensils, and *vice versa*. Thus it is the usual practice for Jewish households to have two sets of dishes and cutlery reserved for milk and meat. Meat dishes are known in Yiddish as *fleishig*; milk dishes are *milchig* (milky). Food as well as utensils that are neither *fleishig* or *milchig* are referred to as *parave*. A pot in which forbidden (*terefah*) food has been cooked should not be used for cooking *kosher* food until it is thoroughly scoured. Here the principle is that the taste of the forbidden food remains in the pot itself, but the pot can be made *kosher* by boiling water in it. If a utensil has been used for forbidden food on a naked flame or in a fire, it can be made *kosher* by heating it over a fire. China, however, cannot be made *kosher* since it is so thoroughly absorbent that the *terefah* cannot be eliminated; on the other hand, a number of contemporary authorities argue that Pyrex dishes can be made ritually fit.

In formulating these regulations, the principle of neutralization is that *terefah* food becomes neutralized in a ratio of one to sixty. Thus if a piece of *terefah* meat is cooked in a pot of *kosher* meat and can no longer be identified, it is *kosher* as long as there is sixty times as much *kosher* meat as *terefah*. Another rule maintains that if food is cooked in a utensil that was used for *terefah* more than twenty-four hours previously, the food is *kosher*. Here the principle is that when *terefah* food has been in a utensil for twenty-four hours or longer its taste becomes flawed and cannot contaminate food later cooked in that object.

Although the Bible does not attempt to explain the origin of these various dietary laws, it does associate them with holiness in three passages: (1) Exodus 22.31: 'You shall be consecrated to me: therefore you shall not eat any flesh torn by beasts in the field; you shall cast it to the dogs'; (2) Leviticus 11.44–5: 'For I am the Lord your God: consecrate yourselves therefore, and be holy, for I am holy. You shall not defile yourselves with any swarming thing that crawls upon the earth. For I am the Lord who brought you up out from the land of Egypt, to be your God; you shall therefore be holy, for I am holy'; (3) Deuteronomy 14.21: 'You shall not eat anything that has died of itself; you may give it to the alien who is within your towns, that he may eat it, or you may sell it to a foreigner; for you are a people holy to the Lord your God. You shall not boil a kid in its mother's milk.'

Similarly, the rabbis of the *Talmud* and *midrash* explored the rationale of the system of *kashrut*. Generally they believed that the observance of such laws aids the development of self-discipline and moral conduct. Maimonides argued in the *Guide for the Perplexed* that the laws of *kashrut* teach mastery of the appetites as well as discipline. In addition, he feels that all forbidden foods are unwholesome. Subsequently, other writers have suggested that there is a humanitarian basis to these laws as reflected in the revulsion to blood, the requirement that an animal be killed painlessly, and the rule that only herbivorous animals be eaten.

Until modern times the rules of *kashrut* were universally practised by Jewry. Yet in the nineteenth century the Reform movement in Germany broke with tradition, decreeing that the dietary laws were connected with Temple ritual and thus not integral to the Jewish tradition. On this basis the Pittsburgh Conference of the Reform movement declared in its statement of principles that the laws of *kashrut* 'fail to impress the modern Jew with the spirit of holiness . . . their observance in our days is apt rather to obstruct than to further modern spiritual elevation.' For this reason, most Reform Jews have largely ignored the prescriptions of the dietary system. Conservative Judaism, however, adheres to the laws of *kashrut*, although allowance is made for personal selectivity. Orthodox Judaism on the other hand strictly follows the tradition, and in recent years the observance of the dietary laws has undergone a revival in various Jewish communities, particularly in the state of Israel.

37

Death and Mourning

Concerning death the Bible declares that human beings will return to the dust of the earth (Gen. 3.19). According to Scripture, burial – especially in a family tomb – was the normal procedure for dealing with the deceased (Gen. 47.29–30; 49.29–31; 1 Kings 21.19). In a number of biblical passages human beings are depicted as descending to a nether world (*sheol*) where they live a shadowy existence – only in the later books of the Bible is there any allusion to resurrection (such as in Dan. 12.2).

The rabbis of the *Talmud* decreed that death occurs when respiration has stopped. However, with the development of modern medical technology, this definition has been subject to alteration. Today it is now possible to resuscitate those who previously would have been regarded as dead: thus the modern rabbinic scholar Mosheh Sofer in his *responsum* declares that death is considered to have occurred when there has been respiratory and cardiac arrest. Another halkhist, Mosheh Feinstein, however, has ruled that a person is considered to have died with the death of his brain stem. Despite such disagreements, it is generally accepted that a critically ill person who hovers between life and death is alive. It is forbidden to hasten the death of such an individual by any positive action; none the less, it is permitted to remove an external obstacle which may be preventing his death.

Jewish law accepts that no effort should be spared to save a dying patient; in this regard the *Talmud* lays down that a change of name may avert the evil decree, and hence the custom developed of altering the formal name of an individual who is seriously ill. Yet despite such an attitude, traditional Judaism fosters an acceptance of death when it is inevitable. The *Tzidduk ha-Din* prayer which is recited by mourners at the funeral service describes God as a righteous Judge and accepts the finality of his decrees. On his deathbed, the dying person is to recite a prayer accepting God's will:

217

I admit before you, God, my God and God of my ancestors, that my cure and my death are in your hands. May it be your will that you heal me with a complete healing. And if I die, may my death be an atonement for the sins, transgressions, and violations which I have sinned, transgressed, and violated before you. And set my portion in the Garden of Eden, and let me merit the world to come reserved for the righteous. Hear, O Israel, the Lord our God, the Lord is One.

The Jewish tradition maintains that utmost regard should be shown for the dying person. Such an individual is not to be left alone. When informing someone who is dying of the duty to confess sins, he should be told: 'Many have confessed, but have not died; and many who have not confessed have died. And many who are walking outside in the market-place have confessed. By the merit of your confessing, you live. All who confess have a place in the world to come.' All those who are present at the moment of death should recite the blessing: 'Blessed be the true judge'; relatives are to recite the prayer, *Tzidduk ha-Din*. The arrangements for care of the body and burial are referred to as *hesed shel emet* (true kindness), because they are made on behalf of those who are unable to reciprocate.

Once death has been determined, the eyes and mouth are closed, and if necessary the mouth is tied shut. The body is then put on the floor, covered with a sheet, and a lighted candle is placed close to the head. Mirrors are covered in the home of the deceased, and any standing water is poured out. A dead body is not to be left unattended, and it is considered a *mitzvah* (good deed) to sit with the person who has died and recite psalms. An individual who watches over a person who has died is exempt from prayers and wearing *tefillin*.

The burial of the body should take place as soon as possible. No burial is allowed to take place on a Sabbath or the Day of Atonement, and in contemporary practice it is considered unacceptable for it to take place on the first and last days of pilgrim festivals. After the members of the burial society have taken care of the body, they prepare it for burial; it is washed and dressed in a white linen shroud. The corpse is then placed in a coffin or on a bier before the funeral service. Traditional Jews only permit the use of a plain wooden coffin, with no metal handles or adornments. The deceased is then borne to the grave face upward; adult males are buried wearing their prayer shawl – one of the fringes having been removed or marred so as to render the prayer shawl unfit. In some Eastern communities, the dead person's *tefillin* are also buried with him. A marker should be placed on a newly-filled grave, and a tombstone should be erected and unveiled as soon as permissible (either at the end of the thirty-day mourning period in Israel, or after eleven months have elapsed in the diaspora). A limb severed or amputated from a person who is still alive should also be buried – this is true also of bodies on which autopsies or dissections have been carried out.

Among Reform Jews, burial practice differs from that of the Orthodox. Embalming and cremation are usually permitted, and Reform rabbis commonly officiate at crematoriums. Burial may be delayed for several days, and the person who has died is usually buried in normal clothing without a prayer shawl. No special places are reserved for priests, nor is any separate arrangement made for someone who has committed suicide or married out of the faith.

Despite differences in procedure between Ashkenazi and Sephardi Jews, there are a number of common features of the burial service: in both rites mourners rend their garments, and biblical and liturgical verses are chanted by the rabbi as he leads the funeral procession to the cemetery. It is customary to stop on the way, allowing mourners to express their grief. Often a eulogy is given either in the funeral chapel or as the coffin is lowered into the grave, which the male mourners help to fill with earth. Memorial prayers and a special mourners' *kaddish* are recited; mourners present words of comfort to the bereaved; and all wash their hands before leaving the cemetery.

The Jewish tradition provides a specific framework for mourning which applies to males over the age of thirteen and females over the age of twelve who have lost a father or mother, husband or wife, son or daughter, brother or sister. From the moment that death takes place until the burial, the mourners are exempt from positive commandments (praying, reciting grace after meals, wearing *tefillin*, etc); in addition, a mourner is not allowed to participate in festival meals or engage in pleasurable activities. Instead he must rend a garment – this is done (depending on the custom) on receiving the news of death, just prior to the funeral, or after the funeral. Once the burial has taken place, mourners are to return to the home of the deceased or where the mourning period will be observed, and consume a meal consisting of bread and a hard-boiled egg which should be provided by others.

The mourning period, known as *shivah* (seven), lasts for seven days beginning with the day of burial. During this time mourners sit on the floor or on low cushions or benches and are forbidden to shave, bathe, go to work, study the *Torah* (except subjects related to mourning), engage in sexual relations, wear leather shoes, greet others, cut their hair, or wear laundered clothing. Through these seven days, it is customary to visit mourners – in some places it is the practice to bring prepared food. Those comforting mourners are not to greet them but rather offer words of consolation. On the Sabbath which falls during the *shivah*, it is forbidden to make a public display of mourning; in some communities mourners do not occupy their normal seats in the synagogue. Among the Sephardim members frequently sit near the mourners for part of the service.

Shivah concludes on the evening of the seventh day and is followed by mourning of a lesser intensity for thirty days known as *sheloshim* (thirty). At this time mourners are not permitted to cut their hair, shave, wear new clothes or attend festivities. Some traditions consider that the *sheloshim* constitutes the full mourning period for relatives other than parents; other traditions continue the period for one year for all relatives. Mourning for parents should take place for nearly a year, and mourners are not supposed to shave or cut their hair after *sheloshim*. Those who mourn are not permitted to attend public celebrations or parties. Mourners are to recite *kaddish* daily throughout the period of mourning – in the case of those whose mourning continues for a year, it is at times customary to recite *kaddish* one month or week before the anniversary of death. If the holy days and festivals of *Rosh Hashanah*, Day of Atonement, *Sukkot*, Passover or *Shavuot* intervene, the *shivah* is terminated; if a burial takes place during the middle days (*Hol Hamoed*) or *Sukkot* or Passover, the laws of *shivah* take effect once the festival ends.

If one hears of the death of a relative while other mourners are observing *shivah*, the person may end his *shivah* with these individuals. However, if news arrives within thirty days after death, *shivah* must be observed in its entirety. On the other hand, if the news arrives after thirty days, mourners are required to observe only a brief period of mourning. When news arrives of a parent's death, the mourner shall rend his garment; however if he learns of the death of another relative after thirty days, he need not do so, although he is to recite the blessing of *Tzidduk ha-Din*. If the deceased was a violator of God's law or had committed suicide (unless it was the result of insanity), the laws of mourning are not carried out. It is a general practice to mark the anniversary of the death of a relative (*yartzeit*) by reciting the *kaddish*, a memorial prayer, studying the *Torah*, chanting the *Haftarah* (reading from the Prophets), and lighting memorial lights.

38

Ethics

In the Jewish religion, ethical values are of primary concern. For Jews moral action is fundamental – it is through the rule of the moral law that God's kingdom can be realized. From ancient times the synagogue liturgy concluded with a prayer in which this hope was expressed:

> May we speedily behold the glory of thy might,
> when thou wilt remove the abominations from the earth,
> and the idols will be utterly cut off;
> when the world will be perfected under the kingdom of the
>   Almighty,
> and all the children of flesh will call upon thy name;
> when thou wilt turn unto thyself all the wicked of the earth.

This is the goal of the history of the world in which God's chosen people have a central role. In this context the Jewish people have a historical mission to be a light to the nations. Through Moses God addressed the people and declared: 'You have seen what I did to the Egyptians, and how I bore you on eagles' wings, and brought you unto myself. Now therefore, if you will obey my voice and keep my covenant, you shall be my own possession among all people; for all the earth is mine, and you shall be to me a kingdom of priests and a holy nation' (Exod. 19.4–6). Election was to be a servant of the Lord; to proclaim God's truth and righteousness throughout the world. Being chosen meant duty and responsibility – it was a divine call which persisted through all ages and embraced the whole earth.

In this quest Judaism did not separate religion from life; instead Jews were called to action, to turn humankind away from violence, wickedness, and falsehood. It was not the hope of bliss in a future life but the establishment of the kingdom of justice and peace that was central to the Jewish faith. Moral action is thus at the heart of the religious tradition. The people of Israel as a light to the nations reflects the moral nature of God –

each Jew is to be like the Creator mirroring the divine qualities revealed to Moses: 'The Lord, the Lord, a God merciful and gracious, slow to anger, and abounding in steadfast love and faithfulness, keeping steadfast love for thousands, forgiving iniquity and transgression and sin' (Exod. 34. 6–7).

God as a moral being demands moral living, as the Psalms declare: 'The Lord is righteous; he loves righteous deeds' (Ps. 11.7); 'Righteousness and justice are the foundation of his throne' (Ps. 97.2); 'Thou hast established equity; thou hast executed justice and righteousness' (Ps. 99.4). Given this theological framework, Jews are directed to obey the revealed will of God, which serves as the basis of the covenantal relationship between God and the Jewish nation.

In the Bible, deeds and events involving moral issues can be found in abundance: the punishment of Cain for murdering his brother, the violence of the generation that brought on the Flood, the early prohibition against murder, the hospitality of Abraham and his pleading for the people of Sodom, the praise of Abraham for his moral attitudes, the condemnation of Joseph's brothers, Joseph's self-restraint in the house of Potiphar, Moses' intercessions on the side of the exploited.

But it is pre-eminently in the legal codes of the *Torah* that we encounter moral guidelines formulated in specific rules. The Decalogue (Ten Commandments) in particular illustrates the centrality of moral action in the life of the Jew. The first commandments are theological in character, but the last six deal with relationships between human beings. The first commandment describes God as the one who redeemed the Jews from Egypt; the one who forbade the worship of other deities and demands respect for the Sabbath and the divine name. These commandments are expressions of the love and fear of God; the remaining injunctions provide a means of expressing love of other human beings. The Decalogue thus makes it clear that moral rules are fundamental to the Jewish religion.

Such ethical standards were repeated in the prophetic books. The teachings of the Prophets are rooted in the *Torah* of Moses. The Prophets saw themselves as messengers of the divine word: their special task was to denounce the people for their transgressions and call them to repentance. In all this they pointed to concrete moral action as the only means of sustaining the covenantal relationship with God. The essential theme of their message was that God demands righteousness and justice.

Emphasis on the moral life was reflected in the prophetic condemnation of cultic practices that were not accompanied by ethical concern. These passages illustrate that ritual commandments are of instrumental value – morality is intrinsic and absolute. The primacy of morality was also reflected in the prophetic warning that righteous action is the determining factor in the destiny of the Jewish nation. Moral transgressions referred to in such contexts concern exploitation, oppression, and the perversion of justice. These sins have the potential to bring about the downfall of the nation.

The Book of Proverbs reinforces the teaching of the *Torah* and the Prophets; wisdom is here conceived as a capacity to act morally; it is a skill that can be learned. Throughout Proverbs dispositional traits are catalogued: the positive moral types include the *tzaddik* (righteous person), the *hakham* (wise person), and the *yashar* (upright person); evil characters include the *rasha* (evil person), the *kheseil* (fool), the *letz* (mocker), and the *peti* (simpleton). Thus here as in the rest of the Bible the moral life is seen as the basis of the Jewish faith. Theology is defined in relation to practical activity – it is through moral activity that humanity encounters the Divine.

Rabbinic literature continued this emphasis on ethical action. Convinced they were the authentic expositors of Scripture, the rabbis amplified biblical law. In their expansion of the commandments, rabbinic exegetes differentiated between the laws governing human relationships to God (*bain adam la-makom*), and those that concern human relationships to others (*bain adam la-havero*). As in the biblical period, rabbinic teachings reflected the same sense of the primacy of morality. Such texts as the following indicate rabbinic priority:

> He who acts honestly and is popular with his fellow creatures, it is imputed to him as though he had fulfilled the entire *Torah*.

> Hillel said: 'What is hateful to yourself, do not do to your fellow man. This is the entire *Torah*, the rest is commentary.'

> Better is one hour of repentance and good deeds in this world then the whole life of the world-to-come.

In the classic texts of Judaism, then, moral behaviour is the predominant theme. By choosing the moral life, the Jew is able to complete God's work of creation. To accomplish this task the rabbis formulated an elaborate system of traditions, which were written down in the *Mishnah*, subsequently expanded in the *Talmud*, and eventually codified in the *Code of Jewish Law*. According to traditional Judaism, this expansion of the pentateuchal law is part of God's revelation. Both the Written Law and the Oral Law are binding on Jews for all time. Such a conviction implies that the entire corpus of moral law is an expression of the divine will and must be obeyed.

For Jews the moral law is absolute and binding. In all cases it was made precise and specific – it is God's word made concrete in the daily life of the Jew. The commandment to love one's neighbour embraces all humanity. In the *Code of Jewish Law* the virtues of justice, honesty and humane concern are regarded as central to community life; hatred, vengeance, deceit, cruelty, and anger are condemned as anti-social. The Jew is instructed to exercise loving-kindness towards all: to clothe the naked, to feed the hungry, to care for the sick, and to comfort the mourner. By fulfilling these ethical demands, the Jewish people are able to help bring about God's kingdom on earth in which exploitation, oppression and injustice are eliminated.

Such a system of ethics – as enshrined in the Bible and in rabbinic literature – embodies a number of essential characteristics. First, there is an intensity of passion about the moral demands made upon human beings. For sins of personal greed, social inequity, and deceit, the Prophets denounced the people and threatened horrific catastrophes. Such shrill denunciations of iniquity continued through the ages as the rabbis attempted to stir the Jewish people from spiritual slumber.

Second, Jewish ethics require that each person be treated equally – biblical and rabbinic sources show a constant concern to eliminate arbitrary distinctions between individuals so as to establish a proper balance between competing claims. On the basis of the biblical view that everyone is created in the image of God, the *Torah* declares that false and irrelevant distinctions must not be introduced to disqualify human beings from the right to justice. The fatherhood and motherhood of God implies human solidarity; the *Torah* rejects the idea of different codes or morality for oneself and others, for the great and the humble, for rulers and ruled. Further, since all of humanity is created in the image of God, Judaism maintains that there is no fundamental difference between Jew and non-Jew: God's ethical demands apply to all.

A third characteristic of Jewish morality is its emphasis on human motivation. The Jewish faith is not solely concerned with actions and their consequences; it also demands right intention. As the rabbis explained: 'The Merciful One requires the heart'. While it is true that Judaism emphasizes the importance of moral action, the Jewish faith also focuses attention on rightmindedness: inner experiences – motives, feelings, dispositions, and attitudes – are of supreme moral significance. For this reason the rabbis identified a group of negative commandments in the *Torah* involving thought. The following are representative examples:

> Thou shalt not take vengeance, nor bear any grudge against the sons of your own people (Lev. 19.8).

> There are six things which the Lord hateth . . . a heart that devises evil plans (Prov. 6.16, 18).

> Take heed lest there be a base thought in your heart (Deut. 15.9).

In the *Mishnah* the rabbis elaborated on this concern for the human heart:

> Rabbi Eliezer said, '. . . be not easily moved to anger.'

> Rabbi Joshua said, 'The evil eye, the evil inclination, and hatred of his fellow creatures drives a man out of the world.'

> Rabbi Levitas of Yavneh said, 'Be exceedingly lowly of spirit.'

A fourth dimension of Jewish morality concerns the traditional attitude towards animals. Since God's mercy and goodness extend to all creatures, 'a righteous person should show consideration to animals' (Ps. 145.9; Prov. 12.10). According to the Jewish faith, human beings are morally obliged to refrain from inflicting pain on animals. Thus the Pentateuch stipulates that assistance be given to animals in distress even on the Sabbath: 'You shall not see your brother's ass or his ox fallen down by the way and withhold your help from them; you shall help him to lift them up again' (Deut. 22.4). In rabbinic Judaism this same theme was reflected in various *midrashim*.

A final aspect of Jewish ethics is its concern for human dignity: the Jewish faith continually emphasizes the respect due to all individuals. This concept, found in various laws in the Pentateuch, was developed by the rabbis who cautioned that one must be careful not to humiliate or embarrass others. Maimonides (twelfth century), for example, wrote:

> A man ought to be especially heedful of his behaviour towards widows and orphans, for their souls are exceedingly depressed and their spirits low, even if they are wealthy. How are we to conduct ourselves toward them? One must not speak to them otherwise than tenderly. One must show them unvarying courtesy; not hurt them physically with hard toil nor wound their feelings with harsh speech.

Throughout the biblical and rabbinic tradition, then, moral behaviour is a predominant theme. Continually the Jewish people have been God's suffering servant, yet inspired by a vision of God's reign they have been able to transcend their own misfortunes. The Jewish tradition points to God's kingdom as the goal and hope of humanity; a world in which all peoples shall turn away from iniquity and injustice. This is not the hope of bliss in a future life, but the building up of the divine kingdom of truth and peace on earth.

39

Conversion

Though there is no formal term for the process of conversion in
the Hebrew Bible, there are several biblical terms which are
suggestive of such an act: *hityahed* is used to describe persons
who are said to have converted to Judaism for fear of the Jews;
amilam (Ps. 118.10–12) may well refer to the circumcision of
foreign nations; *nilvah* (Isa. 56.3) refers to the alien who has
joined himself to the Lord. Such terms as these illustrate that
conversion was practised during the biblical period in order to
assimilate conquered peoples as well as those who came to live
within the Israelite community.

During the period of the tannaitic and amoraic periods AD
100–600) conversion was frequently extolled by various rabbinic
authorities. According to Elazar, for example, conversion was
viewed as part of God's salvationist scheme: 'The Holy One,
blessed be he, dispersed the people of Israel among the nations
in order that they might acquire proselytes.' According to
Hoshiah, God acted righteously towards Israel when he scattered them among the nations. In another passage in the *Talmud*
it is asserted that the proselyte is dearer to God than the Israelite
since he has come of his own accord, while the Israelites are
believers as a result of the miracles exhibited on Mount Sinai.
Resh Lakish noted that the person who oppresses the convert is
as one who oppresses God. In the *midrash* it is maintained that it
is never too late to convert; to teach this Abraham did not enter
the covenant until he was 99, when he was circumcised. As with
Abraham, so every Israelite had the obligation to bring men
under God's wings. In another *midrash* we read that God loves
proselytes exceedingly: 'So spoke the Holy One: "I owe great
things to the stranger in that he has left his family and his
father's house, and has come to dwell amongst us; therefore I
order in the Law: Love the stranger" '.

This positive attitude to proselytes is echoed by the historian
Josephus who, in *Against Apion*, describes the openness of

Hellenistic Judaism to converts: 'The consideration given by our legislator (Moses) to the equitable treatment of aliens also merits attention. To all who desire to come and live under the same laws as us he gives a gracious welcome.' As a result of such openness to converts, a number of Gentiles converted to Judaism during the early rabbinic period. However, the rise of Christianity led to the cessation of Jewish missionizing. Nevertheless, during the talmudic and post-talmudic period occasional conversions did take place in accordance with rabbinic law. Eventually the regulations governing conversion were drawn together and edited by Joseph Caro, the compiler of the *Shulhan Arukh*, which since its publication in 1565 has served as the authoritative Code of Jewish Law.

In the section *Yoreh Deah*, the requirements for conversion as laid down in the *Talmud* and other codes are outlined in detail. When one presents himself as a candidate for conversion he is asked: 'What motivates you? Do you know that, in these days, Jews are subject to persecution and discrimination, that they are hounded and troubled?' If he replies: 'I know this and yet I regard myself as unworthy of being joined to them', he is accepted immediately. The root principles of the faith, namely the unity of God and the prohibition of idol worship, are expounded to him at considerable length. He is taught, too, some of the simpler and some of the more difficult commandments, and he is informed of the punishment involved in violating the commandments. Similarly he is told of the rewards for observing them, particularly that by virtue of keeping the commandments, he will merit the life of the world to come. He is told that no one is considered wholly righteous except those who understand and fulfil the commandments. Further, he is told that the world to come is only intended for the righteous. If he finds these doctrines acceptable, he is circumcised immediately. After his circumcision has completely healed, he undergoes ritual immersion: three learned Jews stand by while he is in the water and instruct him in some of the easy and some of the difficult commandments. In the case of a female proselyte, Jewish women accompany her and supervise her immersion. The three learned male Jews remain outside the baptismal chamber and give the convert instruction while she is in the water.

Concerning the candidate's motives, the *Shulhan Arukh* states:

'When the would-be proselyte presents himself, he should be examined lest he be motivated to enter the congregation of Israel by hope of financial gain or social advantage or by fear. A man is examined lest his motive be to marry a Jewish woman and a woman is questioned lest she have similar desires toward some Jewish man.' If no unethical motive is found, the candidate is told of the heaviness of the yoke of the *Torah* and how difficult it is for the average person to live up to the commandments of the *Torah*. This is done to give the candidate a chance to withdraw if he so desires. If the candidate goes through all this and is not dissuaded, and it is apparent that his motives are of the best, he is accepted. Once a person is circumcised and ritually immersed, he is no longer a non-Jew, although he continues to be under suspicion until he proves by his righteous living that he is worthy of respect. The central feature of these regulations governing the traditional conversion procedure is the emphasis on joining the Jewish community and accepting the Law – conversion is viewed as a legal rite of passage through which the convert takes his place within the Jewish community.

Up until the present day the procedure outlined in the *Shulhan Arukh* has been rigorously followed. Within modern Orthodox Judaism, the emphasis is on living a Jewish way of life within the community. For this reason converts are meticulously given extensive religious instruction before conversion takes place. Although Conservative Judaism follows these legal requirements, Reform Judaism has departed from the traditional practice in a variety of ways. Emphasizing the universalistic mission of Judaism, Reform Jews very early in their history abrogated the necessity of ritual immersion for converts. On the question of circumcision, opinion was at first divided. In 1869 the Pittsburgh Conference took no definite stand, but a particular case of conversion without circumcision brought this question to the forefront of rabbinic debate. As a result, the Reform rabbinate decreed in 1892 that any rabbi, with the concurrence of two associates, could accept into the Jewish faith any 'honourable and intelligent person, without any initiating rite'. The only requirements were that the person freely seek membership, that the candidate be of good character, and be sufficiently acquainted with the faith and practices of Judaism. In addition the candidate was required to give evidence of sincere desire to worship only the God of Judaism, to live by God's laws, and to adhere in life and death to the sacred cause of Israel.

In 1927 the Central Conference of American Rabbis published a handbook for conversion along these lines. Among the questions asked of the candidate were queries about his voluntary acceptance of the Jewish faith, his pledge of loyalty to Judaism, his determination to cast in his lot with that of the Jewish people, his promise to lead a Jewish life, and to rear his children as Jews.

In 1961 the Central Conference of American Rabbis issued a revised version of the conversion service paralleling the 1927 format which was recently updated. Unlike the traditional conversion procedure, the Reform service indicates that definite religious commitment is necessary in order to be accepted. The convert must state that he seeks admittance to the Jewish faith. While he is not under an obligation to profess that he worships 'only the One and Eternal God', as in the 1892 procedure, the service makes it clear that conversion to Judaism essentially entails the acceptance of religious belief. For this reason the service is conducted in the synagogue, and throughout the service the convert is told that conversion to Judaism is a religious act performed in God's presence. Thus, both explicitly and implicitly, conversion to Reform Judaism is construed as primarily a religious ceremony expressing the convert's particular religious convictions, rather than as an affirmation of his willingness to accept the yoke of Jewish law as in Orthodoxy.

In modern times the vast majority of conversions have been performed by Reform and Conservative rabbis, particularly in the United States. In accordance with previous practice most Reform rabbis (unlike Conservative rabbis) do not require circumcision or immersion in the ritual bath. Instead a course of study and a ceremony are required. In addition, Reform Judaism – unlike Orthodoxy – encourages conversion to Judaism for purposes of marriage; in this way, reformers believe, the Jewish faith will be strengthened in times of increasing secularism. In most places Orthodox Judaism refuses to accept the validity of either Reform or Conservative conversions. If asked to conduct a religious service (such as a wedding for non-Orthodox converts) or to register as Jews in Israel, Orthodox rabbis frequently require a new conversion under

Orthodox auspices. According to Orthodoxy, non-Orthodox conversion is not valid because it does not take place according to the *halakhah* (Jewish law), nor is there an insistence that the convert live an Orthodox lifestyle; further, Orthodox Judaism insists that since non-Orthodox rabbis are not entitled to sit on a *bet din* (rabbinical court), any non-Orthodox procedure is not legally valid. Faced with such a lack of recognition, Conservative rabbis (as well as a few Reform rabbis) stress that they do follow the *halakhah* of Orthodox conversion, yet this has not persuaded Orthodoxy to accept their converts.

The issue of conversion has been further complicated in recent years by the decision of the American Reform rabbinate to adopt patrilineal descent as a criterion of Jewishness. According to this stance, a child born of a marriage between a Jewish father and a non-Jewish mother who is religiously observant is considered a Jew without undergoing conversion. Following this decree, Reconstructionist Judaism has adopted the same policy. This is radically different from the position of traditional Judaism, which maintains that a child of a non-Jewish mother is not Jewish, as stipulated by talmudic law; 'Your son by an Israelite woman is called your son, but your son by a heathen woman is not called your son.' In this view a child who is born of a Jewish mother is considered Jewish regardless of the religion of the father, whereas the child born of a Jewish father and a non-Jewish mother is not recognized as a Jew.

In response to this new understanding of Jewish descent, Orthodoxy has repudiated the stance of Reform and Reconstructionist Judaism, and the Rabbinical Assembly of the Conservative movement has reaffirmed its adherence to the traditional interpretation of Jewishness. Both Orthodox and Conservative Judaism argue that the concept of patrilineal descent undermines the *halakhah* as well as the concept of *Kelal Yisrael* (the belief that all Jews are part of a communal body). As a result, the Jewish community is deeply divided about who is Jewish, which individuals require conversion, and what procedures should be employed to grant Jewish status to those who wish to convert to the Jewish faith.

FURTHER READING

GENERAL

Abramson, G. (ed.), *The Blackwell Companion to Jewish Culture* (Basil Blackwell, 1989).

Baeck, L., *The Essence of Judaism* (Schocken, 1948).

Baron, S. W., *A Social and Religious History of the Jews* (Columbia University Press, 1952–76).

Bridger, D. and Wolk, S. (eds.), *The New Jewish Encyclopedia* (Behrman House, 1976).

De Lange, N., *Judaism* (Oxford University Press, 1986).

Cohn-Sherbok, D., *Israel: The History of an Idea* (SPCK, 1992).

Cohn-Sherbok, D., *The Crucified Jew: Twenty Centuries of Christian Anti-Semitism* (Harper Collins, 1992).

Cohn-Sherbok, D., *The Blackwell Dictionary of Judaica* (Basil Blackwell, 1992).

Cohn-Sherbok, D., *The Jewish Heritage* (Basil Blackwell, 1988).

Encyclopedia Judaica (Keter Publishing House, 1972).

Epstein, I., *Judaism* (Penguin, 1975).

Gilbert, M., *Jewish History Atlas* (Weidenfeld and Nicolson, 1988).

Jacobs, L., *The Book of Jewish Practice* (Behrman House, 1987).

Jacobs, L., *The Book of Jewish Belief* (Behrman House, 1984).

Jacobs, L., *A Jewish Theology* (Darton, Longman and Todd, 1973).

Jacobs, L., *Principles of the Jewish Faith* (Jason Aronson, 1988).

Johnson, P., *A History of the Jews* (Weidenfeld and Nicolson, 1987).

Katz, S. T., *Jewish Ideas and Concepts* (Schocken Books, 1977).

Margolis, M. L. and Marx, A., *A History of the Jewish People* (Harper and Row, 1965).

Neusner, Y., *The Way of Torah: An Introduction to Judaism* (Dickenson, 1974).

Pilkington, C. M., *Judaism* (Hodder and Stoughton, 1991).

Roth, C., *A History of the Jews* (Schocken, 1973).

Sachar, A. L., *A History of the Jews* (Alfred A. Knopf, 1973).

Seltzer, R., *Jewish People, Jewish Thought: The Jewish Experience in History* (Collier Macmillan, 1980).

Siegel, R., Strassfield, M. and Strassfield, S. (eds.), *The Jewish Catalogue* (Jewish Publication Society, 1973).

Steinberg, M., *Basic Judaism* (Harcourt Brace Jonanovich, 1947).

Strassfield, S. and Strassfield, M. (eds.), *The Second Jewish Catalogue* (Jewish Publication Society of America, 1976).

Strassfield, S. and Strassfield, M. (eds.), *The Third Jewish Catalogue* (Jewish Publication Society of America, 1980).

Trepp, L., *A History of the Jewish Experience* (Behrman House, 1973).

Werblowsky, R. J. and Wigoder, G. (eds.), *Encyclopedia of the Jewish Religion* (Holt, Reinhardt and Winston, 1966).
Wigoder, G. (ed.), *The Encyclopedia of Judaism* (Macmillan, 1989).
Williams, J. G., *Judaism* (Quest Books, 1980).
Wouk, H., *This is my God* (Garden City, Doubleday, 1968).

THE ANCIENT NEAR EASTERN BACKGROUND

Beyerlin, W. (ed.), *Near Eastern Texts Relating to the Old Testament* (SCM Press, 1978).
Frankfort, H. (ed.), *Before Philosophy* (Penguin, 1964).
Hooke, S. H., *Middle Eastern Mythology* (Penguin, 1981).
Pritchard, J. (ed.),*The Ancient Near East: An Anthology of Texts and Pictures* (Princeton University Press, vol.1, 1958, vol.2, 1975).
Winton Thomas, D., *Documents from Old Testament Times* (Harper and Row, 1976).

PATRIARCHY TO MONARCHY

Anderson, G. W., *The History and Religion of Israel* (Oxford University Press, 1966).
Bright, J., *A History of Israel* (Westminster Press, 1972).
Drane, J., *The Old Testament Story* (Lion Publishing, 1983).
Grant, M., *The History of Ancient Israel* (Scribner's, 1984).
Kenyon, K. M., *The Bible and Recent Archaeology* (John Knox Press, 1978).

KINGS AND PROPHETS

Anderson, B. W., *The Eighth Century Prophets* (SPCK, 1979).
Gray, J., *The Biblical Doctrine of the Reign of God* (T. and T. Clark, 1979).
Lindblom, J., *Prophecy in Ancient Israel* (Basil Blackwell, 1962).
Vawter, B., *The Conscience of Israel* (Sheed and Ward, 1961).
Von Rad, G., *The Message of the Prophets* (SCM Press, 1968).

CAPTIVITY AND RETURN

Ackroyd, P. R., *Exile and Restoration* (SCM Press, 1968).
Ackroyd, P. R., *Israel under Babylon and Persia* (Oxford University Press, 1970).
Blenkinsopp, J., *Prophecy and Canon: A Contribution to the Study of Jewish Origins* (University of Notre Dame Press, 1977).
Hengel, M., *Judaism and Hellenism: Studies in Their Encounter in Palestine During the Early Hellenic Period* (Fortress Press, 1974).
Kaufmann, Y., *The Babylonian Captivity and Deutero-Isaiah* (Union of American Hebrew Congregations, 1970).

REBELLION AND DISPERSION

Dodd, C. H., *The Bible and the Greeks* (Hodder and Stoughton, 1935).

Sandmel, *Judaism and Christian Beginnings* (Oxford University Press, 1978).
Schurer, E., *The History of the Jewish People in the Age of Jesus Christ* (T. and T. Clark, 1973).
Tcherikover, V., *Hellenistic Civilisation and the Jews* (Jewish Publication Society of America, 1959).
Zeitlin, S., *The Rise and Fall of the Judean State*, vols 1–3 (Jewish Publication Society of America, 1962–8).

THE EMERGENCE OF MEDIEVAL JEWRY

Abrahams, I., *Jewish Life in the Middle Ages* (Athenaeum, 1969).
Marcus, J. R. (ed.), *The Jew in the Medieval World* (Harper and Row, 1965).
Parkes, *The Jew in the Medieval Community: A Study of His Political and Economic Situation* (Hermon Press, 1976).
Sharf, A., *Byzantine Jewry: From Justinian to the Fourth Crusade* (Routledge and Kegan Paul, 1971).
Trachtenberg, *Jewish Magic and Superstition* (Jewish Publication Society of America, 1961).

MEDIEVAL JEWISH PHILOSOPHY AND THEOLOGY

Agus, J. B., *The Evolution of Jewish Thought, From Biblical Times to the Opening of the Modern Era* (Abelard-Schuman, 1959).
Blau, J. L., *The Story of Jewish Philosophy* (Random House, 1962).
Husik, I., *A History of Medieval Jewish Philosophy* (Jewish Publication Society of America, 1958).
Jacobs, L., *A Jewish Theology* (Darton, Longman and Todd, 1973).
Katz, S. (ed.), *Jewish Philosophers* (Jewish Publishing Co., 1975).

MEDIEVAL JEWISH MYSTICISM

Abelson, I., *Jewish Mysticism* (Harmon Press, 1969).
Dan, J., *Jewish Mysticism and Jewish Ethics* (Washington University Press, 1986).
Dan, J. and Talmage, F. (eds.), *Studies in Jewish Mysticism* (Association for Jewish Studies, 1982).
Scholem, G., *Major Trends in Jewish Mysticism* (Schocken, 1954).
Scholem, G., *Kabbalah* (Quadrangle, 1974).

JUDAISM IN THE EARLY MODERN PERIOD

Katz, J., *Tradition and Crisis: Jewish Society at the End of the Middle Ages* (Free Press, 1961).
Roth, C., *The Spanish Inquisition* (W. W. Norton, 1964).
Scholem, G., *Sabbatai Sevi: The Mystical Messiah 1626–1676* (Princeton University Press, 1973).
Stern, S., *The Court Jew: A Contribution to the History of the Period of*

Absolutism in Central Europe (Jewish Publication Society of America, 1950).

Weinryb, B., *The Jews of Poland: A Social and Economic History of the Jewish Community of Poland from 1100 to 1800* (Jewish Publication Society of America, 1973).

FROM HASIDISM TO THE ENLIGHTENMENT

Ben-Amos, D., and Mintz, J. R. (eds.), *In Praise of the Baal Shem Tov: The Earliest Collection of Legends About the Founder of Hasidism* (Indiana University Press, 1970).

Dawidowicz, L. S., *The Golden Tradition: Jewish Life and Thought in Eastern Europe* (Holt, Reinhardt and Winston, 1966).

Dubnow, S., *History of the Jews in Russia and Poland* (Ktav Publishing House, 1973).

Hertzberg, A., *The French Enlightenment and the Jews* (Columbia University Press, 1968).

Katz, J., *Out of the Ghetto: The Social Background of Jewish Emancipation 1770–1870* (Harvard University Press, 1973).

THE RISE OF REFORM JUDAISM

Jacob, W. (ed.), *American Reform Responsa* (Central Conference of American Rabbis, 1983).

Marmur, D. (ed.), *Reform Judaism* (Reform Synagogues of Great Britain, 1973).

Phillipson, D., *The Reform Movement in Judaism* (Ktav Publishing House, 1967).

Plaut, G. W. (ed.), *The Rise of Reform Judaism: A Sourcebook of Its European Origins* (World Union of Progressive Judaism, 1963).

Plaut, G. W., (ed.), *The Growth of Reform Judaism: American and European Sources* (World Union of Progressive Judaism, 1965).

JEWISH LIFE IN THE NINETEENTH AND EARLY TWENTIETH CENTURIES

Glazer, N., *American Judaism* (University of Chicago Press, 1972).

Laqueur, W., *A History of Zionism* (Schocken, 1976).

Poliakov, L., *The History of Anti-Semitism*, 3 vols. (Vanguard Press, 1965–76).

Reinharz, J., *Fatherland or Promised Land: The Dilemma of the German Jew 1893–1914* (University of Michigan Press, 1975).

Sachar, H. M., *The Course of Modern Jewish History* (Delta Publishing Company, 1958).

HOLOCAUST AND AFTERMATH

Dawidowicz, L. S., *The War Against the Jews 1937–1945* (Holt, Reinhardt and Winston, 1975).

Further Reading

Dawidowicz, L. S., (ed.), *A Holocaust Reader* (Behrman House, 1976).
De Lange, N., *Atlas of the Jewish World* (Phaidon, 1985).
Levin, N., *The Holocaust: The Destruction of European Jewry 1933–1945* (Schocken, 1973).
O'Brien, C. C., *The Siege: The Saga of Israel and Zionism* (Weidenfeld and Nicolson, 1986).

MODERN JEWISH THOUGHT

Agus, J. B., *Modern Philosophies of Judaism* (Behrman House, 1971).
Bergman, S. H., *An Introduction to Modern Jewish Thought* (Schocken, 1963).
Kaufman, W., *Contemporary Jewish Philosophies* (Behrman House, 1976).
Noveck, S. (ed.), *Great Jewish Thinkers of the Twentieth Century* (B'nai B'rith Department of Jewish Education, 1963).
Rotenstreich, N., *Jewish Philosophy in Modern Times: From Mendelssohn to Rosensweig* (Holt, Reinhardt and Winston, 1968).
Rubenstein, R. L. and Roth, J. K., *Approaches to Auschwitz* (SCM Press, 1987).

GLOSSARY

Ab Initio: 'From the beginning'

Adam Kadmon: primeval man

Adar: twelfth month of the Jewish year

Adon Olam: poem which begins, 'Lord of eternity'

Afar Mavet: dust of the earth

Afikoman: part of the middle *matzah*

Agudat Israel: anti-Zionist movement

Agunah: a married woman whose husband's death is suspected but not proved

Akdamut Millin: liturgical poem ('introduction')

Akedah: the binding (of Isaac)

Alenu: prayer at the end of a service

Al ha-Nissim: prayer ('for the miracles')

Al Het: prayer ('for the sin')

Amidah: the eighteen blessings ('standing')

Amilam: circumcision of foreign nations

Amoraim: Palestinian sages (AD 200–500)

Ani Maamin: prayer which begins, 'I believe'

Ashamnu: prayer ('we have trespassed')

Ashkenazic: originating in Eastern Europe

Asiyah: kabbalistic realm ('making')

Attah Yatsarta: prayer ('you have desired')

Atzilut: kabbalistic realm ('emanation')

Av: fifth month of the Jewish year

Avinu Malkenu: prayer ('our father our king')

Avodah She-ba-lev: service of the heart

Avon: crookedness

Avot: sayings of the Fathers

Ayin: nothingness

Ayn Sof: the Infinite

Bain Adam la-Makom: laws governing human relations with God

Bain Adam la-Havero: laws governing human relationships with each other

Baraita: teachings not included in the *Mishnah*

Bar Mitzvah: male adolescent ceremony ('son of the commandment')

Barukh Shem Kevod Malkhuto: response ('blessed is the name of his holy kingdom')

Barukh She-Petaroni: prayer ('blessed be he who has relieved me')

Bat: daughter

Bat Mitzvah: female adolescent ceremony ('daughter of the commandment')

238

Bereshit: 'In the beginning'
Beriyah: kabbalistic realm ('creation')
Besht: Israel ben Eleazer (also known as the Baal Shem Tov)
Bet Din: rabbinical court
Bhr: 'to choose' in Hebrew
Bimah: platform
Binah: God's wisdom
Birkhat ha-Mazon: Grace after Meals
Bor: pit
Cantor: chanter
Cohen: priest
Creatio Ex Nihilo: creation from nothing
Dayyan: judge
Derashah: discourse
Devekut: mystical cleaving to God
Diaspora: outside Israel
Dreydel: *Hanukkah* top
Einsatzgruppen: mobile killing battalions used by the Nazis
Elilim: non-entities
Eli Tziayyon: prayer ('lament, O Zion')
Elleh Ezkerah: martyrology ('these things I remember')
El Nora Alilah: hymn
Elohim: God
Elul: sixth month of the Jewish year
Eretz: earth
Eretz Israel: land of Israel
Eretz Tachtit: nether parts of the earth
Erusin: stage in betrothal
Exodus Rabbah: *midrash* on Exodus
Fleishig: meat foods
Gan Eden: Garden of Eden (or heaven)
Gaon: head of a Babylonian academy
Ge: cursed valley associated with fire and death
Ge Ben Hinnom: cursed valley associated with fire and death
Gehenna: Hell
Ge Hinnom: cursed valley associated with fire and death
Gehinnom: Hell
Gemara: rabbinic discussions on the *Mishnah*
Genesis Rabbah: *midrash* on Genesis
Gerousia: council
Get: bill of divorce
Get Zikkui: get of benefit
Ghetto: residential area where Jews were confined
Gomel: blessing ('he who makes recompense')
Gregger: noisemaker
Habad: Hasidic movement whose name is based on the initials of the
    words *hokhmah* (wisdom), *binah* (understanding), and *daat* (knowledge)
Haftarah: prophetic reading

Glossary

Haganah: Israeli defence force
Haggadah: Passover prayer book
Hag ha-Aviv: Festival of Spring
Hag ha-Matzot: Festival of Unleavened Bread
Hag ha-Urim: Festival of Lights
Hakham: wise person
Hakham Bashi: chief rabbi
Halakhah: Jewish law
Hallel: Psalms 113—18
Hamantashen: *Purim* cakes ('Haman's hats')
Ha-Mashiah: Messiah ('the anointed')
Hanukkah: festival of lights ('dedication')
Ha-Rahaman: the Compassionate One
Haroset: paste of fruit, spices, wine and matzah eaten at the Passover *Seder*
Hashgahah: divine action
Hashkavah: memorial prayer ('cause us to lie down')
Hasid: pious person
Hasidism: mystical Jewish movement founded in the eighteenth century
Haskalah: Jewish Enlightenment
Havdalah: service at the end of the Sabbath
Havurot: informal prayer groups
Hazot: noon service
Heder: school for children
Hesed Shel Emet: true kindness
Het: to miss; to fail
Hineni He-Ani Mi-Maas: prayer
Hinnah: bride's party before a wedding
Hityahed: convert to Judaism who converts for fear of the Jews
Hokhmah: God's wisdom
Hol Hamoed: intermediate days of a festival
Holocaust: destruction of the Jewish people between 1939–45 in Europe
Hoshanah: prayer ('save, I pray')
Hoshanah Rabbah: seventh day of *Sukkot*
Huppah: marriage canopy
Isru Hag: day after the festival of Passover or *Shavuot*
Iyyar: second month of the Jewish calendar
Judenbischof: bishop of the Jews
Kabbalah: Jewish mysticism
Kaddish: prayer for the dead
Kallah: study session
Kapparot: atonements
Karaism: anti-rabbinic sect
Kashrut: dietary laws
Kavvanot: intention
Kedushah: holiness prayer
Kehillot: Jewish communal bodies

Kelal Yisrael: community of Israel
Keter: God's will
Ketubbah: marriage contract
Ketuvim: Writings (third section of the Hebrew Scriptures)
Kheseil: foolish person
Kiddush: sanctification prayer
Kiddushin: stage in betrothal
Kinot: elegies
Kislev: ninth month of the Jewish calendar
Kittel: robe
Kodashim: holy things
Kolel: advanced institute for *Talmud* study
Kol Nidre: evening service which starts the Day of Atonement ('all vows')
Kosher: ritually fit food
Kristallnacht: German onslaught on Jewish property which took place on 9th to 10th November, 1938
Lag Ba-Omer: scholars' feast
La-Shanah ha-Baah Bi-Yerushalayim: 'Next year in Jerusalem'
Latkes: potato pancakes
Lekhah Dodi: Sabbath hymn ('come, my beloved')
Letz: mocker
Levite: priest
Lulav: palm branch (used on *Sukkot*)
Maariv: evening service
Maftir: reader of the *Haftarah*
Malkhuyyot: prayer dealing with God's rule
Malkot: lashes
Mamzer: child of an incestuous or adulterous relationship
Manna: food provided by God in the desert
Maoz Tsur: hymn for *Hanukkah* ('rock of ages')
Mappah: glosses of Moses Isserles on the *Shulhan Arukh*
Marheshvan: second month of the Jewish year
Maror: bitter herbs
Marranos: Jews who converted to Christianity (in Spain and Portugal)
Maskilim: followers of the Jewish Enlightenment
Matzah: unleavened bread used at Passover
Mavet: death
Megillah: scroll
Mekhilta: *midrash* on Exodus
Menorah: candelabrum
Merkavah: divine chariot
Messiah: God's chosen leader
Mezuzah: box fixed to the doorpost of a Jewish home
Midrash: rabbinic commentary on Scripture
Midrash Rabbah: *midrash* on the Pentateuch and the Five Scrolls
Mikdash Meat: minor sanctuary
Mikveh: ritual bath
Milchig: milk foods

Minhah: meal offering (or afternoon service)
Minyan: quorum of ten men
Mi She-Barakh: prayer ('he who blessed')
Mishnah: compendium of the Oral *Torah*
Mitzvah: commandment
Moed: season
Mohar: payment by the groom
Mohel: official who performs a circumcision
Mulhuyot: section recited as part of the *musaf* service on *Rosh Ha-Shanah*
Musaf: additional service
Musar: movement of return to traditional ethics founded in the modern
    period
Nagid: head of Spanish or North African community
Nahamu: 'comfort'
Nashim: women
Nedunyah: money given to the son on betrothal
Neilah: concluding service
Neilat Shearim: evening service
Neviim: Prophets (second section of the Hebrew Scriptures)
Nezikim: damages
Nilvah: alien who has joined himself to the Lord
Nisan: first month of the Jewish year
Nissuin: second stage in the marriage procedure
Olam: eternity
Olam ha-tikkun: world of perfection
Olam ha-tohu: world of the void
Omer: barley offering
Ophanim: lower order of angels
Orthodoxy: *Torah*-observant Judaism
Parashah: *Torah* portion
Parnas: head of the community
Parokhet: white curtain
Paschal: Passover
Pesah: Passover festival
Peshah: breach
Petah Lanu Shaar: hymn ('open the gate for us')
Peti: simpleton
Petor: divorce document
Pidyon ha-Ben: redemption of the first-born
Piyyutim: hymns
Proselyte: convert
Pur: lot
Purim: feast of Esther
Purim gelt: *Purim* coins
Purim Shoshan: 15th of Adar
Rabbi: teacher
Rasha: evil person
Rebbe: Hasidic leader
Reform Movement: progressive modernizing movement

Responsa: answers to specific legal questions
Rosh Hashanah: New Year
Rosh Hodesh: 1st of the month
Sabbath: seventh day
Sandak: godfather
Sanhedrin: central rabbinic court in ancient times
Seder: Passover ceremony at home
Sefirah Malkhut: heavenly archetype of the community of Israel
Sefirot: divine emanation
Selihot: penitential prayers
Sephardic: originating in Spain or North Africa
Seudah Mafseket: final meal
Seudah Mitzvah: meal in honour of a religious act
Seudah Shelishit: third meal
Shabbat Bereshit: Sabbath when the new *Torah* reading begins
   ('Sabbath of Genesis')
Shabbat ha-Gadol: Great Sabbath
Shabbat ha-Hodesh: Spring Sabbath ('Sabbath of the month')
Shabbat Hanukkah: Sabbath during *Hanukkah*
Shabbat Hazon: Sabbath before *Tishah B'Av* ('Sabbath of Prophecy')
Shabbat Hol Hamoed: Sabbath during *Sukkot* or Passover season
Shabbat Mahar Hodesh: Sabbath of the eve of a New Moon
Shabbat Mevarekhim: Sabbath before a New Moon
Shabbat Nahamin: Sabbath after *Tishah B'Av*
Shabbat Nahamu: Sabbath of Comfort
Shabbaton: day of solemn rest
Shabbat Parah: Spring Sabbath ('Sabbath of the Red Heifer')
Shabbat Rosh Hodesh: New Moon Sabbath
Shabbat Shekalim: Spring Sabbath ('Sabbath of the Shekel Tax')
Shabbat Shirah: Sabbath when the Song of Moses is recited
Shabbat Shuvah: Sabbath between *Rosh Hashanah* and *Yom Kippur*
   ('Sabbath of Return')
Shabbat Teshuvah: Sabbath of Repentance
Shabbat Zakhor: Spring Sabbath ('Sabbath of Remembrance')
Shaddai: Almighty
Shaharit: morning service
Shalom Aleikhem: hymn ('peace be to you')
Shalom Zakhor: birth celebration gathering
Shammash: serving light for *Hanukkah*
Shavuot: Festival of Weeks
Sheheheyanu: blessing ('who has preserved us')
Shehitah: ritual slaughtering
Shekhinah: divine presence
Sheloshim: thirty days of mourning
Shema: prayer ('Hear, O Israel')
Shema Yisrael: 'Hear, O Israel'
Shemini Atseret: final day of the festival of *Sukkot*
Shemoneh Esreh: *Amidah*
Sheol: place of the dead

Shetar Pesikta: betrothal document
Sheva Berakhot: seven blessings
Shevarim: three tremulous notes sounded on the *shofar*
Shevat: eleventh month of the Jewish year
Shiddukhin: financial obligations
Shivah: seven days of mourning
Shofar: ram's horn
Shofarot: prayer relating to the ram's horn
Shohet: slaughterer
ShOVaVIM Tat: feast celebrated in January or February
Shulhan Arukh: code of Jewish Law
Shushan Purim: festival of the victory of the Jews of Shushan
Shuvah: prayer ('return')
Siddur: traditional prayer book
Sidrah: section of the *Torah* reading
Sifra: *midrash* on Leviticus
Sifre: *midrash* on Exodus
Sifrei: *midrash* on Numbers and Deuteronomy
Simhat Torah: Festival of the Rejoicing of the Law
Sitra Ahra: demonic realm ('the other side')
Sivan: third month of the Jewish year
Sufganiyyot: doughnuts
Sukkah: booth
Sukkot: Feast of Tabernacles
Synagogue: place of worship
Tahanun: prayer ('supplication')
Takkanah: enactment
Takkanot ha-Kahal: communal statutes
Tallit (larger): prayer shawl
Tallit (smaller): fringed undergarment
Talmud: compilation of the legal discussions based on the *Mishnah*
Talmud Torah: Jewish school
Tammuz: fourth month of the Jewish year
Tanakh: Hebrew Bible
Tannah: Jewish sage (AD 70–200)
Tashlikh: casting away sin
Tefillah: prayer (also the *Amidah)*
Tefillin: phylacteries
Tekiah: long note sounded on the *shofar*
Teku: 'let it remain undecided'
Tenaim: betrothal document
Terefah: not *kosher* ('torn')
Teruot: nine short notes sounded on the *shofar*
Tevet: tenth month of the Jewish year
Tikkanta Shabbat: prayer
Tikkun: cosmic repair
Tishah B'Av: ninth of Av
Tishri: seventh month of the Jewish year
Tohorot: purity

Tohu u vohu: 'without form' (void)
Torah: Law (or Pentateuch)
Torah She-Be-Al Peh: Oral Law
Torah She-Bi-Ketav: Written Law
Tosefta: additions to the *Mishnah*
Tu Bi-Shevat: New Year for Trees
Tzaddik: righteous person
Tzidduk ha-Din: prayer ('justification of the judgement')
Tzimtzum: contraction of the Godhead into itself
Tzitzit: fringes
U-Netanneh Tokef: prayer ('let us declare the mighty importance')
Viddui: confession
Vort: verbal betrothal agreement
Wimple: swaddling clothes
Yaaleh Ve-Yavo: prayer ('may our remembrances rise and come')
Yamim Noraim: Days of Awe
Yartzeit: anniversary of a death
Yashar: upright person
Yehi Ratson: prayer ('it will be God's will')
Yekum Purkah: prayer for schools and sages
Yemot Hamashiah: Days of the Messiah
Yeshivah: college
Yetsirah: kabbalistic realm ('formation')
Yetsiv Pitgam: liturgical prayer
Yetzer ha-Ra: evil inclination
Yetzer ha-Tov: good inclination
Yihud: seclusion
Yikzor: memorial prayers
Yirat ha-onesh: fear of punishment
Yirat ha-romemut: fear in the presence of God
Yirat Shamayim: fear of heaven
Yisrael: Jewish people
Yom ha-Atsmaut: Israel Independence Day
Yom ha-Din: Day of Judgement
Yom ha-Zikkaron: Day of Remembrance
Yom Kippur: Day of Atonement
Yom Kippur Katan: Small Day of Atonement
Yom Teruah: Day of blowing the *Shofar*
Zeman Herutenu: Season of our Freedom
Zeman Mattan Toratenu: Season of the Giving of our *Torah*
Zemirot: hymns
Zerah: animal sacrifice
Zeraim: seeds
Zikhronot: prayer ('proclamation of God's remembrance')
Zikhron Teruah: memorial proclaimed with a horn
Zionism: movement for a Jewish homeland in Israel
Zohar: medieval mystical work

INDEX

Index

Index